PUBLIC RELATIONS FOR MARKETING PROFESSIONALS

STUDIES IN PUBLIC RELATIONS

Series Editor: Norman A. Hart, MSc FIPR FCIM FCAM

The Studies in Public Relations series of books is designed to present public relations in its new and developing role as a strategic function contributing to the achieving and enhancement of business objectives. It represents a 'second generation' of textbooks which will move from the hitherto concentration on press relations into a wider corporate role.

The series is edited by Norman Hart, a well-known international writer and speaker on all aspects of public relations and marketing communications. Author of many books on various communications subjects, he is a Fellow of the Institute of Public Relations, and was the first Professor of Public Relations in the United Kingdom. Norman is a past Chairman of the International Public Relations Foundation.

Public relations for marketing professionals

Roger Haywood

Foreword by Steve Cuthbert

palgrave

Published by
PALGRAVE
Houndmills, Basingstoke, Hampshire RG21 6XS and
175 Fifth Avenue, New York, N. Y. 10010
Companies and representatives throughout the world

PALGRAVE is the new global academic imprint of
St. Martin's Press LLC Scholarly and Reference Division and
Palgrave Publishers Ltd (formerly Macmillan Press Ltd).

ISBN 0–333–68477–X

This book is printed on paper suitable for recycling and
made from fully managed and sustained forest sources.

A catalogue record for this book is available
from the British Library.

10   9   8   7   6   5
07   06   05   04   03   02

Copy-edited and typeset by Povey–Edmondson
Tavistock and Rochdale, England

Printed and bound in Great Britain by
Antony Rowe Ltd, Eastbourne

■ Contents

■ Foreword

Good marketing must mean good communications. Public relations is a vital element in running a successful business yet, too often, what should be a central business discipline is run as if it were all a matter of personal opinion or idiosyncratic judgement. But good public relations should be planned, should be managed and should be appraised. Everyone buying or using public relations services should look at the principles that underpin the craft – and try to develop procedures that produce the maximum benefit and the highest levels of cost effectiveness from the resources and budget that they allocate to this important function. Indeed, as the author of *Public relations for marketing professionals* argues persuasively, there may be opportunities to improve marketing effectiveness through the wiser allocation of such resources – if the marketers know where and how to allocate these.

Roger Haywood is a rare character in that he has chaired with considerable success both the Chartered Institute of Marketing and the Institute of Public Relations. Though he has written and broadcast extensively on business communications, he is more than a theorist. He is a pragmatic experienced professional who cuts through jargon to offer practical and useable advice. How many marketing people really know how to recruit winning public relations personnel: or how to get the best people in the consultancy demanding to work on their account: or the six essentials to remember when setting up a media interview: or the unfailing no-cost way to test the value of a news story: or the critical factor to set in place first when a crisis hits the organisation? As with marketing, learning from mistakes can be a bruising and expensive way to develop essential skills.

Most business people need a better understanding of marketing. And many marketing professionals need a better understanding not just of what public relations is but how to manage it. Used effectively, public relations can help build the company reputation as well as protect it when the going gets tough.

STEVE CUTHBERT
Director General
The Chartered Institute of Marketing
Maidenhead

■ Acknowledgements

My appreciation goes to my many partners within the Worldcom Group for their suggestions, examples and ideas used throughout this book. It has been a privilege to be part of the Worldcom international partnership; I was fortunate enough to be able to play a part in the formation and development of this remarkable organisation – and, in recent years, to have found associates who have become colleagues and then friends as we have built the organisation from nothing in 1988 into the world's largest partnership of independent consultancies, with 120 offices across the business capitals of the world.

I would also like to thank the many public relations and marketing professionals who have given their time in supplying many of the case studies in this book and who, in many cases, have helped check and constructively amend my copy. I cannot mention each here – but every one is acknowledged in the index. Without their expertise and generosity, this book would not have been possible. Particular appreciation must go to the many members of the Institute of Public Relations, the Chartered Institute of Marketing and The Marketing Society who gave me such support and assistance in the creation of this guide.

I would also like to thank my business partner John Dresser for his unfailing good humour through the trials of preparing this book at a time that we were also developing and building our own business.

But above all, my deepest appreciation must go to my personal partner (as the PC terminology suggests is appropriate these days), my wife Sandra, for tolerating an intolerable other half.

Towards the meritocracy

Whilst making acknowledgements, let me say that one of the joys of the media, public relations and marketing industries is the impressive capabilities of so many of the people at all levels in the business. Our sectors must be amongst the most egalitarian, where achievement relates most closely to performance. We are not yet a true meritocracy for the ethnic minorities have not yet fully achieved senior representation – but all the opportunities are open. Women are not a minority, but in some businesses it is taking a long time for them to get the recognition they deserve. Probably more of the best professionals at the top of our business are women than in any other industry. So when I use 'he' in this book, it is because it becomes tedious to say 'he or she' every time. Equally, I am resistant to the fudge of putting everything into the plural to disguise the gender. If this approach irritates anyone, I am sorry. I doubt that any of the many talented women I have worked with and for will take offence.

ROGER HAYWOOD

Marketing: what business is all about

THE MARKETING PERSPECTIVE

Should the bold spirits all dazzle their eyes by the star high above, they may stumble into the crevasse, but fix their gaze on a heavenly body in proximity to the horizon, be it still as distant, and they will navigate safely the closer hazards.
Stig Enstonze (1834–96), Danish explorer, in *Discoveries* (1889)

■ Background to public relations for marketing professionals

■ Start at the beginning

If public relations is all about creating favourable opinion – and that will do as a starting definition – then it obviously should have a very close relationship with marketing, which must be much about managing customer relations favourably and profitably.

Public relations for marketing professionals has been written primarily for those with a good understanding of marketing. It is particularly relevant to executives with experience and senior responsibility, though it has much that should be of value to those entering marketing. There are also suggestions that should be helpful to professionals in public relations wishing to extend the services they are offering to their marketing colleagues or bosses.

■ Balance thought and action

Public relations often has a valuable role to play in areas outside those initially considered by many marketing executives – it can add much in new product development, research, distributor support and so on.

It can also work both as a communications discipline, often in diverse and surprisingly flexible ways, as well as being capable of being applied to business as a management philosophy, much like marketing itself. Indeed, in much the same way that marketing evangelists have argued for their profession, public

1

relations should also be considered at the strategic level and not just thought of as an optional, add-on communications technique.

■ Move towards integrated communications

All the marketing disciplines have a contribution to make and should be balanced in the marketing mix. This does not mean all are equal. Direct mail might be perfect for some aspects of communications but not all. Within some companies advertising can be dominant, perhaps because of the budget spent. This may be understandable but it must not allow all strategic problems to be approached from an advertising perspective. Public relations problems need to be solved through public relations techniques.

To try to get a better balance and greater synergy, some organisations and agencies have moved to an integrated communications approach. This can work well if all the communications functions are considered and each allowed its proper role. It is less satisfactory if it means that the significance of the input is judged by the level of budget spend.

Public relations is concerned about policies that will win public goodwill, even *before* any communications activity is undertaken. For this reason, it can be unwise to think of public relations only as communications or even an element in some integrated communications mix.

Of course, public relations can be highly effective – or otherwise. This book attempts to help those who need to specify, introduce, brief, commission, manage or monitor this (oft-times undisciplined) discipline to ensure both the maximum effectiveness and cost-effectiveness. There is always a better way, a more creative approach, an extra dimension, some added value, a sharper focus – and the author tries to illustrate how to add this public relations *competitive edge* through both procedures (such as checklists, analytical processes and guidance notes) and through the pragmatic step of examples and case studies, used throughout the text.

■ Getting it right

Few marketing professionals will have direct personal experience in public relations, though most will have been responsible for the management of this activity. The performance quality delivered, either by in-house teams or consultancy, may vary considerably. Therefore this text looks at some of the fundamentals from which the best planned and run programmes must be built. There will be variations in the public relations approach according to whether the marketing is targeting consumers, with products or services, or business buyers – indeed, in any other marketing relationship in the commercial or even non-profit sectors. However, the underlying principles will always remain the same.

If some of these factors are too basic for some readers, the author can only apologise. However, major organisations which have suffered public relations disasters in recent years are so many that it has become embarrassing to admit to being a public relations adviser. Such calamities (some noted in this text) have befallen companies as diverse as British Airways, British Gas, General Motors, McDonald's, Marks & Spencer, McDonnell Douglas, Nestlé, Ratners, Sainsbury's, Shell and Unilever – many of these are companies that have also won awards for their marketing and management excellence.

If some of the most respected companies, often with highly regarded marketing capabilities, can make significant but avoidable public relations mistakes, then some of these basics may not be so fully understood or practised as might be advisable. In these cases, either the organisations were let down by their public relations advice, or it was not offered at a high enough level, or it was not listened to, or was overridden.

Certainly, despite significant investment in both marketing and public relations, something serious keeps going wrong with many corporations. It must ultimately come down to the level of understanding and quality of management.

Public relations can be a powerful force and must be managed firmly and actively. Marketing people must be certain that this is an area under control. Even if public relations is not an active force deployed by the organisation, there may be countless issues that can come to the top of the corporate or marketing agenda that will demand attention. Some might arise without warning and over which management will have no control; failure to manage the consequences will demonstrate that the necessary resources and skills are not in place. This can be embarrassing; it can be disastrous. No company has the option to say it has no public relations. It can only choose to be organised or not. As an illustration, any product can be beset by quality or safety issues; the manufacturer, distributor or retailer of these will need to be able to promptly and effectively handle the public relations aspects that will follow.

At the very least, reading this book and putting the principles into practice could be invaluable insurance against calamity, whilst those with a more visionary perspective might find the public relations approach can do more than act as a defence; it can add massively to business success.

■ Public relations is a core discipline in marketing

Marketing professionals know that everything in the business is dependent on effective marketing – for exceeding the expectations of the customers is what every business should all be about. Of course, business success depends on many skilled professionals across the organisation but if this customer satisfaction factor is not fundamental then all the other efforts will be without point – unless you are planning to go out of business or are in a state monopoly or similar.

All company activities should be focused on short- or long-term customer benefit, including communications both within and without the organisation.

Most of these points in this introductory section will be accepted by marketers – but not all will be fully appreciated by some public relations practitioners, particularly those who may come from journalism or through an arts education rather than from the hard-headed world of business.

Even the most evangelical marketer would agree that business would not survive long without effective financial, personnel, legal (and many other) specialist managers. Marketing is the bridge, the interface, the link between the company and the customers . . . and all those who serve the customers which, again, is everyone.

However – and there would have to be a *but* after such a dogmatic statement – the omnipotence of marketing can give the practitioners of this craft a distorted perspective of public relations. Some think that public relations is media coverage or (if they see themselves as visionaries) media relations.

Others think that public relations is part of marketing – which it is not.

If you are a marketing professional and have bought this book, do not despair or demand a refund. There are many flattering and positive comments later about the magical skills of successful marketing craftspeople.

Should you just be browsing through this part of the book, wondering whether to buy it, take courage and blow such a modest sum to find out why public relations is essential in marketing, yet is not *part* of marketing. Also, through the following pages, learn how to get the maximum contribution to your marketing effectiveness (in some areas you may never even have considered), through the canny use of public relations.

■ Marketing moves centre stage

In recent years, marketing has moved from being a sales improvement discipline – getting all the sales influences working together – to becoming a philosophy of business. If shareholders or employees are identified as the primary focus of the business, can it truly be said to be marketing orientated?

Richard Branson of Virgin argues that his staff come first – and this means that happy employees serve the customers best. That may be true in his case, but it cannot be taken as an infallible rule of human behaviour.

Some companies give the impression that their employees would be happiest if there were no customers. In Dixons, I once interrupted a conversation between two sales assistants to ask them if I could help pay their wages. The irony was lost, even when I patiently explained that my custom was what paid them. When they failed to take the proffered opportunity to put *this* customer first, I took my business to Comet. I may not be important but I have the final say, as does every customer, when I am spending my money.

A marketing organisation has to be built around the concept of putting the customers first. This means anticipating and exceeding their expectations. Profits will come from this customer satisfaction. Employee benefits will flow from both the satisfaction of the work and from the rewards that can be distributed through the profits generated. The owners or shareholders can also expect and earn a better return, for satisfied customers spend more, satisfied staff become more effective (and usually are less expensive than a team with a constant turnover), whilst the customer focus offers a better guarantee of short- and long-term profit.

■ Public relations – like marketing – may be a state of mind

In the introduction to the excellent *Companion Encyclopedia of Marketing* (see bibliography), the editor, Professor Michael Baker of the University of Strathclyde, considers that marketing, like medicine and engineering is a 'synthetic' discipline. He points out that it has sound foundations in the long-established and recognised social sciences such as economics, psychology and sociology – but it differs from them in its holistic approach to understanding the nature and satisfaction of human needs. Also, like medicine and engineering, marketing embraces, in addition to a body of knowledge, a professional practice dependent upon that knowledge.

Baker also examines the way that views about marketing polarise into those who perceive it as a philosophy of business and those who regard it as a management function related to a particular activity, comparable to production, finance or human resource management. Most people will see the true essence of marketing as being *mutually-satisfying exchange relationships*.

It could be argued that marketing has always been an intrinsic element of the commercial exchange process – but that its importance has waxed and waned with shifts in the balance between supply and demand. Brian Jones of the University of Prince Edward Island School of Business, Canada, discusses this in the *Companion Encyclopedia* in his chapter on historical research in marketing. He believes there would appear to be at least three main phases in the evolution of the modern marketing concept: the emergence of the mass market around 1850, the articulation of the modern marketing concept, which would be around 1960, and the transition from an emphasis upon the transaction to the relationship, which would be as late as 1990.

Though marketing might be considered a modern concept, its customer-orientation roots go back to the days when businesses began to grow too big for the product-maker to deal personally with each customer. New technologies made mass production possible and so the industrial revolution began. People moved from country areas into towns to work in the new factories – and began to earn the sort of incomes that allowed them to become consumers themselves.

Mass production led to the creation of the mass market and, in those days in the mid-1800s, the manufacturers were king. They had control over the employees. They had mass markets, sometimes at their factory gates, sometimes across the world through cheap transport; also, they often had the benefit of limited competition from less advanced nations. Raw materials were available at minimal prices from global markets; most of the countries of origin for such raw materials had not yet reached the stage of being able to manage their own economies effectively.

■ Marketing brings business closer to the consumer

But today the picture is different. Both manufacturers and retailers ensure that, through research and other techniques, they keep close to consumers.

For example, the movement towards large-scale retailing both in food and variety store sectors (the multiple market) has increased their power, their influence – and both their understanding of and responsiveness to the moods of the public. In each market, retailers leapfrog each other with innovations and better customer services.

For example, in the UK, when Tesco and Safeway introduced a loyalty card, Sainsbury's declined to participate and, for that year, saw its profits decline for the first time in some twenty years of trading. The two factors may not have been connected . . . but Sainsbury's rapidly introduced its own version of a loyalty scheme.

This closeness of the retailer to the consumer puts considerable emphasis on the need for effective public relations to help align the retailer's ambitions with the aspirations of its customers. Significantly, in most markets around the world, leading retailers have highly professional public relations departments; these are responsible for maintaining relations with customers, prospective customers, suppliers and other key audiences – continuously and regardless of whether the organisation happens to be advertising at that particular time.

Yet it is important to appreciate that advertising by the retailers is of great influence. In the UK, it grew from £85 million in 1985 to £523 million in 1992, according to an Economist Intelligence Unit report. The leading UK retail advertiser in the mid-1990s was Tesco with an estimated £26 million spend, compared with a little over £6 million just four years earlier.

In analysing the expenditure figures, some estimates have worked on different criteria. Is public relations counted as part of the advertising expenditure? Is sponsorship, for example, part of advertising, public relations or a separate communications discipline? Or maybe it is sales support or corporate relations and not communications at all?

Sponsorship may be publicity or entertainment or both. Certainly the right sponsorship can deliver a high level of attention or awareness; the Littlewoods' Cup sponsorship generated in excess of five hours of prime television coverage time in its first year. Though this airtime cannot be directly compared with conventional advertising, it clearly presented the Littlewoods name on many occasions to many potential and current customers.

■ 'Marketing public relations' must be controlled by marketing

Marketing is seen by some only as a consumer-related activity; but this approach to business is just as relevant to a charity, a pressure group, a business service provider, trade union, government department or, indeed, a company selling satellites, bridges or ships.

As noted earlier, business is about nothing if it is not about marketing. Indeed, there can be few organisations that do not have some form of marketing focus at the centre of its activities – even if it does not use this term to describe the activities. For all organisations exist to serve the interests of some group of people, even the KGB or London cabbies; they cannot meet these needs unless they have such a market orientation.

If the organisation needs to meet customer requirements then it needs marketing, whatever it may call the mix of skills it deploys. Similarly, it cannot meet these needs unless it has processes of two-way communications in place – in other words, public relations. And, rightly, the public relations that is responsible for supporting marketing should be managed and directed by marketing, even where it may be undertaken by communications professionals outside the direct responsibility of marketing. It would be intolerable for marketing management to have to work with colleagues influencing marketing audiences – customers, wholesalers, retailers, for example – but operating independently and uncontrollably.

At the same time, marketing management has to understand and accept that, in most organisations, there are audiences where public relations has responsibilities which are not traditionally considered part of marketing – shareholders, government, factory neighbours, employees, may be examples. Clearly, communication with marketing and non-marketing audiences needs to be consistent and co-ordinated. Later, we look at the advantages and otherwise of marketing public relations being run within the marketing function or outside.

■ Marketing communications covers many disciplines

Marketing communications is sometimes used by managers outside marketing as a term interchangeable with public relations. Many would be uncomfortable with that blurring of the roles. Keith Crosier, senior lecturer in marketing at the University of Strathclyde, draws a strong distinction between public relations and marketing communications. In his view, public relations is an expression of corporate strategy rather than marketing strategy and hence belongs outside the marketing discipline.

The author agrees with this contention: public relations techniques have much to contribute to marketing; the expertise of public relations professionals needs to be deployed in the marketing arena, even if these professionals are not responsible for all aspects of marketing communications; whilst, of course, public relations has responsibilities outside marketing.

Crosier believes that there are seven aspects of marketing communications: advertising, publicity (editorial promotion), packaging, personal selling, direct marketing, sponsorship and sales promotion.

■ Public relations works where market forces do apply

Of course, an organisation can be held artificially in a market place through monopoly or state control. Clearly, if a business is defying the basic laws that govern market forces, then it will need to be subsidised, protected or supported in some such unnatural way if it is not to collapse. In such cases, the rule that public relations is an essential part of the company/customer communications may not apply. If there is only one take-it-or-leave-it train service, or the choice of bread is the state loaf, then what the customer experiences and what the management think about that will be irrelevant.

The world of business has changed dramatically in recent years, not least in those countries where the state controlled markets and production. External pressures from liberalisation and the inevitability of market forces have often forced change – and not only in totalitarian states.

Some state airlines in western Europe – Italy, France or Spain, for example – used to employ five or more times as many people per mile flown as their privatised competition on international routes, such as BA or the more progressive US airlines. Once EU protection was removed and an open market created, then this overhead could not be supported – fares would either be uncompetitive or the state would foot a lunatic subsidy bill that taxpayers (not airline passengers) would have to pay – even were that allowable under European competitive practices.

Organisations that move from a position of protection and find themselves working in a marketing environment rapidly have to learn to re-write both their objectives and their operating procedures in terms of both marketing and public relations. The state airlines, in the example, competing internationally would have to find ways to improve productivity and reduce excessive employment.

■ Open markets demand more effective communications

Or consider the example of all those protected industries that existed within the Soviet Union. One of the world's largest manufacturers of fork-lift trucks, a little unexpectedly, was based in an East European country, supplying the captive market across the whole of the Soviet Union.

Before *perestroika*, if you ran a factory or warehouse in any of those nations and needed a fork-lift truck, you had no choice but to buy from this source. And you had no influence over the price that was paid. There was no choice, no option and no negotiation. In those less liberalised days, marketing played little part in the business and customer communications, as we might understand it, did not exist. *Glasnost* would eventually create the openness that would lead to freedom of speech – from which both marketing and public relations could develop.

Even under the communist regime, the fork-lift truck company tried to compete in countries where market forces applied; they had to change policy. Indeed, in at least one western European market the company set up a factory to take the Soviet-assembled product to pieces – and then put it back together properly, adding all the components that had been left off on the original production line. Often they also had to re-paint the vehicles.

The managing director of this plant – an urbane and wise East European who could see the oddity of the situation – ruefully showed me an example of the incredible craftsmanship of his factory colleagues on the production line. A curved exhaust less than half a metre long was impressively welded from fourteen pieces of cut, straight pipe.

On a good day, and when the welding operatives did not have a hangover, the workmanship could be quite impressive. However, even with the most meticulous welding of these exhaust pipes, there were fourteen opportunities for leaks. The company sadly had to remove and throw out these magnificent examples of the welders' art; each was replaced with a single curved piece of steel tube . . . the product of capitalist technology, more reliable, less labour intensive – but requiring sophisticated machinery for its manufacture. As a piece of engineering art this may have been less impressive, but which would you have preferred on a fork-lift truck that you depended on to keep your production line busy? The managers of this enterprise were decidedly uncomfortable about improving efficiency at the expense of jobs – a perspective that even survives in western Europe.

The philosophical executive boss told me that it was possible for fork-lift trucks to be delivered to his re-assembly plant without gearboxes or engine controls; in some cases, there had not even been the most rudimentary attempt to test drive the product before shipping. Heaven knows what the customers in the Soviet Union did under these circumstances. What the subsidiary did in western European markets was to cannibalise these production models and raid the spares stores to build complete products that were saleable.

The products were supplied so cheaply from source that they could still be rebuilt and sold at a margin. Clearly, no one had ever calculated the real costs at the factory. The boss in charge of this strange re-assembly operation could spend money on rebuilding the products but not in getting the problem resolved at source. Communications that proposed such change was just too threatening. It is all different now.

After my factory tour, the managing director took me to his office to toast the future over a glass or two of East European champagne.

He noticed my quizzical look at the curious yellow colour of the wine. Taste it, he assured me. Of course he was right and it was a splendidly delicious, dry champagne that totally belied its rather sickly colour. Again, why bother to filter or process the champagne the way that western producers might have to (or whatever other technique might be deployed) if the market had no choice and simply had to take it or leave it? Both were examples of products from organisations that were then largely insulated from normal market forces.

■ Marketing creates the open market – as does *real* communications

So what is marketing and what are these market forces? How do they relate to public relations?

Marketing is defined by the Chartered Institute of Marketing as 'the management process responsible for identifying, anticipating and satisfying customer requirements profitably'.

Though this book focuses on the commercial world, these principles apply in any area of human activity where people have a choice, even in non-profit organisations such as charities, churches, hospitals, universities, or trade unions.

Every marketer understands that, at its simplest, business is all about satisfying customers. In an open market, if the business does not have satisfied customers then it will soon be out of business. The CIM definition implies the need for credible marketing communications, for how could an organisation identify or satisfy customer requirements without an effective two-way exchange of information and views? Of course marketing communications include public relations, as well as advertising, market research and other skills.

What is an open market? Some countries are more open than others. Even liberal nations may be less liberal in sensitive areas. For many years, the UK kept tight control over transatlantic flights from London. Germany, Spain and Switzerland held to restrictive rules on foreign ownership of national companies. Even the USA has disallowed foreign ownership of some companies in aviation and other sectors – and has also prevented the usage of non-US satellite communications equipment within its borders.

Many governments have chosen an option somewhere between outright socialism and total capitalism. These countries have favoured a mixed economy, where state-owned and state-directed enterprises work alongside (sometimes in competition with) commercial businesses. Until the early 1990s, the politicians may have felt they had found the best of both worlds. Sadly, this was rarely true. Why should a state own the airlines or the banks? National pride may have been a factor but there is no logical reason why any airline or bank should not be owned by ordinary shareholders, as any other business. If a business focuses its primary efforts on prestige and is not driven by the need to satisfy customers, it will be doomed to failure.

■ Marketing becomes part of the economic democracy

Though China still maintains high levels of state control, the best known example of a system designed to ignore the needs and rights of customers was the Soviet Union. Indeed, there used to be an old saying about Russia – why did it have such great athletes and such poor cars? The answer was that there was competition for athletes and no competition for cars.

Some countries uninhibited by tradition, such as the United States, have considered that all markets (or almost all, with one or two exceptions noted above) should be open and competitive. This has even extended to those markets that provide services which other nations have viewed as being part of the social remit of government. As we all know, in the USA, hospital treatment and university education are largely in the private sector.

In other parts of the world, as the cost of providing social services rises and the willingness of the populace to support these declines, many governments have looked to see what they could shift out of the public, state-owned sector and into the private sector. Some of these initiatives were led by Mrs Thatcher who, as prime minister of the UK, successively moved state-owned local authority housing, the electricity industry, steel manufacturing, broadcasting, water and waste treatment into the private sector.

Even those services that needed to be retained as a national responsibility, because of their social function, were exposed to the pressures of the market place and open competition. University funding by the state was significantly cut back, polytechnics were encouraged to upgrade themselves to universities and all in the sector expected to compete both for government funds and for educational fees, particularly from students from within the business or overseas sectors. Similar moves in the health service gave doctors the opportunity to 'buy' services and obliged hospitals to become competitive and, so the theory ran, put more emphasis on both customer care and customer service.

■ Communications can build competitive edge

Regardless of the political wisdom of such moves, it is certain that most nations across the world have been looking to self-funding for many of their social services. This inevitably means that those who achieve the highest level of customer satisfaction will be those that generate the most revenue. And whether it is a university or a hospital, that involves marketing – in which public relations will play a central role in communicating with customers.

Marketers sometimes argue over what is the market. These points should be reviewed with the public relations professionals supporting the marketing initiatives – as is discussed in Chapter 6 on briefing them. Clearly the modern meaning of the word market derives from the old concept of a mart where goods were bought, sold or exchanged.

Today, the market is the arena within which the products or services are offered in direct or indirect competition with other offers. Direct competition, such as one restaurant in comparison with others, and indirect competition, say, a meal out in comparison with a trip to the cinema, will each require different marketing communications. Properly deployed public relations can help establish the necessary competitive edge, as well as building the most favourable environment within that market.

As marketing academics like to point out, the key deciding factor in open competition is always value. Of course, value is a perceived factor rather than a tangible reality, such as price. A meal in a four star restaurant might cost £100, whilst in a more modest establishment it might cost £50. One is arithmetically twice as much as the other. Whether it is twice the value or no better value or ten times the value will depend upon the skill of the offerer and the perception of the potential customer. Value may be in the eye – or wallet – of the beholder. Some sectors of the market will rate superb food and be indifferent to the surroundings – whilst others will want an elegant ambience and not be too concerned about the food as long as it reaches a certain minimum level.

Public relations should always be working closely with marketing in trying to present and project competitive edge. This can be even more important where product differences may not be major – or in the area of forced or distress purchases.

■ Customers make buying decisions on perceptions

A motorist may be obliged to buy new tyres for his or her car – and have no choice because the present ones are worn out, dangerous or illegal. If he perceives all tyres as being more or less the same, then he may well go for the cheapest. Few people will derive great satisfaction from buying a new set of tyres – though manufacturers may well try to position their product as offering specific benefits that set themselves away from the competition.

Tyre manufacturers are likely to use public relations and advertising techniques to establish this differential. Not just the enthusiast but many average motorists might believe that Michelin is considerably superior to Pirelli or vice versa. Indeed, Michelin was one of the first companies to recognise that people did not enjoy buying tyres; therefore, the company's marketing professionals urged design and production colleagues to produce tyres with customer benefits. In parallel, they strengthened the branding in advertising and at point of sale.

The first product to be produced to meet this marketing brief was the Michelin X. Advertising for the new product – a branded tyre! – presented satisfied customers saying that they *drove* Michelin X, almost as if the choice of tyre was a more important decision than the car which rode upon them. Other manufacturers followed suit with stronger branding and an attempt to move the tyre out of the 'distress purchase' area.

■ Marketing and public relations people are the same – but different

What makes a good marketing person? Or a good public relations person? Both must be able to perform effectively so they can bring professional skills to the work. Marketing and public relations are broad disciplines so there will be a wide range of skills, expertise and personal attributes relevant to the different roles. Some of these will be common – analytical and planning skills, for example.

However, there is one key area where marketing professionals and the public relations professionals will bring different qualities to the marketing mix – or, perhaps, more accurately these will be different facets of the same set of qualities.

Usually marketing professionals will be driven by the need to achieve and continually build customer satisfaction. This will enable them to generate the best possible prices for the product or services.

Generally, marketing skills have less of a role to play in commodity sectors. Imagine that you are a seasoned marketing person with a responsibility for marketing, perhaps, building sand. It is a commodity and it has its price in the market place which probably varies little. It ends up being used with cement in construction and the finished product (used with one supply of sand or another) will be indistinguishable to anyone except the handful of world building sand experts.

So you can't do much about price – but you can work on distribution, technical advisory service, customer satisfaction, customer relations, loyalty schemes, builders' merchants events, joint promotions with cement makers, contract deals with large customers, plus sponsorship, entertaining, advertising, and public relations to promote all these added extras.

But, as a marketing evangelist, how long before you start trying to develop product differentiation and, even, a little branding? If there were only some way to make your building sand distinctive from other building sand then, with a little branding and the right sort of promotion, a premium price might be obtained in the market. . .

And so your marketing instincts come to the fore; you are driving towards customer satisfaction which leads to higher sales and better prices. Of course, many marketing professionals believe there is no better measure of the effectiveness of their work than the sales figures. And they are generally right.

■ The development of reputation motivates communicators

So, marketing people tend to be commercial and profit-driven. Given the choice of long-term or short-term results, many will find the attraction of the short-term results just too much to resist. Few marketers will jeopardise short-term benefits for the sake of long-term returns; many will put the long-term situation in second place on their agenda.

How does that compare with public relations professionals? Theoretically, they are also driven by the goals of customer satisfaction, improved price and better profitability. But that may be only the theory. Though they may have learnt the language and can mimic the motivations of their colleagues in marketing, few of them are ultimately *really* driven by this key profit dimension. They may know that they are expected to be concerned about sales, costs and margins but, unless it is a requirement of the job, they will soon lose interest in such areas and focus more attention on the one thing that really does motivate them – goodwill. This is not universally so, but is too often true to risk ignoring such motivations.

For whilst even the most uncommercial public relations person will concede that profitability is important (and that public relations can make a major contribution in this area), it is not usually what gives them a buzz. They want people to respect the organisation. Some may be prepared to fight to get management to change policies to those that are more likely to win regard. Admiration and respect are often higher up their agenda than sales and performance. They want the best company reputation that they can achieve – for many will feel that this is much more what their work is about than anything that appears on the bottom line. It is not uncommon for a public relations practitioner not to know the turnover and profits of his company or client.

Of course, if they are even moderately disciplined, then they will want this reputation to be at its highest levels amongst those publics that the organisation depends upon for its success – such as, customers, employees, legislators, factory neighbours, shareholders and so on.

■ Focus the public relations personnel on the objectives

To get the best out of public relations people, the marketers need to keep them firmly focused on the marketing objectives. This cannot be repeated too often – nor can the public relations results be checked against the original objectives too often. If public relations professionals are invited and constantly encouraged to work within this framework, they are more likely to deliver the performance.

On the other hand, for public relations professionals to get the best out of the marketing team, they will need to keep repeating that they have responsibility to address a broader audience than those just directly impacted by the marketing. Typically, they may have responsibilities for employees, for the community within which the company operates, local and national legislators, shareholders and city analysts, plus many others.

It may be part of their job to warn marketing colleagues about any proposed marketing initiatives which might be damaging to the reputation of the company. As an illustration, some years ago, a member of Philips marketing department proposed a promotion for a business system that was built around a gambling theme: a free set of poker dice for business enquirers was one of the incentives.

At a planning meeting, the public relations person asked whether a proportion of the market might feel uncomfortable about gambling. If national indicators applied, a small but important proportion would be actively opposed on conscientious grounds. This view was reinforced by the coincidental discovery that the purchasing director of a key customer was a Methodist lay-preacher who had firm views on the topic. After discussion, the main elements of the scheme were retained but the incentives were adapted to business desk items – something less likely to cause offence.

The marketing director of Vent-Axia once stopped his public relations consultant from developing an impressive and effective programme of government relations. He was right: it bore no relation to company objectives. I know because I was that public relations consultant. It was many years ago, at an early stage in my career, but the constant driving of all activity by that marketing director towards achieving the marketing objective produced some remarkable results – sales growth year on year, profits up, an excellent trade and consumer reputation, literally tens of thousands of enquiries generated through the public relations which, at one stage, represented 85 per cent of all sales enquiries generated by all methods then deployed.

■ Key corporate audiences are outside marketing's brief

If you accept traditional definitions of marketing being about satisfying customer needs profitably, then it is clear that the discipline is responsible for part of the business – but not all of the business. Clearly, this part of the business will be the absolute core and is essential to operating success. Indeed, without this central marketing focus, nothing else matters.

There are many audiences of importance that are outside the traditional marketing area of responsibility. Many employees may play a minor role in company/customer relations and some will play virtually no role at all. It might be stretching logic to claim that the fork-lift truck driver, the lathe operator, the maintenance engineer or the canteen assistant have a direct contribution to make to company marketing beyond their responsibilities to make the product to the best possible quality. Even in a total-quality organisation their contribution to better customer relations may be limited. All may be an active part of the public relations team of the company but some will only be observers of marketing at work.

Other audiences that may be important to the organisation but not central to its marketing might include investors, suppliers, factory communities, city analysts, legislators, trade and professional bodies and many others.

Of course, all have some influence upon the market and the credibility of the organisation. If shareholders are unhappy about performance, city analysts have gloomy predictions for the future, suppliers are late delivering raw materials because of poor payment records, factory neighbours are picketing the plants, employees are constantly on strike, then obviously these will not have a beneficial effect on the marketing. Such actions could create negative comment. However, that is not the same as saying that these groups of people have a primary responsibility for marketing, or even are part of the marketing resources of the organisation.

■ Marketing must be the core but not the only discipline

Recently some definitions of marketing have tried to embrace all the relationships between the organisation and groups of importance to its success. However, many feel that this is stretching the responsibility too far and may even dilute the power of the marketing area of responsibility. Even senior marketing people question whether this is a credible approach. Often the view is that marketing is the core business discipline with primary responsibility for the marketing audiences and that is quite enough for marketing professionals to handle.

In contrast, public relations professionals believe that their discipline has a responsibility for relationships with all audiences. For this reason – and the fact that perceptions are shaped by what the organisation does as well as says – public relations is a strategic force.

Few (though some) claim that marketing is part of public relations. Most public relations professionals believe that public relations is (or should be) an essential part of the marketing mix, able to contribute in ways that are not quite matched by any other of the communications disciplines. Yet they accept that public relations is not the *only* communications discipline; other areas such as advertising and sales promotion have a level of specialised expertise that only a tiny minority of public relations people would claim to have the skill to be able to manage – unlike their marketing colleagues who must manage and co-ordinate all such disciplines within marketing.

However, most public relations people would point out that the non-marketing audiences are also important to the success of the organisation and that ensuring that they have positive attitudes is part of the public relations brief.

■ Get advertising and public relations people co-operating

Public relations and advertising have so much in common that you would imagine that the professionals in these two areas would get on well together. This is not always the case.

Advertising and public relations are both important disciplines in the support of any marketing initiative. But one area for potential friction between the respective professionals arises from the unavoidable fact that advertising is a tactical communications technique (however important it may be to the corporate destiny) whilst public relations is a strategic philosophy (however tactically it may be managed by some less visionary practitioners).

Public relations is all about the development of policies that are sensitive to public concerns and that will win public goodwill and support; it involves listening before speaking. Advertising can attempt to cover these areas but when it successfully does so, it has become public relations; for advertising is all about projecting agreed messages. Indeed, when it is a one-way process, it is not strictly communications.

However, the two disciplines come together in marketing where each projects messages through channels of communication to target specific audiences. Each (properly planned) is based upon research to gain a full understanding of existing perceptions to ensure the communications efforts are directed with maximum efficiency towards creating the most positive attitudes and the most constructive actions by those targeted. Each discipline demands skills in objective analysis, clinical planning but also emotive creativity. Each discipline is managed through departments or agencies that employ some of the most talented and committed people in business today. In each, the top practitioners are almost household names and are highly rewarded. And both advertising and public relations demand instinct and flair – yet can rarely work without critical standards of organisation and logistical control. They have so much in common. . .

And yet, and yet. Mutual feelings between advertising and public relations professionals are more likely to be suspicion and hostility than co-operation and admiration.

Consider the differences. Often, advertising is a marketing function reporting to some level of marketing management. Public relations is more likely to be corporate and frequently will be reporting to the chairman or chief executive. Few chairman play much of a direct role in advertising decisions but, equally, few chairmen delegate the management of the corporate reputation amongst investors and shareholders to anyone other than a public relations professional reporting directly to them.

Advertising often carries responsibility for shifting volumes of product or service – or, at least, creating the environment within which these products and services can be sold. To do this, advertising usually commands a substantial budget.

Public relations professionals may have the responsibility for the corporate reputation, may report directly to the chairman, may be on first name terms with cabinet ministers and newspaper editors – but are likely to be operating on budgets that may be minus one or more noughts in comparison with that put at the disposal of their advertising colleagues.

■ Differing access and budgets can cause friction

Understandably, sometimes advertising professionals resent the access that public relations colleagues have. In some cases, they will see the public relations preparation as being informal or even casual. The size of the budget means that research discipline must almost always underpin advertising; yet the modesty of the public relations budget often makes this research base too large a proportion to be the norm.

Public relations professionals often feel that their planning and preparation – as well as the implementation – can be limited by the smaller budgets usually available. These may not allow them to undertake the level of research that even the least significant advertising campaign would justify. They may look ruefully at the advertising expenditure where, perhaps, a five-point cut might go almost unnoticed, yet this small percentage could be doubling, or more, the total public relations spend.

A famous international electronics company bought a specialised company to extend its product range and paid some £50 million for this opportunity. It allocated £4 million for advertising.

This was a new product in a new sector with new technologies that were not understood by the market. The company allocated £35 000 to the public relations task of explaining the acquisition, the relationship to the company's corporate objectives and educating the market to a new technology that it did not understand.

■ Resolve friction by improving the briefing

Yet, as many effective, well-managed companies have shown, this friction is completely unnecessary. There are some simple steps that need to be taken to get these professionals working effectively together. This will offer potential to substantially multiply the effectiveness of each's work – or 'leverage the communications investments', as our American friends would say.

In practice, these basics should be applied to ensure smooth and effective co-operation between *everyone* working in a discipline within the marketing mix. A good department may not be a democracy, but it will be run to ensure that all feel valued and can contribute their best, understanding even those decisions that do not go in their favour.

- *Objectives*. Ensure all members of the team have an input to the marketing objectives and that the specific objectives for each discipline become a subset to these.

- *Briefing*. Before any new initiatives, brief managers together, allowing them to propose support programmes which, in turn, should be presented to the whole team.
- *Planning*. Ask each discipline to propose the timetable and resources necessary for their suggested programme *before* allocating budgets and responsibilities.
- *Approvals*. The boss decides the final programme, but make sure that all receive the same document so that all understand the roles and responsibilities of the others.
- *Reporting*. Set up a standard procedure for progress reports and circulate a consolidated version of these to all, on a weekly or monthly basis.
- *Recognition*. Criticise in private and praise in public, recognising outstanding performance in the covering notes to the consolidated progress report.
- *Evaluation*. Expect each discipline to suggest the best procedures for measuring performance and adjusting the activity but, over time, get these harmonised and discussed by all.
- Then back to the start again.

Public relations in action

Performance criteria set the agenda for change

Appraisal central to AEA communications planning

Public relations was a central discipline in the process of changing the trading company of the Atomic Energy Authority to AEA Technology which was eventually privatised. As Andrew McCree, director of corporate affairs for the company explained, the organisation always had a strong culture based on scientific, research and public service values. Through the periods of change, the staff (for the most part highly qualified and committed to the old values of the organisation) had to learn to come to terms with commercial practices and realities. And for many this was hard.

Whilst corporate communications within the new organisation has not had to justify its position, it has had to produce results. The measure of the change of the body is indicated by the reduction in manpower from 40 000 people in the early 1960s to a staff of around 3500 at the time that it was privatised in 1996. A central task was informing groups outside the organisation of the changes – and these included City audiences, media commentators and government.

Targets needed to measure change

McCree believes that commitment from the top to the use of communications as a strategic tool for the management of change was absolutely vital.

Members of the corporate communications group were expected to work with senior management to help them to clarify and achieve organisational objectives. This process of discussion helped management to become clearer in its thinking. Communicators brought their own perspective to the organisation, as well as feedback to management on the perception and understanding of policies, both from within the company and from external groups.

In addition, to achieve commercial success, it was important to clarify the interface between the public relations and the marketing functions.

Over the 1980s and 1990s AEA Technology was growing international business and changing the composition of its customer base. Corporate communications had to assist marketing by helping to create an environment in which such marketing activities could be more successful. A plan was developed to establish a more visible and recognisable single corporate identity for the company and this was developed through corporate advertising and continuity relations work with audiences such as the media, customers, opinion leaders, City analysts and commentators.

In AEA Technology, corporate communications and marketing are kept as separate departments each, according to Andrew McCree, with their own unique perspective. This would not have produced harmonised efforts if there had not been close and trusting collaboration between these professionals.

Appraisal must be a discipline

To measure the effectiveness of the contribution, AEA Technology approaches planning, implementation and appraisal in a disciplined way. Research is used as the means of understanding what AEA Technology's publics understand and feel, but it is also used to develop programme approaches, to modify programmes in progress and to evaluate what is being achieved.

Public relations objectives are drafted to directly support business objectives. The planning process for communications involves an analysis of the organisation's business plans in order to help develop such matching and supporting communications objectives. Research is also undertaken to determine the behaviour of central audiences, as well as changes in perceptions, opinions and attitudes.

The management believes that it is easier to justify expenditures when it can be shown that the activities supported are having demonstrable results. Achievements should bridge the communications and marketing areas, showing tangible improvements in both reputation and in sales. Measurable results, Andrew McCree believes, should be the start of the communications process and not just its end.

CHAPTER 2

Public relations: the management of reputation

SOME PUBLIC RELATIONS FUNDAMENTALS

To listen, to understand and to exchange views in mutual persuasion through gentle reason, that is the especial, elevating quality that makes people human.
Mimi Rabachage (1889–1974), philosopher, in *Bouffée* (1939)

■ The audiences control the organisation

Customers are the key audience for marketing. So they are with public relations – but alongside employees, shareholders, neighbours, regulators and many others.

One marketing philosophy is that the customers 'own' the organisation. And, in many ways, they do. With customers the organisation may be able to do almost anything, but without them, nothing. Public relations across the organisation will have responsibilities for all audiences and not just the customers and prospective customers.

Within the marketing framework, public relations approaches to ensure effective two-way communications with different types of customers will clearly vary – from the internal customers and sales personnel, through to the end users of the products and services; with intermediaries such as wholesalers, distributors, importers, exporters agents and retailers; from specifiers, orderers, authorisers and to users – who may be different people with different purchases. Of course, the techniques to support the marketing of consumer durables or business services may need to be adapted, but they will work to the same fundamental principles.

■ Public relations is the ambassador and conscience of the enterprise

It would be difficult today to find a leading corporation that did not have a formalised marketing function – though that would not have been the case forty or fifty years ago. Yet if marketing is seen as being the function of satisfying customer needs profitably, then it has existed ever since commercial organisations began trading, from the first market stalls and barrows. Until the latter part of the twentieth century, marketing has been a function waiting to be discovered, often carried out by many different people with different job titles.

In many respects, public relations is a business discipline in a similar position to marketing a decade or two ago. The need to manage the relationships between the organisation and the many publics upon which it depends for success has been a fact of business life from the year dot. Similarly to marketing, this craft was always practised long before it adopted the title of public relations.

Every organisation has public relations whether it likes it or not. In recent years the need to draw these diverse skills together into one managed function has been recognised, often adopted with enthusiasm; virtually every one of the *Fortune 500* and the *Times Top 1000* companies now has formalised public relations in its operations.

This acceptance may not be quite as universal as you move further down the scale but, as with marketing, it will come. Also, at present, public relations is less likely to be recognised in the boardroom, with a professional sitting alongside his or her marketing colleague – but that also will come.

As public relations has been gaining acceptance within commercial companies, so too has it been winning recognition in other organisations, such as trade unions, charities, government departments and professional bodies.

■ Apply discipline in managing public relations

In creating or managing a public relations function, it is important to remember this relatively short history. Some of the best practitioners may have no formal qualifications and may even have spent part of their career in other, though related areas such as journalism, advertising, sales, even marketing.

Although public relations has been developing its own body of theory and case experience it is still in a process of evolution. It has often been practised – and still is by some – in an unstructured way, much as marketing was just a few short decades ago. This means that, in some respects, the discipline is rather undisciplined. Some practitioners may have no management training and their idiosyncrasies may not always make them good team players. This is becoming less true, particularly for younger professionals; indeed many consultancies and departments are run by people setting entry standards that they could not meet themselves.

■ Look for qualified personnel

Many colleges and universities are now running courses in public relations, some to a high level. This will increase the quality of many new entrants to the business and allow marketing directors to set similar qualification levels as they do for other professionals on their teams.

There are few other professional management disciplines experiencing such a fast rate of development, particularly, according to the Institute of Public Relations (IPR), in areas such as the management of reputation, issues and crisis management and the fast-changing skills demanded by the introduction of new media. All this underlines the importance of qualifications. Public relations is management discipline, comments the IPR in its *Guide on Qualifications*, parallel with finance, personnel, marketing and quality management. One benchmark for qualifications was the introduction of the public relations education and training matrix. This is believed to be unique in the UK for a professional body and charts five levels where differing elements of professional knowledge and communication techniques, management and business skills are required by public relations practitioners. The stages range from new entrants through to the most senior, experienced practitioner.

Coincidentally, the author was the initiator of this matrix, as vice-chairman of the Public Relations Consultancies Association and one of the small group of people keen to see practitioners behaving in a disciplined way. Though most professionals believed that this was a positive step in the right direction, some of the older hands still argued that public relations was an art that could not be taught.

Fairly typically, the author began his career as a journalist, moved into advertising copywriting and then was offered a 'promotion' to run the public relations department of a small advertising agency; I was well into my career before, untypically, I gained marketing and CAM diplomas in advertising and public relations.

Of course, there are many outstanding practitioners – including some without formal qualifications – and they are at work both in-house and within consultancies. Some excellent graduates and qualified professionals from other disciplines are moving into public relations because of the opportunities that it offers. In some universities, public relations is now first or second career choice.

Public relations is a fast growing business with rising standards; the UK market is the second biggest in the world after the United States – and even many American practitioners believe the standards that apply in the UK are better than in the US. The increasing skill and discrimination that are being deployed in appointing staff or consultancies are separating the good from the not so good.

■ Professional bodies set industry standards

The professional bodies for public relations are well established across the globe. In the UK, the Public Relations Consultants Association (PRCA) is a trade body representing consultancies and the Institute of Public Relations (IPR) is the professional body representing individuals. Many of the principals of PRCA consultancy members are also members of the IPR. Similar bodies to the institute have been established in each country across the world which has an organised public relations market – close to 100 at the last count.

The PRCA has taken the lead in helping many countries to set up their own equivalent bodies and many are now joined in an international consultancy associations' federation, ICO. The professional body across much of Europe, CERP, is the Centre Européen des Relations Publiques. Also at the international level, the International Public Relations Association (IPRA) is the professional body representing some of the foremost practitioners operating in the world.

In the United States, public relations has long been offered as an academic course in many universities, such courses often growing out of the schools of media, journalism or communications. Much the same development, although coming from a later start, has been seen in countries such as Australia, Canada, Germany, India, the Netherlands and the UK.

Public relations has grown in effectiveness and importance partly because of the parallel growth in the public's demand for information. In the business sector, the consumer has become extremely well-educated and demands more information about both the products or services available and the organisations that are offering these. People prefer to invest in, work with and buy from organisations that they hold in high regard.

Public relations has become part of the freedom of choice where manufacturers and suppliers can present the best case possible – and the public can decide in the court of public opinion. In that sense, public relations (and marketing) are part of our commercial democracy, offering choice in the competition for the goodwill, support and (and in the case of marketing) the purchasing power of the public.

■ Develop and project the corporate personality

Public relations has been described as the projection of the personality of the organisation; this echoes some of the philosophies that drive marketing.

Used properly, public relations can help to define and then to project the personality of the organisation to its key audiences. The corporate personality is what the organisation is all about; it reflects its beliefs, values and aspirations. In the well-planned organisation, senior executives will want to define and control this personality and ensure that all aspects (particularly communications) are consistent with this. They will not want the corporate reputation to be shaped by chance or distorted by third parties working to a different agenda. For this reason, public relations is often allocated the primary responsibility for building, projecting and protecting the corporate reputation.

Even if a major part of the public relations activity is in support of the marketing function, it will still have responsibilities to the chairman or chief executive for communications with other publics outside marketing. Because of this central management role in the relationships between the organisation and its publics, 'management of reputation' has become the most useful, popular definition of public relations.

Consistency in what the company does and what it says is critically important if this personality is to be strongly established. As in personal relations, we expect those we trust to behave in a consistent way. If they do not, this causes us to be concerned, uncertain and possibly wary, even hostile.

We might doubt whether a company that cannot handle telephone calls in a brisk, efficient, yet friendly way can really manage any of the other relationships we might wish to have with it – whether as investors, employees, neighbours or customers. We may be impressed by the cleanliness and good design of a Shell petrol station, the warmth and friendliness of the staff and the obvious investment in customer services and training – but if that company cannot manage the disposal of its disused oil production facilities – or, worse, cannot intelligently inform us as interested members of the public what its policies are in these areas, we certainly become confused and hostile.

If Cunard see its customers on the cruise of a lifetime who complain about travelling on a floating building site, beset by noise and mess, as 'whingers', it is no surprise that the management runs the organisation into financial difficulties.

■ Marketing plans can be ruined by unrelated public issues

The best possible marketing programme can be completely undone by public relations failures – including problems which may not even be in the marketing arena or even under the control of public relations. If there is a risk of this happening, then the marketing professionals have the right – indeed responsibility – to ensure that the most senior members of the company take the necessary action. Usually only the marketing personnel can foul up company marketing but almost anyone can make a mess of company public relations, from the chairman to a single lorry driver or salesman.

As an illustration, it was the incompetence of Excalibur's operational personnel – not its marketing – that forced the company to fold, despite having come through a successful period of trading. It was the crass ineptitude of the speech writers for Gerald Ratner which brought about the ultimate collapse of that company – not the marketing people; he famously quipped at an Institute of Directors' conference that some of his products would not last as long as a Marks & Spencers' prawn sandwich.

Case after horrifying case could be cited. Indeed, if the marketing people cannot convince the chief executive or the chairman to take personal responsibility for the ultimate control of corporate public relations, then the marketing people might consider putting the processes in place themselves. Whatever structure might be set up, one central factor will decide success or failure – getting the public relations responsibility carried by a credible and competent professional.

A useful working definition of public relations is: those efforts used by management to identify and close any gap between how the organisation is seen by its key publics and how it would like to be seen.

Of course, there are many other factors that are essential to success, above all, marketing itself. The best public relations will not compensate for weaknesses in production, quality, service or personnel and many other important business areas. It is likely that an active public relations policy will expose rather than hide such weaknesses.

The official definition of the craft given by the Institute of Public Relations (1994) is: 'the planned and sustained effort to establish and maintain goodwill and mutual understanding between an organisation and its publics'.

Some definitions of public relations only cover 'mutual understanding'. This is not satisfactory for such definitions focus on the public's knowledge but not necessarily on its opinions and attitudes. Clearly, information is only part of communications, in the same way that communications is only part of public relations. For what the company does is as important as what it says.

Marketing as the management process responsible for satisfying customer requirements profitably implies the need to create the best business environment within which these products or services can be sold and supported. It is not unreasonable to extend this to the creation of goodwill between the organisation offering the products and services and the purchasers of these. This is the normal situation within an information democracy.

■ Make public relations work across the organisation

Organisations can attempt to win the reputation they would like; whatever they do, they will get the one they deserve. Current public relations practitioners do not see themselves as just as publicists but as custodians of the public reputation of the organisations they represent. Their craft may involve publicity functions – but it should also include the responsibility for advising on and helping develop the stance the organisation takes towards issues: strategic policy-making. If the organisation is to win the goodwill and support of those publics upon whom it depends for success, then what it does matters as much as what it says. Its attitude to these publics will shape *their* attitudes to the organisation and its products and services.

True public relations starts before communications and should be all about company policy – and not just the brands. This has not always been the case. In Europe, as an example, for many years Unilever policy was that the corporate reputation should be carried by the brands. The company felt its corporate policies were of little interest to its customers. More recently, as with many large corporations, it has realised that the organisation behind the brands is important.

Marketing presents and develops the brands and their values while, in a sense, the corporate public relations is 'marketing the company'. This was brought to the forefront by the detergent wars when claims and counterclaims on product performance and damage to clothes as well as worries about dermatological hazards made the public deeply concerned about the corporate philosophies behind those famous brands.

A similar shift in public focus towards the senior executives who run the corporations happened when IBM and Apple ran into trouble; when Pepsi-Cola challenged Coca-Cola; when ICI split off Zeneca as a separate company; when Ford and General Motors faced major legal challenges over product safety that brought their corporate policies under scrutiny.

'Marketing public relations' can be one of the most powerful and effective influences within the broader craft of marketing. It should work in harmony not only with other marketing communications disciplines such as advertising and sales promotion but with other elements of public relations targeted at those audiences that are not always considered part of the marketing respon-sibility – including , employees, shareholders, suppliers, factory neighbours and government.

■ Corporate reputation can affect commercial success

However these responsibilities may be allocated, the success of all business activities – including marketing, sales and, therefore, profit – are dependent to some extent on how the company is regarded. Corporate reputation can be the most valuable asset. To quote George Washington: 'With public opinion you can do anything – without it, nothing.'

Attitude is a critical factor in virtually every decision. In business there is an understandable pressure to focus only on the tangible factors that make business sense – asking, for example, is the price competitive? Are the working conditions acceptable? Will this earn the right return for the shareholders? Might the factory neighbours accept this planning application? Most of the audiences upon which every company depends for business success are not in business with the company. They may have a different agenda: employees may be looking at security or career options; shareholders comparing investments for their pensions; local politicians seeking a vote-winning business/community alliance.

One aim in many public relations programmes will be to win the hearts and not just the minds of these key audiences. Sometimes managers rely too much on logic and believe all decisions are made on a rational basis alone. The factor they may overlook is that decisions can be influenced by opinions and attitudes. One of the prime functions of public relations is to manage company policies and associated communications to build the regard in which the organisation is held.

When Shell was challenged by Greenpeace over its plans to sink the Brent Spar oil platform in deep sea, the share price dropped and customers began to boycott company products. Obviously neither the products nor prices had changed, but the public either did not like what they were hearing or, at least, were confused. The failure to manage the public issue, regardless of who might be right or wrong, was immediately reflected in shareholders' perceptions of the value of the company and consumers' inclination to buy the products.

When British Airways explained to its staff that customers were number one – and trained employees in how to make their travellers *feel* that they were number one – sales soared. Customers liked being treated as if they mattered. In many cases, this approach proved to be more important to flyers than the ticket price.

■ Policy must be supported from the top of the organisation

Public relations is an essential top management responsibility – not an optional extra, or a mechanical function that can be delegated to administrators.

Public relations must be a two-way activity – listening to what the public thinks, as well as projecting the organisation's messages. It follows that public relations efforts can only be effective where the aims of the organisation are compatible with the aims of the public. The concept of the hidden persuader does not make sense.

Any failure of the directors to be on top of communications could be most damaging. Should the company experience difficult times, it is likely that shareholders or statutory bodies might become interested in how the public relations aspects of key issues were being considered at board level, as they unfolded.

Sometimes it transpires, at a time of crisis, that critical questions on public relations have been raised but ignored. Companies that do not review their corporate communications at board level are taking a risk. Yet with proper planning, the review of a responsibly run programme takes little time. Indeed, the fact that the board signs off policy may be one vital element in ensuring that the programme is responsibly run.

When Sir Adrian Cadbury, chairman of the UK Committee on the Financial Aspects of Corporate Governance, was gathering evidence, he confirmed that communications, particularly investor public relations, was an essential and integral element within proper corporate governance, as was well appreciated by the City of London. When it was subsequently published in 1993, the *Code of Best Practice on the Financial Aspects of Corporate Governance* specifically required that the board should have a formal schedule of matters for decision to ensure that control of the company was firmly in its hands. This referred, of course, to financial matters where communications were central. In addition, the Code also said that it was the board's duty to present a balanced and understandable assessment of the company's position. Again this focused on financial communications.

■ Support for the company has to be earned

The responsibilities of directors are extending steadily to encompass all aspects of corporate communications. However, few companies produce written communications policies and fewer publish them. Such policies can be an invaluable way to help define the responsibilities of the board and senior executives.

The ideal reputation for the organisation will not be earned by accident. It will be won through application, direction and commitment. Therefore, managers should ensure that the public relations implications of all company operations are considered in all appropriate policies and plans. Ideally, the mission statement (or the corporate objectives) will include an appropriate commitment to the development of the corporate reputation. This will also need to be reflected in all business and marketing plans.

As an illustration, marketing may be all about satisfying customer needs profitably, but it also has a responsibility to develop and reinforce the reputation of the organisation. A suitable statement in the marketing plan about the reputation objective will help avoid the adoption of unacceptable sales techniques or promotional activities – say, those that may be better for short-term results than they are for the longer-term perceptions among those who matter.

Despite fluctuating fortunes, IBM, as an illustration, follows policies that reflect its belief in behaving properly. People relate to such decent values. Being well regarded by the public creates a good reputation. People like to buy from and work for those that have good reputations. Companies which people like to deal with have an advantage over those which are not popular. If IBM products and prices are as good as its promised services and proven values, it will have a competitive edge.

Companies with shorter-term horizons may risk being more cavalier with customers, but those with long-term aims need the goodwill of those who can make or break them – as IBM proved when they traded through the difficult times.

Many companies are choosing to define and publish their mission. They make a formal commitment against which individual managers and employees can measure their own performance or, indeed, direct their staff, peers or even their bosses when standards appear to be in conflict with some of the points in the mission statement.

■ Reputation is a board responsibility

One of the weaknesses of some corporate mission statements is that companies will tend to write them to be broad enough to cover most eventualities; this means they do not have quite enough focus. One recommendation might be to start with a general mission statement but to refine it over a period of time. Certainly no company should be publishing the identical mission statement year after year in, for example, the annual report unless they are convinced that this is the definitive version. It can always be improved and the sharper the focus of the mission statement, theoretically, the sharper the focus of the organisation.

The only satisfactory reporting method must be for public relations to be a regular and routine board item. Directors should not just be concerning themselves with communications when there is a problem. Perhaps winning a good company reputation is a little like building a good marriage – it requires constant work, through the good times and the bad. When problems strike, it may be too late to apply remedial treatment. Effective relations between the organisation and its various publics require constant attention.

Public relations strategy might be reviewed once or twice a year with marketing management on those matters relating to marketing support and with the board on the corporate areas. A strategy review paper might cover the following areas:

- *The present position.* What are the attitudes of those whose goodwill the company needs for success? What are the perceptions of customers, employees, shareholders and others?
- *The ambitions.* What is to be achieved over the coming period? What objectives have been written and are these quantified and set to a timetable for achievement?
- *The strategy.* What approaches do we propose to use to turn the objectives into reality? How might these impact on other aspects of company operations?
- *The tactics.* What communications methods are to be used? Who is directing and implementing the programme? Are there company contingency plans in place to deal with the unexpected?
- *The themes.* What messages will be projected through the planned campaigns? What gaps are there between reality and perception? Are all the communications activities reinforcing agreed messages?
- *The timetable.* Are there significant activities in the corporate calendar that have public relations implications? Is the programme scheduled realistically to manage communications initiatives?
- *The issues.* What might be coming up over the horizon for which we should have plans? Have we checked the input we might need from other departments?
- *The competition.* Are there current or anticipated activities by competitors that should be countered? How is their public relations effectiveness, say in the tone of media coverage?
- *The resources.* What manpower and budget will be deployed to achieve the objectives? Does the activity require manpower or budget from other departments?
- *Evaluation.* How effective is the programme? What are the achievements to date and expected, measured against the objectives?

■ Create the optimum business environment

Public relations as a marketing support technique is well understood. It is less often appreciated as a strategic approach to undertaking business, creating the environment within which the marketing efforts can be most successful.

Major business successes have been built on the strength of effective public relations. Brand awareness and loyalty can be more credibly developed through communications channels.

McDonald's identified public relations as central to the business strategy originally developed by the founder of the company, the late Ray Kroc. His policy, continued by the company, was to make a significant commitment to local community relations, consistently year after year, market by market, to build a deep consumer trust in the business. For McDonald's, public relations is not an option. As senior executives have commented, the payback is there for all to see.

Get the corporate projection right and the company will have the business environment in which to thrive with the right products, service, prices and people. Get it wrong and, whatever the quality of the rest, the company may not survive. So, where does public relations fit in and how does it relate to marketing?

Public relations is an essential element in the building of goodwill. Any marketing plan that does not consider public relations is likely to be dangerously deficient. One MORI survey confirmed that goodwill towards the company is closely linked to public perceptions of product quality – a central element in marketing. Some 70 per cent of a sample of the general public believed that reputable companies do not sell poor quality products.

Also, shoppers are more likely to try something new from a trusted name. Such an advantage, built through marketing techniques (including relevant public relations and advertising) can be significant in sales and market share terms.

Other studies have demonstrated the direct relationship between familiarity and high regard. All such evidence confirms the importance of the brands as well as the company behind the brands. The credibility of public relations as a communications technique which tends to be trusted by consumers can be important in the marketing mix – and certainly able to justify its own significant proportion of the spend.

The goodwill of a company may well be its largest single asset. With consumer goods companies, this goodwill is often represented as the value of the brands. In recent years there has been much debate about whether these should be shown on the balance sheet.

■ Public relations and marketing contribute to asset value

The Accounting Standards Committee in the UK suggested that a brand value should be written off against profits over an agreed period of twenty or more years. Of course, this makes no sense as high-profile brands such as Heineken, Mars, Range Rover, Stella Artois or Tide may be of vastly increased value and some of these have been around for fifty or more years. Of course, in some cases it becomes difficult to separate the brand value from the company – particularly where the same name is in use, as in the cases of Ford, Hotpoint, Kellogg and Olivetti.

Consider the commercial value that brands can have and, therefore, the potential return on the marketing effort that can build those brands. Nestlé bought Rowntree Macintosh for a sum in excess of £2.5 billion in 1988 when the physical assets represented only 20 per cent of this price. The balance was to pay for marketing expertise, distribution capability and the range of brands. In other words, Nestlé were prepared to pay five times as much as the assets to acquire these brands and the mechanics that had been perfected for delivering the brands to the market. Similar deals carried out in the late 1980s valued companies at four or five times the asset value.

Whatever company policy, it is still important that the public relations keeps the brand statements separate from the values of the company. Ideally, there should be two public relations programmes, promoting the products and projecting the corporation – separate but co-ordinated.

The marketing approach to the corporation can put a fresh perspective on the management of one very important asset: the company name. Sometimes companies can create a whole aura around an organisation. The statement that 'We try harder' was credible and worked hard for Avis around the world.

Good public relations not only builds brand loyalty but can reinforce customer relations efforts, backing both the salesforce and customer services operations. In the car rental industry, Hertz built a world brand using marketing and public relations policies that were consistent around the world, even where local management were resistant to global branding. Public relations was used to promote the customer experience.

The thinking was that a brand should spell consistency wherever it was developed. Business travellers and holidaymakers alike were more reassured at the prospect of hiring a car which would be prepared to conform everywhere to the same high standard – and was provided on comparable terms through identical payment methods. Above all, the customers' relationship with the company would be recognised, even if this was the first time they had visited Manhattan, Madras or Madrid. Local variations may be attractive in food, fashion or shopping but not in car rental.

Avis later fought this challenge through similar harmonising of operations, plus an appealing, impertinent challenge to the leader – effectively, 'we're number two so we have to try harder'. A decade later number three in the Europe market merged some ten or so operations – one owned by Volkswagen and one by Renault – to form Europcar. Various old brands were dropped, such as Inter-rent and Godfrey Davis. Co-ordinated public relations, working within a clear marketing framework, across all operating markets helped project the new offer and establish the new brand with customers.

■ Monitor all issues that can affect marketing credibility

The best laid marketing plans can sometimes be devastated by factors that are outside the control of marketing management. Confidence in products has been shaken by health, safety or pollution scares which often attract wide news coverage.

A couple of angry shareholders at an annual general meeting have been known to attract more attention than the announcement of a massive new production facility. A few neighbours have been influential in stopping planning permission for extensions to factories. Public relations for the company, its values and aims will be important, but this will be most effective if it is consistent with the messages projected through marketing.

An historical problem with mercury pollution at one site created poor local media coverage for international chemical giant, Rhône–Poulenc. Under an enlightened management, the company developed possibly some of the finest environmental policies in the industry and called in professional public relations resources to improve community relations. These joint initiatives were so successful that, with the full co-operation of local communities, the company has since invested over £50 million on that site in new research and manufacturing facilities. Community relations was essential to enable the products to be properly marketed; a poor community reputation is equally damaging to sales.

A chicken production facility jointly owned by a leading feed company and a large retailer had such a smell problem that local residents successfully blocked planning permissions for extensions which would have created many new jobs. The problems could not be solved by technical improvements alone. The goodwill and support of the local people had to be won through a public relations programme to show that the company listened and acted vigorously to end the nuisance and become a good neighbour.

Cargill corn-milling plants have been threatened with closure through complaints from neighbours over smells. When Union Carbide suffered the tragic accident at Bhopal in India, planning permissions for many factory developments at locations around the world were blocked, even where the processes were unrelated to the chemicals involved in the Bhopal incident. With both companies, technical improvements were successfully introduced in parallel with effective communications to win community support.

■ Some campaigns should be led by public relations

In all these cases, the product marketing could not solve the problem and sales were threatened by issues remote from the normal responsibilities of the marketing function.

Some marketing campaigns will be led by advertising. Everyday products of limited news value and which are frequently bought may need the strength of advertising to lift them above competition, stress their special features and benefits, remind the purchaser of their brand values. Examples might include soft drinks, coffee and most grocery products. Public relations may be used in support to reach both trade and consumer audiences. Coca-Cola has an active involvement in soccer, as a case in point.

Yet many products and services can best be supported with public relations, with this discipline taking the lead. This will be particularly relevant where the product or service has a broad interest because it is new or affects the quality of our lives. For example. First Direct, Europe's first telephone home banking service, established its position of strength almost entirely through public relations.

A useful exercise is to ensure that the advertising, sales, promotion and public relations professionals identify the balance and the priorities for each craft. Of course, advertising and public relations should not be viewed as competitive but should be run as complementary, reinforcing communications techniques. Therefore, liaison between the advertising and public relations must be close and effective.

Public relations alone cannot win orders, generate profit or reduce costs. However, used skilfully, public relations can substantially enhance the effectiveness of marketing, helping to develop the goodwill of the key corporate audiences. In essence, along with the other communications disciplines, it can create the business environment within which the marketing offer can be presented.

To paraphrase the famous McGraw-Hill advertisement: I know your company, you have a good reputation, your products and services are well regarded. What is the proposition you wish to put to me?

Public relations in action

Strategy to change perceptions of Rover

Marketing and public relations project consistent messages

Effective marketing campaigns can deploy public relations to win customer support for major changes – where the marketing itself is part of the process of change.

Yet, even today, some companies think that their marketing strategies must be kept confidential from their customers – as if marketing is 'being done to them' rather than involving them in a process of mutual benefit.

But in progressive companies marketing is a discipline that defines how they feel about their customers and other publics. In Rover, as an example, marketing has been combined with a programme of corporate and product communications which, believes Bernard Carey, corporate affairs director of Rover Group, has been responsible for a complete change of perceptions of the company. 'Our new position has been the subject of so much positive comment, it is difficult to remember the "bad old days" when BL, as the company was known then, was seen as an industrial basket case. For our continuing reputation, public relations plays a central role and we are firm believers in keeping marketing and public relations messages consistent.'

The Rover Group took the philosophy of openness one stage further than co-ordinated programmes. Management developed a strategy based upon detailed research with customers and had the vision to publish the resulting strategies as a document, freely available to customers.

The director of Rover Group marketing, Rod Ramsay, believes that marketing is a partnership between the company and the market. He illustrates the crucial role that the customer plays when he quotes the experience of the launch of the new Range Rover.

The company needed to replace a classic which had been around for the previous 25 years – a premium brand which had acquired extraordinary levels of customer loyalty, imagery and affection; it also represented a crucially important profit contribution to the business. The company therefore had to get the launch of the new Range Rover right first time and, in particular, ensure that it involved their loyal customers.

Marketing management developed a launch strategy which was almost completely 'below the line' and which featured virtually no advertising in the traditional sense. Rover set out not only to launch the product but to achieve a breakthrough in the quality of customer relationships, wherever in the world they happened to be.

Central to the plan was the simultaneous launch of the new vehicle to 50 000 customers in over 50 markets worldwide. Range Rover used innovative direct marketing to invite small groups of customers to exclusive dealer previews of the new car; these used satellite television links to give customers the opportunity to share the insights of guests participating in what were called 'The Epic Experiences'. Five groups of individuals (including celebrities such as Richard Branson) embarked on five different journeys in the new vehicle – in Japan, Africa, the USA, South America and the UK. These journeys were broadcast live into customer previews. The footage produced was also used to create six short films or 'documercials' which were run on Channel 4, replacing conventional television advertising.

In this way, Rover gave each customer a unique, one-off experience, successfully establishing the new Range Rover in the marketplace.

Background

The last ten years have witnessed the turnaround of Rover as a company, and effective marketing has been central to that change.

In the early 1980s Austin Rover was pursuing a strategy of re-establishing itself as a major volume manufacturer. By the mid-1980s it was becoming clear that this product-led recovery was not enough. A new strategy was needed which was *customer-led*.

Consumer research

Customers' opinions had to be sought on the improvements they wanted. Rover started the most comprehensive consumer research programme the industry had ever experienced. Thousands of people were asked to compare each Rover product with its competitors. The objective was to find the correct target markets, and the most motivating marketing and model propositions.

Changing the image

The research revealed a fundamental problem of perception versus reality. Their perceptions were clouded by their image of the company, particular associated with the name Austin.

Rover set out to transform the image of the company and its products. The aim was to move from the image of a publicly owned manufacturer of an unfocused range of brands, to a successful privately owned producer of a range of top quality cars – accompanied by premium standards of marketing, sales and service.

Roverisation

It was a bold aspiration, which grew into a plan known as 'Roverisation' – the re-positioning of the company as:

- A more specialist manufacturer, using the Rover name.
- Producing vehicles claiming a premium position in the market.

Roverisation involved raising the image of the Rover dealer, as people who deliver unmatched, premium standards of customer service.

Marque values

Key to the Roverisation plan was the understanding of what Rover stands for with consumers. These values had to be put into practice by everyone, including Rover's workforce, its dealers and suppliers. Roverisation not only involved a change of marketing strategy; it also brought about a fundamental change of philosophy.

The public face of the company's transformation involved a new name – Rover Cars – and a new identity. The burgundy and cream of Rover was created, and a new livery replaced the old.

The new generation

The new company was launched, heralding a total revitalisation of the product range, which began with the launch of the Rover 200 that year. It was followed by the Rover 400 and Rover Metro, the new Rover 800, the Rover 600, the new Range Rover and the MGF. All increased consumer awareness and market share.

Critical success factors

The success of the new generation of Rover products can be attributed to key factors such as:

- Rover cars are clearly differentiated from their competitors – mainly by their 'Britishness'. Rover has successfully combined the use of wood, leather and quality materials to give a unique feel to the interiors. Distinctive exterior styles, incorporating the Rover grille, have given stronger identity.
- Rover cars are good to drive; with modern, powerful and refined engines, responsive handling and a smooth ride.
- The Rover dealership is a place where consumers will experience extraordinary customer satisfaction, through standards of service second to none.

The future

Rover has established a clear premium position in the marketplace.

The link of Rover with BMW has created the world's largest specialist car manufacturer, with combined worldwide sales of one million vehicles a year (excluding sales of four-wheel drive vehicles). Rover and BMW will retain their respective strengths and traditions.

CHAPTER 3

Managing public relations

THE POLICIES, THE PEOPLE, THE PLANNING

We for a certainty are not the first
Have sat in taverns while the tempest hurled
Their hopeful plans to emptiness, and cursed
Whatever brute and blackguard made the world.

A. E. Houseman (1859–1936), *A Shropshire Lad* (1896)

■ Planning harnesses the power of effective communications

Public relations is the one business discipline that, above all, needs a direction; the best programmes that have achieved the best results are always those built on a clear plan – as demonstrated by winners of the PR Week or the Sword of Excellence awards from the Institute of Public Relations. Such schemes – and the Silver Anvils in the USA and others – recognise that good public relations is both strategic *and* tactical and always results from thought. Programme effectiveness should be measured by achievement and not activity.

Coverage in relevant (or irrelevant) publications, issues of the company newsletter, open days at the factory and briefings for the analysts are not public relations but the by-product of public relations. For public relations has to be all about how perceptions have been favourably changed, to the benefit of the organisation and in line with organisational objectives.

Some philosophers have explored the concept of planning as learning. The view is that people learn by playing and that toys are models of real objects. A plan can be seen as a model of the future – perhaps a toy to help managers learn?

■ The plan is not the solution but the thought process

Generals from Napoleon through to Eisenhower (and later) recognised that the planning process is essential to get everyone heading in the same direction – but the plan itself is often of little consequence. Indeed, too much planning can inhibit creativity, even initiative, as well as absorbing a disproportionate share of management resources. Marketers tend to be results-orientated and can be wary of those who seem planning-obsessed.

This planning torpor used to be called *management by analysis.* I once worked with the managing director of a consumer goods company who was extremely well-intentioned, but eventually had to be removed because of his indecisiveness. He had managed to hide this failing for years by approaching each decision with the observation that the team needed more information. The marketing department – with the exception of the researcher – dreaded this response. It always sounded logical, even prudent, but simply postponed decisions, often until they had lost any point – the competition had moved in, the market had moved on, the proposer of the idea had moved out.

Over-detailed plans can also be reassuring to a mediocre manager, unable to achieve the results of the truly talented but able to use the detailed plan to restrain his more visionary, ambitious colleague. Again, and this is a danger with public relations planning, the complex and detailed plan may not be the best. Do not imagine that someone is ill-prepared because he or she has not dotted every i or crossed every t. Such details are rarely necessary in the plan for approval, certainly in the initial stages. Leave the detailed planning to those who have to carry out the details.

Often, the most useful starting point for public relations planning will be the corporate philosophy. The one management tool that allows public relations to show its paces and, at the same time, creates the framework within which these efforts can be measured is the mission statement of the organisation.

■ The mission is the foundation for public relations

Mission or vision? Either is better than neither – though they are different and should not really be used interchangeably. The mission is why the organisation exists, what it is trying to achieve and a justification for all the activities that take place from day to day. As with most other missions in life, it represents a path or a progress rather than a specific point. A company that is rated as number three in its market in terms of service might well identify its mission as being to provide excellent services to its customers in its business sector. Even should it achieve the number one position in the market, that mission will still continue to be relevant to maintaining its position of leadership.

In the CIM *Marketing Dictionary*, Norman Hart defines the mission state-ment as a carefully drawn up statement by an organisation of 'what we are, and we aim to do', that is 'our unique ethical stance and strategic objectives'.

Managers sometimes wrestle a little too much over the concept of 'unique-ness' in the mission for their company. If there were ten companies making bricks or ten companies making cornflakes, it would not be too much of a surprise if there were elements in their mission statements that were similar in spirit, if not in wording.

The real skill in drafting a mission is to make it credible and relevant to the company. This will demand some research; if a company does not have such a statement and considers it might help unify the team then it can be a sensible task to allocate to the public relations people.

The mission statement may relate to how the company aspires to be – in other words, a few steps further on from today. But there are certain words that need to be treated with great caution. One of these might be 'excellence'. There is nothing wrong with the concept, nor is there much wrong with the practice of pursuing excellence, but it is a term that has become devalued; one company's view of excellence may be very different from another's. One company may think that excellence in customer care is answering the telephone reasonably promptly, whilst to another it is getting customer satisfaction to 100 per cent and complaints to zero. If that is their aim, then that is the wording that should be used.

The test of the appropriateness of the wording is simply to ask: how will this help members of the company work more effectively? Certainly, if they laugh when it is unveiled – as happened with at least one high street name – then you have either got the words wrong or the team wrong!

■ Make the mission practical

Mission statements may help to give a focus to the organisation's ambitions. They also set targets that have to be achieved – and should be reflected in the behaviour of all personnel. Organisations that do not live up to bold aims may find that it would have been better to have made no such claims in the first place. Also, should there be a lapse in the standards, then the handling of complaints becomes critically important.

Most people in marketing understand that a complaint can be the best new business opportunity. The converted complainant can become a true ambassador for the organisation. However, a disgruntled complainant (whose problems are aggravated by the treatment that he or she receives) may well spread the bad news far wider than someone who is satisfied.

One example, quoted by a senior marketing director, led to his extreme disappointment with American Express. It is an organisation that had always impressed him with its attention to its customers and the quality of everything that it tackled. That was until he needed to make a purchase that was somewhat bigger than normal – though still modest – and found a whole range of complications he had not anticipated.

His first shock was when the credit card transaction was rejected by American Express on the curious grounds that the amount was more than his normal level. It proved impossible on the telephone to get any indication from the person handling this problem what might be an expected or unexpected level. However, worse was to follow. Interminable delays on the customer service line were bad enough. Eager representatives keen to sort out the problem could not overcome the fact that they seemed to have no authority and were invariably reading from a computer screen with out of date information.

The system simply did not seem to be geared to what he considered to be a reasonably normal transaction. Personnel had ineffective training in dealing with anything out of the ordinary and constantly had to refer to someone in authority who was always unable to talk to a mere customer. The problem ran on for hours, involving many phone calls and constantly broken promises. One of the representatives who promised to resolve the problem turned out to have finished his shift and gone home less than half an hour after making his promise.

Everything was resolved ultimately. And to the credit of American Express, a senior executive did telephone the unhappy client and write with his apologies. Indeed, American Express had the good grace to explain that the problem was caused partially through a failure in the system, which they now claim to have rectified, and partially through poor training, which they have also addressed.

The problem illustrates the dangers of claiming to provide a high level of customer service – unless you can guarantee to meet this standard at all times, even with the hazards of human fallibility.

■ The vision sets the tone for communications

In contrast to the mission statement, a vision (not defined in the *Marketing Dictionary*) is less immediate. It is the ideal, the 'what-if' position to which the organisation might strive. It is not current, there is no guarantee that it is achievable but it can be just as real and as important to the organisation as this month's sales figures or this morning's share prices. The vision might be to become the biggest or the most profitable or the organisation with the most diverse range or the highest quality products. It can be quite specific in this context, for example . . . *to be the world leader in* . . . *to be number one* . . . and so on. British Airways' vision was to become the best managed company in Britain.

When reviewing the public relations management processes, check activity back to both the mission statement and the vision; these can provide a springboard for the public relations objectives – the former to be reinforced by what the company is doing and saying today and the latter as a basis for public relations initiatives that move the company towards the future.

You've got to have a dream, or how you gonna have a dream come true?

Perhaps the best dreams are those that never do come true – you get closer and closer to them, they get clearer and clearer, more and more obtainable yet always seem to be just that elusive bit ahead of you. That is the vision of an organisation.

So why might these little statements be of such importance to public relations? Because the core of business is achievement and public relations should be helping to create the environment within which all other disciplines are able to notch up new levels of achievement.

■ The best way to manage is to employ the best people

Good public relations people will tend to be ambitious, if not for themselves, for the organisation. Even in conservative industries, the view of what might be possible – not just of what is impossible – is invaluable in a public relations colleague. Of course, you need a pragmatist with his or her feet on the ground but this is not the same as a dullard.

I once worked with a client marketing manager in a construction company; he always had ten good reasons why something would not work before the idea had even been fully explained. I could cope with this because I was able to put ideas into operation without approval – but it used to upset his younger colleagues, who rightly were concerned that the only public relations activity that he would allow them to undertake was desperately cautious.

He unbent a little when some of the ideas that were pushed through worked. He relaxed completely after I presented an idea I was supposedly putting together for the UN, on which I said I wanted his opinion.

> 'Every country in the world', I explained, 'will send a full team of delegates to this event at their own expense. Major cities will bid competitively to build special accommodation and facilities to hold this. We will negotiate television coverage, with the aim of making this a top global event with an audience in billions.'
> 'What sort of crazy idea is that? It will never work', he commented.
> 'It already has. It's called the Olympic games! '

To his credit, he laughed and agreed to listen to the whole presentation before deciding future ideas would not work.

The nature of the work demands someone of confidence and courage, someone who thrives on challenge, someone who wants to change the world and whose energy and commitment will be part of what they bring to the job. As I say to young people I am interviewing for a possible job where I suspect there may be a hint of timidity: No one wants a reserved or retiring public relations professional. No one will buy hesitancy or lack of confidence or ambivalence. If you want to be shy, fine. Practise that on Sunday as your hobby, but don't bring it to work.'

Of course, this does not mean that the public relations professional has to be brash, insensitive, unheeding of others and, especially, someone more likely to talk than listen. But the practitioner who is hesitant about putting a contrary view when the decision is being made, or reluctant to step in to sort out a potential disaster, or unwilling to burn the midnight oil to get the project right, may well simply ensure that all public relations activities deliver below their real potential.

The advice to marketing professionals might be to ensure that any public relations staff or consultancy personnel they employ or brief to undertake a programme on their behalf have the personal qualities to be able to offer advice and get it listened to, even when it is what is not what they want to hear.

■ Try to find professionals with sympathetic attitudes

Rather obviously, the single most important rule in managing public relations personnel to get the best from them is to recruit the right ones in the first place. A good person may not work well in the wrong position. Therefore, the personality of the public relations people must be matched to the business environment. Get it right and it adds an extra dimension.

Compatability is important. I learned that lesson early in my career when I thought I was sharper than my boss. At that time, the great British tradition of helpful advice to foreigners had become something of a national sport – *in the UK, remember on public transport always shake hands with everyone in the bus or train carriage.*

When Hap Wagner took over as my boss as managing director of Air Products, I led the members of the marketing division in stringing him out for two or three weeks with invented traditions in the local pub where we used to meet after work. Hap was fresh out of California and, at that time, young and inexperienced in the ways of Europeans.

The first time we all pushed through the door to line up the bar, I invited him to get the drinks in. He complied, though a little bemused. I explained to him that the third man through the door always got the drinks. A few days later we met again one evening after work. On that occasion he made sure he was not third through the door and waited, grinning, for his beer. 'Sorry, Hap,' said one of my colleagues with a flash of inspiration. 'A green tie always takes precedence over the third man through the door.' Hap looked down and realised he was the only one in the group wearing a green tie and he reluctantly called up a round.

This sport went on through several ever more complicated rounds until Hap, with the mildest of tones, quietly pointed out that salary review time would be coming up shortly.

But Hap, now chief executive of the global Air Products company, taught that arrogant young public relations person some important lessons with the same good humour. For example, when I complained that my track record should justify a proposed plan of action without complicated evidence, he commented mildly that anyone of value in business should expect to be constantly presenting his or her credentials.

On another occasion, when I was reluctant to lose a good person on my team, he quietly explained that one measure of a good manager was his or her ability to develop the skills and contribution of those who worked for them; it was an indicator of success to have others from other divisions in the company keen to offer promotion opportunities to such people.

Such was the style of the company and the skill of the management of a brash but energetic and committed youngster such as myself, that I feel I gave them my best. The truth was that I was compatible with the personality of the company and that must be the most important factor.

■ Set the framework for outstanding performance

Tom Brannan is director of communications for Unichema International, the oleochemicals operation within ICI. He comes from a marketing background but is committed to the potential contribution that good public relations can make to business development – even speaking at an Institute of Public Relations conference on the opportunities that public relations people should be developing with top marketers. He believes that effective public relations is an invaluable marketing tool.

In an era of increasing product similarity, he suggests that public relations should be working to deliver corporate reputation effectively, at the same time as enhancing brand perception – part of the total communications package.

Corporate behaviour can have a significant effect on marketplace success; it can make a real difference in a potential crisis. The behaviour of the senior executives in the business can make or break the company, can significantly shift the share price and shape perceptions of key audiences, such as customers, towards the organisation. A good public relations professional can help design the ground rules and handle the inevitable mishaps when they occur from time to time.

However, in practice, he finds that too many practitioners cannot meet the challenge. 'Public relations advisers are in the perfect position to gain the ear of the most senior people in the client company, yet often they fail to make that access really pay. This is largely because many of them are weak marketers.

They should understand that companies do not exist to use public relations services; management tries to take an overview and look at how best communications can help build brands and business. Often marketing professionals are not comparing one public relations option with another – whether consultancy or in-house – but with other techniques for achieving a business return.'

All disciplines within a progressive company have to compete for budget and other resources, Brannan points out. Public relations is not alone in having to prove that it can make a better contribution to the bottom line than an additional salesman or a new piece of machinery. The fight should not be to win the public relations business but to win input into the strategic thinking of the bosses or client company.

An essential requirement, he feels, is that the public relations professional must have a good grasp of the implications of the many aspects of the problems and challenges which businesses face. Professionalism is ultimately all that any external adviser has to sell.

He quotes the example of a meeting in an Arab embassy in which the director of a public relations agency – one which claimed expertise in the Middle East – mentioned the 'Persian Gulf' on several occasions during the presentation. If the advisers can make such simple but breathtaking mistakes, it is no surprise that management do not invite them into the boardroom to help develop strategy.

And yet, observes Tom Brannan, when public relations works well it makes a massive contribution. Quality public relations, delivered well, commands a premium price and guarantees the advisers access to the most senior people within management. From his own experience, strategic well-structured public relations can deliver measurable results in both awareness and goodwill.

■ A corporate position on ethics is not optional

An area of some importance that can get overlooked in managing public relations is company policy on sensitive issues. A later chapter looks in more detail at reviewing potential issues and developing a stance towards these. When the company is in the middle of a public row about, say, its environmental attitudes, is not a good time to find out that there is dissension at board level – or, worse, that the public relations people are innocently pursuing angles that seem reasonable but are totally contrary to some policy that no one had bothered to explain to them.

This can be worse than embarrassing. It can be devastating to reputation if the company has to make an about-turn. Such misunderstandings can also be frighteningly expensive.

The French public relations manager for a US aerospace company working across Europe was deputed to handle the closure of a small subsidiary, only acquired a few years before. He handled this on the basis of many other corporate activities, quoting to enquiring journalists the company's policies in such areas; this was that they made the maximum settlement for employees and not the minimum.

In fact, the company was planning to recover redundancy costs from the previous owners, who had been economical with the truth about the strength of the orderbook of the acquisition, in contravention of clauses in the purchase agreement. But no one had told the public relations spokesperson. His media comments cost the company over $30 million in additional payments; as soon as they saw the news reports, the company vendors simply put their operation into liquidation to avoid their liabilities. These, therefore, neatly but painfully passed to the US corporation whose spokesman had already told the world they would be treating all employees honourably.

The ethical stance of the organisation needs to be reflected in its published policies, annual reports and in any mission statements. It may not be enough to deliver excellent services, if this happens at the same time as the company is polluting the environment, putting the employees' health at risk, or keeping the plant neighbours awake all night with the noise of production or excessive smells.

■ Areas of possible contention must be resolved

Any areas where there might be different views should be resolved before any problem arises. As an illustration, a common area of conflict is when the legal advisers or insurers try to prevent any apologies or expressions of sympathy by company representatives after an accident. This is not universal but it still happens.

Those with this attitude claim that such comments may increase the company liability. Of course, the public, seeing the company failing to express regret for polluting the river, injuring employees, poisoning customers or terrifying neighbours, does not appreciate these niceties. They see insensitivity. The company's reputation is damaged and sales often plummet. But the legal adviser or insurance manager has protected the position of the company in any court action or claim.

That is not the way to do it. Methods of handling crises and of behaving with decency and feeling need to be worked out in advance should, heaven forbid, the unthinkable happens.

■ Ethical stance can give competitive edge

Of course, in line with the concept of accentuating the positive, companies can use ethical policy to develop strategies that give competitive edge. All parties can play a part in shaping such policies, for the company that treats its employees, its neighbours, its customers and its suppliers with care and consideration may well be the company that gains that extra percentage when it comes to being viewed favourably. And that edge can make the difference between winning the business or not, gaining the customers or not.

Positive and imaginative ethical, environmental and community policies are developed by great companies because they believe in doing what is right. At the very least, the pragmatic company might consider working out what it is going to have to do anyway – and then undertake this ahead of the game and, perhaps, to some level above the legal, statutory or social minimum.

■ General Electric use ethics to give edge

One company that has viewed ethics as an essential element in the development of a responsible business is General Electric of the USA. It may be no coincidence that this is the largest company in the world in capitalisation terms.

The company has reviewed and defined ethical stances; these help employees understand the issues that might face them in their jobs and how they should make decisions that the company can support. It is clearly rewarding to employees, customers, suppliers and all others involved with the company to be associated with an organisation that believes it has a responsibility in the world to behave properly. It seems likely that although these policies represent a cost, they can also bring the company benefits that contribute to its competitive edge – it sets the standards in many of these areas – and ultimately to its commercial success.

GE has developed these policies so that they become part of employee induction, part of training and a constant factor in the lives of those who work within the company across the globe. The ethical policies are produced in a document that is available in local languages. Extracts of this document are featured on internal noticeboards and within periodic poster campaigns.

Of course, a policy of ethics has to be consistently and rigorously followed through. Ethics are of no value where they may be bent to suit the practicalities of an immediate situation.

As an illustration, one of the GE companies had to consider a product recall when it discovered the line it was manufacturing was not up to its highest standard and could potentially be dangerous. Although the company was just reaching the close of its financial year and all sales and marketing personnel were looking forward to exceeding their targets, management had the courage to decide to undertake recall activities; this won the full and immediate support of all sales and marketing personnel, as well as the country managers. This meant that the sales budget went by the board. It was a tough decision but taken without hesitation.

The reputation of the company and the safety of its customers (and employees) was of paramount importance; it was inconceivable that the achievement of sales figures would be put ahead of this. Perhaps the managers would have made this decision anyway. But, certainly, the ethical policies of the company and the publicly declared responsibility it expected to show to all its publics will have been of considerable support.

As often happens, in the event, that last month's sales were badly affected – but the reputation of the company was so enhanced that the sales chart line bounced back within a few months of the start of the new financial year and actually lifted above the previous levels. The explanation was simple. During the crisis, the company had to contact senior people within the customer organisations they were servicing; these executives were fully able to understand the possibility of a crisis – it could happen in their own companies. Such senior managers were impressed by the professionalism of the individuals handling the exercise and the ethical stance of the company behind these decisions.

This had not been the intention, but the opportunity to talk to senior people and demonstrate the professionalism of the company created positive attitudes from a crisis. But of most importance, the products at risk were identified, located and recovered without risk to customers.

■ Public relations strategy must be driven from the top

In the case just discussed, the ethical strategy was driven from the top. Increasingly, the most senior company executives – chairmen, chief executives, managing directors – are not only involved in communications but often set corporate policy. This sets both opportunities and challenges for those running marketing when company communications are likely to be divided between the corporate and marketing levels – each having a significant impact in the company's 'market', in the broadest sense.

In the US, research has confirmed that senior executives spend up to 60 per cent of their time on corporate communications. John Smith of General Motors has said, 'The modern top business executive is a quasi public figure, representing the company not only in the traditional market place where goods are sold but in the market place of ideas where the forces shaping society are determined.'

Top executives are following the US example and taking more responsibility for communications – which means they need to understand the world in which the company operates. In his introduction to Sir Adrian Cadbury's *The Company Chairman* that notable one-time chairman of ICI, Sir John Harvey-Jones, says, 'While the responsibilities of the chairman do not alter, the role varies with the changing social, economic and political environments in which we operate. Moreover, it behoves a chairman not only to be aware of the massive changes occurring in his own company and his own country but also those in many other parts of the world. There is no company that is immune to the changes which are occurring all round us.'

Sir John made the comments a few years ago but they are probably even more relevant today. If the chairman is the ultimate arbiter of strategy, the representative of the shareholders' interests, the link between the company and top opinion formers in the City, government, professional bodies and customers, (and customer bodies where these exist), he or she is also likely to be the ultimate company spokesperson.

This puts a responsibility on the marketing director. Corporate communications must be co-ordinated closely with marketing communications. The potential for difficulty or even conflict is considerable.

The chairman will not usually want to manage marketing communications (though he will be likely to take a keen interest in broad policies); at the same time, marketing may wish to control corporate communications but will be unable to manage what the chairman is saying when he is representing the company in conversations with politicians, bankers, institutional investors and even on the conference platform or in the press, on radio and television.

■ Marketing can take responsibility for company briefings

One effective way in which marketing can play a constructive role in co-ordinating these two important but separate areas of communications is for the department to take responsibility for briefings. Some extend this to writing the speeches that will be given by all top executives.

Whether marketing controls public relations or not, it does have resources for research – and will be close to many audiences of great commercial importance to the company. It can use these facilities, in co-operation with the public relations professionals, to prepare regular briefs for senior management on the issues of the day and how company policy relates to these.

These are probably most helpful as a monthly headline service, with weekly updates (or more frequently, when necessary) on topical matters.

When Marks & Spencer found itself facing media allegations over the use of child labour in the manufacture of pyjamas, the chief executive and chairman of every clothing manufacturer and retailer in the country should have received *that day* not just the relevant news cuttings, but a briefing on the company's position in relation to this issue plus any recent history and recommended responses to public, customer or media enquiries.

It is probable that few such briefings were prepared. And, if so, many marketing departments may have lost an opportunity to control a central area of their company communications. If the marketing department is to take such a role, then it has to have the resources in place, for this cannot be an off/on service.

■ Build change on an understanding of current perceptions

Before attempting to plan the programme of public relations activity, it is important to have a proper understanding of present perceptions. Of all the communications disciplines, public relations should be research-based, but this is not always the case. Surely if you plan to change perceptions, how can you do this effectively if you do not know what they are at present?

You need to know the views of the key audiences if you wish to undertake activity to move these more favourably towards the organisation. This may require formal research or simpler forms of evaluation, sometimes just asking the right question or two of the right people.

The UK managing director of a Japanese company making small electrical appliances was disappointed with the customer reaction to an innovative new product. He authorised a public relations programme to stress the UK design and manufacturing content in the model.

Wisely, the consultancy selected for the task undertook some simple research and found that resistance was not because of the Japanese origin but concern over the complexity of the technology. A campaign stressing the testing and reliability of the system and the no-quibble guarantee proved effective in reducing these concerns.

Good public relations is dependent on such accurate intelligence. The views of senior executives may be helpful but are rarely enough, alone, on which to make decisions. As everyone in marketing appreciates, the only sound base for planning should be research.

In Britain, it has been estimated that over 90 per cent of *The Times* top 1000 companies regularly use research to find out more on subjects about which (it might be supposed) they already know enough. Such research is often aimed at understanding perceptions of key publics and how these perceptions developed.

What factors create such perceptions and how do they affect reputation? The most common reason why companies commission research is that they suspect that subjective views, which they acknowledge to be imporant, do not always reflect the reality. Even where the research merely confirms such suspicions, it is still worthwhile, as decisions about the corporate reputation can be made with greater confidence.

■ New research studies sharpen the focus of public relations

A study sponsored by the International Public Relations Association and supported by a number of communications bodies as well as individual practitioners and academics in the field, recently identified sixteen areas of research priority. These were:

1. The measurement and evaluation of public relations.
2. The definition of public relations.
3. The need to integrate public relations with other communications functions.
4. Strategic planning and public relations.
5. The relationship of top management to public relations.
6. Professional skills in public relations.
7. The impact of technology on public relations.
8. The image of public relations.
9. The expectations of users of public relations.
10. Public relations' role in organisational change.
11. Quality of public relations services.
12. International issues in public relations practice.
13. Ethics in public relations practice.
14. The impact of media content.
15. Gender issues in public relations practice.
16. Features of the market for public relations service.

However, at a symposium to discuss this list, general feeling was expressed that not enough progress had been made in addressing the use of research in public relations practice. In addition, ways to research the public relations impact on the bottom line could be usefully developed.

■ Challenge erroneous board views of where the company stands

Experienced managers know the dangers of basing decisions upon personal observation. We all know that we tend to see what we want to see, hear what we want to hear. As anyone in public relations will confirm, it is almost a truism that each company thinks it is better known, better understood, better supported than it actually is.

Keeping in touch is central to public relations and the chief executive may often have to accept that he is not closest to the key audiences. The higher up the company an executive moves, the more remote he or she may get from the publics upon whom the organisation depends for its success. Often, managers of vision recognise this and set up procedures to ensure they get a full feedback of views. Happily, some successful company chairmen and chief executives make particular efforts to keep in touch with feelings that matter.

All senior executives of McDonald's spend time behind their counters, and that includes, on their appointment, non-executives like Sir Bernard Ingham. And why not? The fact that this simple policy received media comment shows how rare it is.

All top managers must be in touch and understand the points of view of those that their decisions will affect. The chairman of one large plc – sadly, now a shadow of its former self – was asked by a television newsman to talk to a lathe operator during a board visit to its largest regional manufacturing site.

Desperately searching for a topic of conversation, he remembered he was in the country and asked the bemused man, 'What's the hunting and shooting like round here?' Fortunately, the television reporter did not hear the reply above the machine room noise – but the chairman did, and reddened. Later, in private, he commented on worker hostility and their failure to appreciate their jobs, without any hint of irony.

Cabinet minister John Gummer carried the responsibility for London as well as his better known portfolio on the environment. On one *it-could-not-possibly-happen* day, he berated Londoners for whingeing about the collapse of the capital's services. Incredibly, this was on the day that 20 000 of his fellow Londoners were to spend frightening hours trapped underground in crowded, claustrophobic tube trains, crippled by maintenance failures. More than one or two reporters pointed out that Mr Gummer travelled by government car with chauffeur and was not known as a regular tube traveller.

How could they be so cruel? But do not laugh. It could be your chairman next!

■ Marketers must think before accepting corporate responsibility

As those battered by the ironies that abound in the world of public relations say, 'Never say never'. Murphy's Law really does seem to apply – if anything happens, it will always be the most embarrassing or, even, damaging eventuality imaginable. This can be an important lesson to remember if marketing has taken over senior executive speech writing. Read all such pronouncements carefully to make sure that you are not forecasting something that cannot possibly happen. It just might.

Indeed, marketing professionals need to seriously consider all the implications of taking over *any* corporate public relations responsibilities – that is, those that may be outside normal marketing areas.

Many senior public relations professionals believe this can be highly risky. If the company handles a situation badly or is involved in an incident that hits the headlines, far-reaching decisions may have to be taken, including the resignation of the chairman or other senior executives – remember Exxon and the Alaska disaster, Cunard and the QE2 floating building site, Cedric Brown and British Gas, Gerald Ratner, plus countless others.

Whoever takes on the corporate role may find they have to say, one day, 'Chairman, we cannot pursue that policy. It is the route to disaster.' This corporate adviser may find that all other directors fall silent and he or she holds the loneliest post in the company. Later, the adviser might even have to say, 'Chairman, I am afraid you will have to resign. You refused the advice and so must carry the responsibility, if anything is to survive of this company.'

If keen candidates for this corporate role do not feel they could handle this, then they are unlikely to be right for the responsibility.

Consider this. UK government papers published in 1997 showed that the prime minister in the late 1960s fought to keep Lord Robens as chairman of British Coal after the Aberfan disaster. Recklessly casual policies had allowed massive spoil heaps to be built and one, through rain and underground springs, turned to slurry and engulfed a school, killing almost all the children and staff in horrific circumstances that shocked the world. In an incredibly aloof and pompous style, Robens told the media his organisation was not responsible. The television interviews are so breathtaking in their insensitivity that they will be shown 100 years from now.

Times have changed. Do not rely on the support of the prime minister, or any other public figure, when things go wrong. No chairman dare be arrogant. The media control the agenda. And those in responsibility know they cannot survive if they make far smaller mistakes that those of the board of British Coal.

■ Without feedback, communications can become shouting

Every public relations plan will include some measure of feedback from important groups. All communications must be based on a two-way flow of information or views. Effective communications needs to be built up from an understanding of all points of view.

Often, a lack of knowledge of an issue amongst an important public has been mistakenly interpreted as resistance. As noted earlier, you cannot be certain you will change opinion or influence attitude in the way you intend unless you know what these are in the first place. Yet, too many commercial communications plans make assumptions about the knowledge, opinion and attitude – and do not always put these to the test.

At best, this will be a considerable waste of money. At worst, it may actually produce hostility in the audiences supposed to be being wooed. Even the language acceptable to the audiences you wish to influence can be a factor.

One of the Worldcom Group partners in the USA, Epley Associates, uses a sophisticated computer-based system which allows selected representatives of any audience to show instant reactions to any case being presented to them.

Even the reaction to individual words can be analysed. One business presentation for a new car from a US big-three maker was achieving high acceptance scores – until the voice-over reached the phrase 'The ultimate driving experience.'

Audience approval scoring instantly dropped to a minimal level, never to recover. Interviews with members of that audience showed that they rejected that phrase. The ultimate driving experience for most people might be a Ferrari, a classic racing car or a vintage Rolls-Royce. It was not a popular family saloon, however good it might be. The rejection of the rest of the film followed because the audience felt that if the company could 'lie' about that, maybe all the rest of the claims were exaggerated.

■ An opinion-leading chief executive is a great public relations asset

Consider the view expressed by the Sir Clive Thompson, chief executive of Rentokil, summarising the philosophy behind the vigorous growth and diversification of the company: 'Our corporate identity is red, white and quality.'

In comparison, a study of awareness of the logo of a high-profile business group failed to produce any intelligent result because so few could recognise the recently-changed company name, including some 50 per cent of its existing clients! Fortunately, the positive outgoing approach of a business leader like Thompson is widely appreciated and respected. Senior executives making decisions on matters relating to public relations need to be certain that they have the right independent input.

The top director may not need constant, day-to-day contact with customers. But, if this is so, equally he should not be deciding the approach for marketing communications, or managing the public relation programme of activity. The high public profile of some directors does mean that what they may be saying, sometimes at no notice at all, must be consistent with what is being said through marketing and public relations spokespeople.

The corporate relations director must be trained to take a detached view. He or she should also be well in tune with feelings towards management through the best internal and external grapevine of anyone in the organisation. Get the personal chemistry right and the public relations professional will be uniquely equipped to handle sensitive and critical areas.

Indeed, this relationship of trust is essential if the board is to agree the correct objectives for the company public relations programme. This can be an 'inside track' of considerable importance to the marketing professionals. Management pays for advice; to get value, it must create the atmosphere in which honest and objective advice can be offered.

■ Keep your management tough but fair

As most chief executives appreciate, good public relations people are still rather rare. Good writers there are aplenty. Good journalists (in or out of journalism) there are aplenty. Polished public relations salespeople there are aplenty. Strategic advisers who want to philosophise (and do no work) there are aplenty. But the public relations professional that can be trusted for his or her wisdom, judgement, and solid advice and, importantly, the practical follow-through are few and far between. They should be sought out, cherished . . . and challenged.

Whether you need them to work on your staff or whether you want them to advise you through a consultancy role is a different question. It is probably far less important whether they are in-house or not than whether they can win your confidence and deliver. Above all, can they tell you not just what you want to hear but, sometimes, what you need to hear . . . and may not actually want to hear?

Whatever other decisions may be taken, make sure that the senior manager of the public relations function is close to hand. Public relations factors are involved in many company decisions and the marketing director (and the chief executive) will need regular input. This will not happen if the public relation executive has to be 'called in' from some distant office.

■ Encourage advisers to give the advice you do not want to hear

Overpowering management can bully advisers into submission. Perhaps some marketing and communications professionals see there is more profit in being diplomatic to the point of compliance. Any failure to agree what the public relations plan is supposed to achieve can also mean that different elements within the marketing and communications mix can be working to different agendas.

Public relations people will tell you that this is not a rare occurrence. Good advice can be unpopular. It takes a confident, professional and courageous management to accept advice from a confident, professional and courageous public relations professional. Of course, this problem is not peculiar to the public relations arena. Management has to appoint good advisers with no bias. They have to have honesty, skill and vision. The company needs to be certain their advice is considered, independent, honest and presented with the best interests of the company at heart.

Curious how some human resources professionals do not seem to like people. But then, many teachers can't stand children. Make sure you do not appoint a public relations adviser who does not like business or hates journalists; they exist!

When the framework is set for the public relations adviser, it should ensure that he or she has the freedom to offer advice under all circumstances. The marketing professionals must support him in this, particularly when he has to advise top management.

■ Ensure that senior managers listen as vigorously as they speak

If the chief executive truly wants an atmosphere in which colleagues can be outspoken, then he or she has to listen and to be seen to listen. Equally, those offering views or advice should not take advantage. All are equal but the boss is the boss because he is more equal than the rest – that is how he got there!

Heaven protect us from the manager who sees his role as being the professional bluntman! The Scottish managing director of one of the electricity companies prided himself on telling colleagues what was what, as he put it, without mincing his words. The trouble was that he could not cope with anyone else talking directly and rarely listened to anything unless he had already decided he agreed. He regularly ignored the briefings of his public relations director and constantly invented policy, on the hoof, in front of the radio microphone or television camera.

His senior colleagues soon learned what was acceptable. Of course, he became surrounded by compliant managers, the company ran into trouble and he was eventually fired. What a tragic waste of all his talents.

Once in Brussels I was presenting a concept to a Commissioner with a dozen of his team in the room. Discussing the approach, I pointed out an important anomaly in one of his assumptions, the result of some research that we had undertaken. He listened and accepted the point and later commented, mildly, no one on his own staff had made any observation about such a curious matter.

Perhaps he failed to notice that none of his senior colleagues had made any comment during the whole of the presentation. They had learned not to debate issues with Commissioners. There had only been enthusiasm and words of approval at the end, once he had made it quite clear that he was happy with the proposition.

■ Creativity needs a framework of discipline

Public relations may be flexible, organic, responsive and creative. It may well be handled effectively by some of the most talented people – but the need for creativity must never be used as the excuse for a lack of discipline. Though reputation is specific, clear and tangible, it is extremely difficult to quantify. How good is a good reputation? Does the company have a good reputation in all areas: products, financial performance, environmental responsibility and so on?

In reality, it is the comparative value of the reputation that matters, as well as whether it is improving or deteriorating. Both formal and informal research methods can be used to establish this comparative position. Of all the professionals in the company, marketing advisers have by far the best understanding of research. Even if the head of public relations does not report to marketing, there is still some logic in the marketing discipline providing the research services to public relations.

Qualitative studies are often sufficient to provide a simple benchmark against which any changes or developments in the reputation can be measured at the end of a year – or two years, or any other period that the management chooses.

Alternatively, how such publics rate the reputation in comparison with other organisations can be appraised. It can be helpful to check this against competitors in the same sector and/or the companies in other industries that are viewed as being leaders.

Of course, in such studies, it is important to remember that what is being measured are perceptions and not realities. Any anomalies between the perceptions and the reality may suggest an area for management attention.

Normally, there is considerable information which can be gathered by your public relations team through informal research. Talking to people can be invaluable. The head of public relations might be encouraged to put together a committee to represent the various operating sectors of the company. The chief executive may like to attend an occasional one of these or check the agenda and any debrief notes, every so often.

■ Informal research may give a snapshot perspective

Make sure this panel convenes on a regular basis so that it performs a continuous monitoring operation. Each member of this discussion group will or should be discussing public relations issues within the company. As a result, this group will be getting representative views from a far wider spread than could ever be achieved by one manager.

Organisations have available a large number of sources of valuable information about the attitudes of important publics; many of these are never tapped. These may be the professional advisers and trading partners who observe reactions to the organisation.

Confidential discussions with such specialists as banks, accountants, solicitors, union leaders, the advertising agency, suppliers, professional bodies, financial analysts, trade editors, stockbrokers, careers officers, even government officials and civil servants – all can put a fresh perspective on many aspects of the organisation's operations.

Marketing is constantly checking the company or brand position against the competition. Public relations should be encouraged to do the same. Your public relations adviser should be getting a view of how competitors and other peer organisations are performing in their public relations activities. Get members of the team to develop this habit of asking and listening. Make sure they carefully read reports, literature and brochures. Get them to check on complaints received by customer services and talk to personnel about the reasons people give for leaving the company.

Ask them to collate all such information into an informal report, say quarterly. The objective of this research will be to establish the gap between how the organisation is seen and how it would like to be seen.

Public relations managers should be expected to undertake their own desk research. They should know how to identify the basic statistical information that is available from dozens of public, industry and professional sources.

Your marketing research manager may wish to help co-ordinate this effort. He or she must make sure that the public relations practitioners build up their own library of statistical industry information, company data, trends and product information, available for media and company use. Key data should be collated into briefing sheets and held on the computer.

■ Informal evaluations of reputation provide direction

For many major projects, formal studies may be essential; these can be planned to provide the basis on which the programme of activity will be built. In addition, with the right questions, they may provide information that is directly usable in the public relations activity.

Such studies can also provide a useful benchmark on the progress of the programme, recording the changing perceptions of the company or its products amongst selected audiences.

Even where expensive, formal studies may not be appropriate, the public relations professionals should always be expected to present evidence of the value of their work. With some projects, reviews that give a snapshot perspective, without being statistically valid, may still be useful; simple questionnaires can be circulated to management, put in salary notices, made an element in annual performance reviews, featured in the company newsletter, raised amongst attendees at the annual general meeting or the national sales conference, and so on.

The advantage of these simple studies is that they can be undertaken at virtually no cost. As researchers will advise, these respondents are self-selecting and will not be representative of the larger universe; but they may give some indication. At the least, these studies demonstrate that a company cares about its reputation enough to want to find out what people think and take the necessary steps to make any appropriate improvements.

In managing public relations professionals, it is wise to encourage their natural curiosity, irritating though it may be on occasions. Many may not have the discipline of their marketing colleagues, but most have a wide view of the world, breadth (if not depth) of company knowledge and, usually, some wisdom. It is one reason why they can often make lateral and radical contributions to planning meetings. It is a quality shared by most with some entrepreneurial flair.

I remember once being invited to fly to Pennsylvania to interview the late Leonard Paul, the founder and chairman of the world leading industrial gas company, Air Products, for whom I worked at the time. It was a fascinating interview which confirmed in my mind why he had achieved so much in such a short lifetime. He asked almost as many questions at the interview as I did. The one I remember best was: 'Tell me, Roger, what companies do you admire most and why?'

Similarly, early in my career I worked at Dexion, the international materials handling company. Some time after I had joined the company, I was introduced to the founder, Demetrius Comino, who had built an international empire on the basis of the slotted angle concept that he had invented. His first question to me was simple but wise: 'Why did you choose to come and work with us here at Dexion?'

The boss of such a large and successful organisation might have been forgiven for concentrating on what I was going to contribute to the empire. His perspective was different, more original and much more intriguing. He wanted to know what his company had done that might have attracted me to want to further my career by joining them.

This question made me think deeply and explore views that had certainly not been at the top of my mind or come up in the number of interviews before I had got the job. But then, perhaps that was why he was where he was.

■ The fundamentals of any public relations plan

Regardless of the campaign, there always are seven or eight questions that need to be addressed in planning the activity. These have been gathered into a form that the author recommends to help remember them and to use as a checklist:

Who	– the publics or audiences to be reached.
What	– the messages to be projected.
Why	– the aims or objectives of the activity.
Where	– the geographical location of the key audiences.
When	– the timetable for the activity.
How	– the techniques to be deployed
How much	– the budget and other resources to be allocated.
How appraised	– the evaluation, monitoring and refinement processes for the continuing activity.

And a final thought on motivating public relations staff: impossible – they can only motivate themselves.

CHAPTER 4

Communications and issues audits

THE OBJECTIVE BASE FOR PLANNING

*Mr Podsnap settled that whatever he put behind him he put out of existence . . .
(he) had even acquired a peculiar flourish of his right arm in clearing the world of
its most difficult problems . . .*
Charles Dickens (1812–70), *Martin Chuzzlewit* (1844)

■ Plans must be based on reality not supposition

Many of the techniques now firmly within the responsibility of public relations
have been borrowed from other communications disciplines. For example,
hospitality events, public opinion surveys, sponsorship, business seminars,
newsletters, corporate videos are all activities that would now be considered
part of public relations in most companies.

However, there is at least one technique which has been developed exclu-
sively within public relations and which is making a valuable contribution to
intelligent corporate planning. More accurately, there are two linked techniques
– the familiar communications audit, which has led to the broader, and even
more important, issues audit.

Communications audits have been around for some years, although the more
formal terminology and the structured procedures came into general acceptance
in the last decade or so. The first fullscale issues audit – the first undertaken as
far as I am aware, but I await correction – was run by my company on behalf of
Rhône–Poulenc, the French chemicals multinational. This was in 1984 and is
described in my book *All About Public Relations*. Many such early audits were
carried out independently of the marketing departments. They tended to be
seen as operational, relating more to potential crises that could arise through
production accidents, transport incidents, unintentional product contamina-
tions and so on. For these reasons, issues tended to be considered as negative,
but that is far from the reality.

Of course, the importance of issues (more often negative than positive) to
marketing should have been obvious to all, through such incidents as the

Distillers' Thalidomide, later the deliberate poisoning of Johnson & Johnson's Tylenol, the suspect research that sank the first synthetic sweeteners designed to replace saccharin – and others.

■ The issues audit can be built from the communications audit

The issues audit is an invaluable aid to marketing planning and should be considered by all companies that like to have the maximum control over the agenda that influences the business in which they operate.

Most marketing professionals will use some form of downside analysis when planning new initiatives (even if they do not use that term for the process). They analyse what could go wrong with this plan and how might we prevent this or minimise the risk? Does this proposal impact on other audiences such as trade and professional bodies or government departments and, if so, how should we best get their input before going public? How will our competition react to this and what might they do to foil our intentions? Are there any disadvantages to our retailers and/or customers that might cause negative reactions?

And (if they are sensitive to at least the media relations part of public relations) how might journalists react and could some try to create mischief, perhaps aided by our competitors? . . . and so on.

Such wise evaluations are routinely undertaken by business – though rarely by governments, which is one reason why public communications by those who would govern us have been in such disarray. Though that is another story . . .

However, some marketing managers only look at the downside of marketing initiatives and do not give proper weight to those issues outside their control that can seriously disrupt or even destroy marketing plans. If you feel I exaggerate, consider this. Shell has significant and professional marketing resources. Where were they when the company decided to sink the disused Brent Spar oil platform in the deep ocean? Or when the company reversed this policy, dramatically embarrassing the government and the prime minister who were vigorously defending the very policy that had just been abandoned?

I am not observing whether Shell was right or wrong. But undeniably something went seriously awry that resulted in massive and hostile media coverage – and, inevitably, a significant impact on company marketing. I do not know where the marketing professionals were but it is certain they were not delighted with what happened.

■ Consider what could happen to damage your marketing plans

So, what might be happening in your company today, perhaps in some area outside your control, that will make a nonsense of all your efforts? Months later, could this impossible possibility still leave you apologising to editors or your peers in the industry: 'It was nothing to do with me'? Or could you still be dreading that first question when you meet someone new or talk at a meeting? Or bitterly resenting the millions spent on rectifying a problem that might never have arisen with a little more forward planning?

The *Daily Mail* reported estimates that Marks & Spencer spent £2 million a week on crisis efforts after the television programme that alleged that they were selling pyjamas, mislabelled and supposedly made by child labour.

Accusations may be true or false but the cost of damage limitation is always massively more than undertaking the audits to try to identify areas of potential risk

None of us wants to have to apologise that it was 'nothing to do with us'. If you are responsible for marketing, then *everything* is to do with you. Even if you do not control such areas of public relations, you need to be certain that the right processes are in place to anticipate possible problems. And to get the full machinery of the company in place to resolve these.

■ The unexpected is perhaps what you should expect

If you think it cannot happen then it probably can. Let me recount just a few random but coincidental examples from my own experience.

- The day after we had tested emergency procedures at an electrical appliance manufacturers, a real accident happened and several employees were injured, happily none seriously.
- Product contamination processes at a famous food manufacturer were rigorously checked and tested as the result of an issues audit I undertook; a few months later these were by-passed by a rogue building firm, working on a new extension, using substitute solvent-based paints, which led to the contamination – and recall – of product.
- A high-security, bomb-proof chlorine production and storage facility near London where my company was training managers in crisis communications survived what could have been a serious incident when an airplane luggage door landed in the neighbouring field, prompting the embarrassed production director to admit that he had never considered the safety of the roof of his plant.
- The storm-proof roof of a computer warehouse in a typhoon-prone area of the States, insured by a client of mine, collapsed under the weight of snow in a freak cold spell no one had predicted.

■ Emergency resources need to be agreed in advance

If a mishap should happen, do not think that everyone in the company will understand the urgency or allocate it the same priority that you might – *unless* the procedures are properly set up in advance! Which is, of course, the first rule.

Our team was once called in by a UK-based international chemicals company to help handle a highly significant health hazard issue, in the headlines because of a damaging report. The biggest frustrations in the first day or two were getting the top managers to take it seriously and then obtaining the resources necessary to deal with the crisis.

The boardroom was 'booked', no secretary was available, all the PCs were 'in use', the company had no spare telephone or fax lines, security locked the building at 7 pm and no one could get in until 8 am, although members of the crisis management team needed 24 hour access . . . It was a great time to find out that the operation was run by bureaucrats and jobsworths.

Worst of all, the key people at board level who were needed for policy issues and to act as spokespeople were unavailable (with the honourable exception of the production and human resources directors). We manoeuvred our way through all the problems but, in the calm after the storm, I told the managing director that active support by the board would have been helpful, as our biggest obstacle had not been hostile media (we could deal with them) but unco-operative staff. We explained that this was a disappointment, for most of those at middle management levels were extremely professional and motivated.

We successfully resolved the problems but, not surprisingly, relationships were a little strained at times. It was no coincidence in my view, nor consolation, that the company was later bought at a knockdown price by a US corporation – which promptly sacked all the directors. And, incidentally, through the whole process we never did see the marketing director, who was always in some meeting or conference whilst the world was conspiring to destroy his company and his market.

However, of even greater significance, he was not represented by anybody and decisions were being made that were affecting both marketing and the marketplace without his views being part of that process.

■ Planning for incidents develops the right state of mind

The marketing director rightfully insists on taking responsibility for everything that impacts upon his or her marketing. Usually marketing professionals are pretty good at planning and so it is reasonable to assume that most are well organised to deal with what might be expected. But what is the definition of expected?

As an extension of Murphy's Law might say, the rule in issues and crisis management is to expect the unexpected. It is probably impossible to plan for all eventualities. However, if you have planned for a possible road accident involving one of your vehicles that might run, say, into a bus queue, then many of the most helpful procedures might be in place if an incident involving at least some of the elements of your imagined scenario were to occur. For instance, a vehicle might be hijacked, or there could be an accident involving your product while it was being transported by railway wagon rather than lorry.

The issues audit is based upon a process of interviewing key people both internally and externally and extracting those factors that might appear to have potential significance. From my experience, there are few issues that could impact upon an organisation that are not known and well understood by at least a number of executives within the organisation.

Quite often these views are simply not taken seriously by management.

As an illustration, the enquiries into the tragedy of the sinking of the Townsend Thorenson *Herald of Free Enterprise* established that there were many people within the company who were concerned about the procedures that were being followed in relation to turning round the ferries quickly in harbour. A procedure had grown up whereby each ferry would set sail as soon its cargo of passengers and cars was on board, even if this meant there had not been time to close the loading bow doors. There was no communication between the seamen manning these doors and the captain on the bridge – either by voice, electronic signal or any other means. Therefore, the captain had no idea whether the doors were open or closed. In the tragic accident concerned, the ship sailed into rough seas as it left harbour whilst the doors were still open, and shipped enough water to tilt her. Because of her design, she was soon unbalanced and doomed to sink.

■ Top management often does not know the areas of risk

Many people within the ferry company were concerned about these procedures but these views either did not reach top management or had not been taken seriously.

There is little doubt that if the senior management had had the opportunity to see the news stories that followed the sinking of the vessel some three or four days before it had sunk, they would have spared no expense in instituting proper procedures to prevent it happening.

They did not have this foresight, the dangers were not properly presented to them and they did not take the action necessary. It was pretty certain that nobody at the top in Townsend Thorenson behaved in a reckless or irresponsible way. They simply had no idea of the risks that were involved.

An intelligent starting point for an issues audit might be to look at the effectiveness of existing communications. The communications, both internally and externally in relation to each issue, will be of considerable importance, particularly should a situation arise where the organisation is under some pressure.

There is also another good reason for running a communications audit in parallel with the issues audit. Both would depend to some extent on qualitative interviews with key people in the organisation and outside.

The cost of investigating both areas at the same time can be significantly reduced in comparison with running two separate audits. In addition, the issues audit is almost certain to identify changes that might be necessary in communications and these can be better effected if the existing channels of communication have been effectively audited through such an independent study.

PLANNING THE COMMUNICATIONS AUDIT

■ Analyse the effectiveness of the full communications matrix

Many methods of communications within an organisation have arisen over time. They may have met a particular need that once existed but rarely are these procedures checked to see if they are still currently valid.

An interesting example is the company newsletter. A study that my own company undertook a little time ago suggested that as many as 40 per cent of these may have reached the point where they have ceased to become a credible means of communication. This was not because they were not well produced or had become introspective. In most cases, other channels of communication were viewed as being more relevant – meetings, seminars, cascade communications methods, corporate video and even the internet.

Even with the 60 per cent of company newsletters in the limited survey that were still felt to be valid, over half could be given extra value through a communications audit that might help sharpen their focus.

Communications audits can be as complex as may be necessary. They can range in scale from informal discussions with a dozen people through to opinion surveys involving thousands. Yet the principles are simple.

Identify the audiences that the organisation is trying to reach. List the channels of communications that are being used by the organisation. Analyse the audiences being reached through these channels and set some measure of the effectiveness of the communications through these channels in terms of the reach and influence upon the audiences. From this analysis, identify any weaknesses, any overlap or any gaps in the communications matrix.

■ Basic desk research helps plan the interviews

A proportion of the research work can be done from behind the desk, but the important aspects on the quality of communications do require some form of survey with the audiences identified as being of importance to the organisation. A statistically valid opinion poll can be run across each of the key audiences identified – shareholders, customers, retailers and wholesalers, employees and so on.

It is advisable first to undertake a number of interviews not only to get a snapshot view of possible perceptions but also to help shape the questionnaire and logistical approach that might be deployed in the opinion survey. Focus groups consisting of six or eight interested people brought together to review an area under discussion can be useful. Individual interviews tend to be more helpful. These put less influence on the interviewee and do not give so much of an indication of what may be considered a 'constructive or positive' answer.

Whether you use focus groups or individual interviews, a larger-scale survey which has statistical validity relevant to the broad population will be of importance. Questions need to cover the relevance and quality of the channels of communication in terms of the information that is delivered to members of key audiences – and the feedback processes that may exist. Key representatives of these groups should be interviewed. It will be important to select these people carefully to ensure that they are independent and sufficiently outspoken to give an honest perspective. Their confidentiality needs to be protected to ensure that they do say what needs to be said, rather than what the organisation wants to hear.

■ Plan the issues audit on the basis of the communications review

The communications audit and the issues audit can, of course, be handled separately. However, there can be some economic and efficiency benefits in running these together, as the communications strategy will almost certainly be one of the requirements that will arise from an effective issues audit.

Let us assume that the communications audit has been undertaken and the strengths and weaknesses, the gaps or overlaps have been identified. This might provide a good basis on which to build the issues audit.

As noted earlier, issues are simply those potential areas coming up over the horizon that could have an impact upon the operations of the organisation. The objective of the issues audit is to identify all that might be of consequence and to help the company consider and plan its stance towards these.

In some cases, the company will want to take positive action; in others it will want to be prepared to react, if necessary; and, with a third group, it may simply want to be aware of the issues and consider them as low priority . . . or as items that could be dealt with when they arise and which do not need substantial forward planning.

■ Issues can completely reshape the business environment

To take a few practical examples:

- An issue likely to be of increasing importance to food manufacturers might be the growth in vegetarianism as well as the increased interest in organic or low-chemical food options.
- Retailers might find increasing public concern over the conditions of employment in Third World countries from where they are sourcing food, clothing and other lines.
- A tobacco manufacturer faces the certainty of tougher legislation and the likelihood that social pressures in the developed world will spread across the globe into developing nations which they are currently looking to maintaining sales levels.

Some of these trends are so strong and well established that they are barely issues and more realities.

In all cases, companies would be wise to evaluate the potential impact and consider the options that face them.

For example, how might a high street retailer or grocery multiple respond to concerns over sourcing from Third World countries? It might feel that it needs to give the public more information about the countries and the companies from where it is sourcing food and other items. The company might consider going one step further and setting up a buying policy with criteria for those companies or countries from which they will buy and those (that do not conform to the standards) from which they will not.

After all, as an illustration, Marks & Spencer would not buy from a clothing manufacturer in Manchester that had an appalling environmental or safety record. Could the public (or a consumer group or a trade union or the pressure groups that create public issues) ask why the company should consider different standards to be appropriate in Brazil or in Algeria?

The tobacco company might consider that the people of the world will be so enlightened that in a century or two no-one will smoke. If they were to believe this, then they would not be looking at whether they should be in tobacco or not – but at the timetable for them to get out of the product.

■ Public opinion defines acceptable trading practices

These are all reasonably obvious examples of how tomorrow's trading may be different because of the environment within which the companies will be working. This environment is largely shaped by public opinion, which itself is driven by many motivators, such as pressure groups, the media, politicians, legislation and so on.

The public relations professional is one of those best qualified to work alongside marketing specialists to analyse the pressures that are currently at work in the marketplace and make reasonably accurate predictions on what might happen in the future. Even should these predictions not be 100 per cent accurate, they will give at least a direction to company policy and the opportunity to begin planning.

In some cases, the fact that the company has evaluated its attitudes towards issues can, in itself, be useful. However well organised, companies do not control the public agenda and have no idea what might move to the top of public debate as a result of actions by third parties over which they have no control.

■ The audit is preparation for possible public and media debate

Consider a hypothetical example. Amnesty International decides to run a campaign looking at Someplace and its human rights' records. The media pick this up and journalists start looking at international links to see what the connections might be. They realise that one of these is Someplace trading. They soon find that, as an illustration, coffee brands from Someplace are on the shelves of most supermarkets. Suppose their reporter in Someplace sees there is potential for him to make his name by writing a powerful story about the appalling employment conditions on coffee farms and processing plants in our mythical Someplace.

The first that the retailer may learn about this is the telephone call from a journalist putting together a story for that evening's television news or for tomorrow morning's paper; there will be little time to consider the response. That is the way the media work. Editors cannot wait on a story as they always have to beat their competitors to the headlines. Yesterday's news is often no news at all.

Usually the story is almost finished when the journalist asks for a response, and the company representative will have no idea of the other accusations and scandals that they are about to reveal. They may also not tell the spokesperson that their story is a dramatic exposé of corruption in the Someplace government

– a nasty saga of alleged backhanders, into which the company can become unwittingly involved, if the representative does not have the right information or give the right answers. And, by the way, no panic. Any time in the next ten minutes will be fine. There is a television crew and several reporters waiting in reception.

Suppose the company has audited its buying policies and looked at all the countries from which it is sourcing products. Then it will have some facts and figures relating to Someplace – and, even more important, a policy that has been developed based upon these facts. Immediately, the company spokesperson can respond to enquiries by saying, 'We looked at Someplace in the global review we undertook eighteen months ago and our findings were . . . and for that reason our policy is . . .'

■ Evaluating attitudes to issues sets the media relations stance

At the least, the company looks well informed and responsible. It might even be able to contradict the stories, as these are not consistent with its own information on the country. Or it might be able to confirm that, as a result of its findings, it had written to the government/ministry of agriculture/farming co-operative organisation of Someplace asking them to prepare a timetable for improving the working conditions if the company is to continue trading with them. The company might have decided the situation was unacceptable – and be able to report that, at such and such a date, it had advised that it would be sourcing no more coffee from Someplace.

The answer is less important than the fact that the company is ahead of this and countless other issues. It is not caught by surprise, as so many big names have been The company will be able to answer authoritatively and this will result in a positive story or, at worst, no story, for the media will move to focus on others less well organised.

Those companies that are not prepared are simply setting themselves up as easy targets for the media and pressure groups. Too often, they do not have the answers. And/or are too frightened to answer. Or are inhibited by a structure that simply cannot respond quickly enough. These matters have to be sorted out in advance.

■ Be prepared to respond instantly to media investigations

In relation to the above scenario, compare these two options:

First, the hypothetical company focuses on today's trading and leaves tomorrow to look after itself. A crisis arises and it has no proper up-to-date information, no policy and no agreed stance. It reacts slowly and cautiously to the news story which unfolds over the coming days. Members of the public respond by declining to buy the products. Staff are confused about whether the company has a policy; they all see television and read the papers but it is hours or even days later that they get any policy information from the top. In the meantime, some individual managers have instructed staff to remove the product – but others have not, which causes even greater confusion and media comment.

Both the public relations and marketing departments are in disarray. By now, the company is spending millions with external consultancies in public affairs, legal, international trade, marketing and public relations specialities, all working (supposedly) 24 hours a day and making a fortune from the lack of foresight of the company.

Smart alecs like Roger Haywood (who may have failed to sell an issues audit to the public relations department to prevent such disasters) are sufficiently close to the chairman to try to help him out of the mess. He is keen to get his and his company's position clear and clean. The chairman's reputation (and knighthood) may be at stake. But this admirable, energetic and positive action bypasses the marketing and public relations professionals – and, probably rightly by now, for they have proven they are not on top of the issue. So, are you *sure* you want to manage public relations?

Or alternatively. . .

The company allocates a tiny percentage of what might be required if it had to deal with a crisis – less than 5 per cent of its marketing budget, typically. This sum is put towards an intelligent issues audit. From this audit, it decides priorities and policies. All possible issues are investigated and a clear position on each presented to the board with recommendations on the stance the company might take.

The crisis arises. The spokesperson deals with it effectively and efficiently and the company is seen to be a sensible, responsible, caring organisation. It is the only retailer to be able to respond within the ten minute deadline of the media. It impresses journalists immensely because its spokesperson is able to call up the background on Someplace immediately on its PC.

This produces a couple of modest but positive stories. On the hairier stuff, all the flak and criticism becomes targeted at its competitors. They are in disarray, even possibly associated by implication (however unfairly) with the corruption scandal that is unfolding.

The organised company has substantially enhanced its reputation with its publics, including an embarrassed government, and secures competitive edge as customers unwilling to buy Someplace coffees from competitors' shelves pour into the stores in appreciation of a retailer that seems to understand some of the important aspects of what is happening in the world.

Which position would you prefer? And which would you prefer to be presenting to your boss?

■ Companies that have done their homework do not hit the headlines

The recommendation is fairly obvious. Review and audit the issues *before* considering managing a crisis. Set up procedures to prevent the crisis devastating the company.

We rarely hear of those companies that have taken such an intelligent stance – they have not been engulfed in a crisis because they planned to avoid this eventuality.

We regularly hear of those whose advance planning is suspect or non-existent, or who fail to be able to cope with the impact of the media and public pressure. Remember Cunard and the QE2 refit; Yorkshire Water and its chairman who did not take a bath for three months to help alleviate the water shortage; Eastern Electricity and its inadequate reaction to public criticism of its advanced billing methods; the National Farmers' Union losing control over the BSE issue; British Gas doubling the salary of its chief executive at the same time as cutting incomes to sales staff, and then banning the media from its AGM, thus guaranteeing maximum coverage for any shareholder bright enough to take a video camera into the meeting to record the shareholder fury; everything the whole tobacco industry says and does . . . I could go on.

The key point in crisis management is not the details of the incident but the attention that has been paid to pre-planning and the allocation of appropriate resources within the framework of an agreed procedure. It is no good relying on commonsense or traditional lines of delegated responsibility. When the crisis hits, a brand manager or press officer may be the person who has to take priority in decision-making over someone more senior in the organisation.

■ Many issues provide business opportunities

Traditionally, issues have tended to be seen as problems, but this is not the case. Some issues – such as safety, the environment and industrial relations – may potentially create problems. But some issues may be neutral or, even, positive.

Neutral issues may affect everyone equally. A change in European packaging laws, for example. The skill will be to put up a stance towards such a change which will add competitive edge. Some changes or issues might even be positive. They may well be working to your advantage. A packaging directive might give an edge to a company whose product is cased in soft rubber but whose competitors are using more fragile, hard plastic.

■ Decide what the company stance is on important issues

The issues audit is a broader and more substantial review. It attempts to isolate all those factors that might have a significant impact upon the trading operation of the organisation and how these might be managed.

This audit has less to be statistically valid as it is a review of perspectives. The skill is to try to balance the perspectives across the spectrum to ensure that a fair picture is presented; management will need to make important decisions on the stance the company needs to take towards each issue and how this should be projected both internally and externally.

The power of the issues audit is that it takes all views – popular or unpopular – that might be derived from all members of the management team and presents these for consideration by the top management. They cannot afford to ignore anything. They know that the one item they discount may be the one that could cause the downfall of the company. And it will be on the record that this area was not given serious consideration.

Some public relations people would argue that it is their responsibility to constantly audit the issues that are of concern to members of the management team and to make sure that the chairman and chief executive are aware of these and are taking the appropriate action.

Whether or not the marketing professional believes that this is a reasonable stance for the public relations chief to adopt, it would certainly be wise for members of the management team to assure themselves that they are fully abreast of the issues and are working as partners with the public relations professionals in presenting to top management the approach that they recommend should be adopted towards issues of potential significance.

■ Set the procedure for reviewing key issues

Most of the issues that demand attention will be well known within the company. It only requires candid, confidential interviews with key line managers and directors to identify them. It can be helpful to talk to external bodies such as trade and professional groups, associations, government departments and so on, to get their perspective; clearly, most companies know their own business so these bodies rarely identify practices that are not well known within some department or division within the company.

■ Prepare a list of issues to be circulated

A document circulated amongst top managers which identifies all these issues and the possible impacts upon the company is an effective starting point for beginning to manage activities within this environment of issues.

■ Identify areas of concern – and of opportunity

Clearly, the company has to have a stance towards each of these issues, some of which it will be able to control and some of which will be external. An intelligent issues-appraisal procedure in operation at Heatrae-Sadia enabled the company to identify a trend likely to evolve towards longer guarantees on electric appliances. The company scored a marketing first and scooped a dominant share of the market for its electric showers and heaters by being first with a two-year instead of the traditional one-year guarantee.

External legislation may be a factor over which the company has little control. However, by keeping close to proposed legislation, alternative approaches can be developed. Clearly, such procedures should be run in parallel with lobbying efforts to minimise the possibility of unhelpful legislation.

■ Monitor potential legislation that could affect markets

The process that is sometimes called reputation risk management is close in many ways to the idea of issues management. Reputation risk management is sometimes defined as the discipline designed to protect the reputation against threats.

In other words, packaging trends and public concerns may be issues over which the manufacturer could have a good degree of influence. Industry legislation and competitive activity may be issues where it has not.

To take one of these as an example, the traditional metal electric kettle market was wiped out almost overnight by the introduction of a new product design – the plastic jug type kettle. Manufacturers even with dominant positions in secure markets need to be constantly looking at everything which could endanger their position.

■ Identify the executive responsible for leading on each issue

A sensitive monitoring system is absolutely essential for an effective crisis management programme. Remember too, that some threats to the reputation may begin quite modestly.

One difficulty in such situations is that it can take time to establish the facts . . . and time is not available to an organisation when the media spotlight is glaring on it. Understandably, a strong instinct is to play for safety. Yet to offer no comment can destroy a company reputation by making management look indifferent to the hazard or actual harm that might be created by an incident.

If the company reputation is to be protected, early and sensitive comments are essential. Remember the concept of the corporate personality. Would an individual retain much respect if he declined to comment on a tragedy in which he was involved, whether or not he may have been responsible?

■ Set up a standing crisis management team

The company needs to form a crisis management team. Ideally, this will be composed of a number of individuals, all of whom will have been trained and know how to work together. The company will need more personnel allocated to this team than are actually necessary.

Some are certain to be away, ill or on holiday at the time of crisis.

Equally, there needs to be more than one leader of this team to cover such an eventuality. The crisis management team should encompass a range of skills, other than communications. Thus it might include senior executives from within sales, marketing, customer care, operations, personnel or industrial relations. Ideally, these should be individuals at the most senior level. The advantage of having such a mixed team is that they bring a range of expertise and improve the chances of various aspects of any crisis being well covered. Each member of the team also needs an understudy.

■ Incident facilities are needed at all company locations

There should be an incident room established at every company location. Quite often this will double as some other function room, such as a reception, canteen, briefing or interview room. However, it is helpful if it is equipped to deal with the emergency – generally with a locked cupboard containing all the essential items.

Note that each location may need more than one incident room as these can be closed off or inaccessible when the incident is something such as a fire or an explosion.

■ Develop training based on a policy document

The issues management team will develop a crisis manual. This is a practical document full of essential information, not only to help the team in handling the incident but in providing background material that can be handed out in response to enquiries. Copies of this manual need to be available at all incident locations. It is particularly useful if this can be in electronic form on computer so that high speed print-outs of background to various products, situation, safety records and other items can be available instantly.

The conventional crisis-handling plan which details exactly what should be done in each incident, often prepared by specialists with minimal company input, is unlikely to be used and will sit on the shelf gathering dust.

A document that has helpful and immediate information is much more useful. It should include telephone numbers of relevant staff and external agencies and a simple procedure sheet. Copies need to be kept by each member of the crisis team, both in their offices and at their homes. Members of this flying squad are also advised to hold a packed bag with any emergency items that may be necessary, such as a change of clothing, portable telephone, spare batteries, the crisis manual, a company telephone list, a key media list, even a video recorder with blank tapes, charged laptop computers with modems, action checklists and so on.

In dealing with a serious incident, your company spokespeople will need to be able to handle the media effectively. In many cases, the media will be aware of the incident before the company. The most credible company spokespeople for the media will always be the most senior person; such individuals are not always the most competent or even likely to have the right skills and attitudes.

■ Develop and train your company spokespeople

There are some basic guidelines that should be considered when dealing with journalists in an incident situation.

- Make sure that all your spokespeople are fully trained.
- Give the media the fullest information possible. Even if you do not have full details of the incident, useful background on the company, its record and trading activities will be helpful to journalists.
- Establish a media relations strategy as early as possible and ensure that all are fully briefed on it.
- Make sure that everybody is as helpful as they can possibly can be with the media, dealing with all questions they can cover and logging those they are unable to answer so that they can be called back.
- Get on top of the situation early and maintain control. Decide the agenda and manage the media information to that.
- Use pre-prepared information. With television journalists it is extremely useful to have available maps, plans and aerial photographs of all locations so that they can be used with a spokesman to discuss where an incident has happened.
- Honour all commitments to the media. If information will be available in half an hour then make sure that it is and that it is disseminated to those that have asked for it.
- Get the information out as fast as you can, even if this means it is going out part by part.
- Ensure that you are disseminating information through other channels of communication – telephone and fax should not be forgotten.
- Ensure other audiences such as employees are not totally reliant on the media for their understanding of what is happening.
- The central quality to drill into personnel is their responsibility. Send in the most senior person, fast, in an emergency

When the Exxon *Valdez* split open in Alaska, spilling millions of gallons of oil, senior executives were slow to visit to scene until forced by public pressure. Some 30 000 customers sent back their company charge cards in disgust. The reputation damage to the company was enormous; the financial damage incalculable.

■ Develop policies that clarify how decisions will be made

Perhaps one of the keys to the prompt and responsible approach adopted by Johnson & Johnson when handling the Tylenol poisoning was that the company had a well-published credo – this identified its primary responsibility as being towards its customers.

One visible action that the public can note and respond to is the seniority of manager allocated to deal with crisis. One criticism of the Exxon company was that top executives did not immediately respond and it was some considerable time before anyone in authority actually arrived at the scene of the *Valdez* disaster in Alaska.

In contrast, Warren Anderson, chairman of Union Carbide, immediately flew to Bhopal when his Indian subsidiary suffered an unimaginable manufacturing accident. This produced a poisonous gas cloud which, in one night, had killed 1200 people – and a death toll that was rising hour by hour. He knew he risked almost certain arrest and an obviously hostile reception but believed that it was his responsibility.

He defied the advice of some legal colleagues, accepted responsibility and expressed both regret and concern. This established Union Carbide as a victim of the disaster. It also positioned the company as the leader in establishing what went wrong and what needed to be done to rectify the tragedy that had been created.

Union Carbide may have mismanaged some aspects of the tragedy, but they did have the sense to respond promptly, calling a press conference at their head office on the first day. This contrasted with the Firestone Tyre & Rubber Company, which claimed that nothing was wrong when Firestone 500 tyres first began disintegrating.

■ Behave as if all questions and answers will be made public

It is important to remember the speed of response of the media. Journalists can often be the first to be aware of many incidents – sometimes even ahead of management.

When the Gulf tanker, *Betelguese*, unloading at Bantry Bay, caught fire and exploded at 1.00 am on a January night some years ago, a senior journalist from the *Irish Times* was actually watching the shipping in the bay through his binoculars from his holiday cottage. The ship literally blew up before his eyes. News of the disaster was being flashed around the world on the wire services within ten minutes of it happening. It was over an hour before the public relations people were advised.

What starts as a small story can also become a big story, even if there is no direct single tragedy, accident or incident involved.

■ Plan comment from all spokespeople to reinforce strategy

Lever Brothers had enjoyed a high-profile multi-media launch of its advanced detergent, New System Persil automatic washing powder. A report by the National Eczema Society throwing doubts on the product was quoted in the *Guardian*, and was the start of an escalating problem. It was picked up by the *Sunday Mirror*, later the *Daily Mirror* and virtually all the national UK publications. Market share collapsed.

It is important that the management should remember that many new products will have potentially critical audiences. Some journalists are also interested in manufacturers' problem stories.

In the case of the Persil powder, research eventually undertaken suggested that only one in ten thousand people might have had a dermatological reaction related to its use. However, that was too late and the damage had been done. Better warnings on the packet and more detailed explanation over its enzyme base might have prevented the problem in the first instance. This was a case where an issue audit before the launch might have identified the risk – it would certainly have prepared the company to deal more promptly with a problem before it could cause such damage.

■ Use simulations to test the procedures

An emergency exercise is an excellent way to test the procedures. A simulated emergency will be agreed amongst a small group of people – the smaller the better. To make this an effective test, other members of the emergency and crisis teams must be able to react from it fresh – exactly as they would with the real thing.

The testing will be a good way of evaluating how effective training has been. No set of procedures can work perfectly and any test will identify any number of areas – hopefully, mostly only needing fine-tuning but, occasionally, some needing radical reorganisation.

When he was a senior manager of public relations for British Airways, Peter Jones had had considerable experience of developing and running crisis management systems. On a number of occasions – sometimes the real thing and sometimes tests – he was able to check out practice against theory. One critical factor, he believes, is that you must contain and separate the incident. The rest of the business has to continue or you will have no business.

From his experience, you might only use 50 per cent of whatever the crisis manual says – but you will never be able to tell in advance what that 50 per cent may be. However, one constant factor is that with the speed of modern media you have an absolute maximum of 60 minutes to get the incident communications under control. Broadcasters can be on air in seconds and on many occasions they may be the first on the scene. The tone of those early broadcasts can set the tone for the whole incident.

■ Communicate internally and externally in parallel

Whilst the natural focus is on external communications, it is critical not to forget to keep your own personnel and your business partners fully informed. For example, if a plane is involved in an incident and your counter staff are not briefed then they cannot adequately deal with the naturally concerned enquiries of other passengers. 'Believe me,' adds Jones, '*I don't know* equals *I don't care*.'

Managers need the ability to see the crisis from the public perspective. For Rhône–Poulenc's biggest facility in the UK, we helped run an exercise to test emergency procedures. The aim was to check communications alongside essential rescue and containment operations. The company had simulated an explosion on site in which a number of people had been severely 'injured' and perhaps some may even have 'died'. The test allowed company personnel to identify any weaknesses, sharpen their skills and check co-ordination with emergency services. It ran well and identified some areas where improvements could be made to minimise problems should – heaven forbid – the real thing happen.

The senior site manager was an example of command and authority as the unnerving 'incident' unfolded. Just one factor caught him by surprise. He had dealt effectively with a 'local radio reporter' – in actuality a member of my staff – who had grilled him on the incident. He had forgotten that such comments could be broadcast locally within minutes – indeed, factory neighbours might have heard or seen a real explosion. He was disturbed when the next phone call turned out to be a tearful and very worried local neighbour, convinced that her husband, who was working on that shift, had been killed.

The management, in dealing with the accident and emergency services, had remembered their responsibilities to the media but had forgotten that phone lines would be instantly jammed with calls from anxious friends and relatives. Emergency procedures were adjusted in this and other areas as a result of this experience. Although the woman calling was only a member of the consultancy team, the adrenalin had been running so high that the plant manager was genuinely shocked by the thought that in reality this could be the widow of somebody on his staff who had been killed.

■ Remember that every employee who comments is the company

On another occasion, during a similar test, a consultant posed as an aggressive television reporter and grilled a hapless employee of a leading distributor of hazardous materials at its Thameside plant. He challenged the executive over the hazards of the butane stored at one of their facilities. He bullied the man into admitting that he lived 20 miles away and that he was glad that 'I'm not a factory neighbour, because my family would never feel safe.'

An executive from the nuclear waste reprocessing plant in Sellafield, Cumbria, casually commented after a leak of radioactive vapour: 'This sort of thing happens daily in industry.'

An official in the steel industry protested about what he felt to be unfair reporting of a fatal accident with the comment: 'Our industry is improving standards all the time. We have only killed four people this year.' No doubt comforting news for the widows.

The moral is to think about what you are proposing to say. Run through it. Review your plans and, above all, test any procedure – for each incident has the potential to create new problems and from these come the lessons that bring constant improvement.

■ Polish all the policies and procedures in 'peacetime'

A group safety adviser with the worldwide remit for all aspects of BP's safety awareness, risk management and emergency preparedness is Richard Read. He is responsible for the BP group's emergency management structure and, specifically, for the provision of crisis management response in the group's centre. He firmly believes that the best time to prepare for crisis is when there is none. 'You need to get your peacetime lines in operation so you can use them in war.'

One informal technique that he deploys for evaluating whether a crisis is a significant at an industry or company level is to ask whether it is likely to develop to a point where it might need to be featured in the annual report or whether the company might be asked to explain.

He makes a good point, because after the Union Carbide disaster at Bhopal where several thousand people within the local community were killed as a result of a major chemical incident, the company found that its operations at all plants were affected – even if they were not making any products that were in any way related to those at Bhopal.

BP uses the effective 'two-room' approach to managing a crisis. As Read explains, the inner room is an area of quiet where the most senior managers in the company, representing the relevant disciplines, can consider the information as the situation unfolds; they can make reasoned policy decisions, knowing they are fully informed.

The second room is for the line managers who are directly responsible for operations, with their necessary staff support. This can be a hectic and noisy hive of activity, as information comes in and instructions go out. From here, the updates for management are developed; the relevant manager detaches himself or herself from the activity centre to report to the top executives in the quiet room, there to debate and decide policy.

The handling of a crisis can have an impact on all audiences including, of course, customers. This is an area of great importance in making decisions and where marketing and public relations need to be co-operating closely.

The priorities in handling crises are usually quite clear, such as the protection of life, the environment, investment but, at the same time, reputation. The best policy must be to do what is right because it is right. Happily this is also likely to win at least the understanding of the public, even where an organisation may have made a mistake.

CHAPTER 5

Public relations budget and resources

APPOINTING AND HANDLING PROFESSIONALS

The lyf so short, the craft so long to lerne
(Ars longa, vita brevis)
　　Geoffrey Chaucer (1340–1400), translating from Hippocrates (460–357 BC)

■ Recruit public relations professionals compatible with corporate ambitions

In many companies, public relations will be run as a separate operation, often in parallel with marketing – possibly reporting in to different board directors. Marketing is more often accepted (and often more accepted) as a business discipline than public relations – certainly as one contributing to the bottom line.

As a consequence, there will be few companies of any size where marketing is not represented on the board, particularly where the organisation has a consumer orientation. Equally, there will be few companies where public relations *is* directly represented on the board – even where its practitioners are given honorary titles such as director of communications or of corporate relations. Yet public relations in larger companies will nearly always report to the chief executive or the chairman.

Ironically, many marketing policy decisions will be made within the marketing function. Few significant public relations policy decisions will be made within the public relations function; though the senior adviser may not be seen to be senior enough for a position on the board, the function is so critical that the chairman will be involved in the decisions.

As someone once said, aye there's the rub. For though in some companies public relations is seen as part of marketing, in others it is separate because of its broader responsibilities, particularly at government and investor levels, where the chairman and chief executive often wish to (and should) have a direct involvement.

Even if the marketing professionals do not recruit directly the public relations team, they need to know the processes involved in selecting people of the right compatibility and quality; at the least, they will have to work closely together. These notes suggest procedures that have worked well in this selection lottery.

It is far more likely that marketing will appoint consultancies. Many companies have senior staff professionals to handle corporate relations and advise the board. Marketing may be supported by staff responsible for supervising marketing public relations, often with the support of one or more consultancies. Sometimes one consultancy will handle all marketing public relations but, more often, specialists will be appointed to handle brands or divisions, wholesaler or retailer relations, new product launches and so on.

For this chapter, we look at a company making its first public relations appointment. (The principles involved are relevant to adding people to the team. Then we look at the appointment of consultancies.

Once an organisation has established that it has a public relations need, there may be a number of options on how this can be covered. The three main methods are:

- the nomination and training of an existing executive and a support team;
- the recruitment of professional (in other words, experienced) public relations staff;
- the appointment of one or more consultancies.

Sometimes the ideal solution may involve more than one of these options.

A company in a competitive market, under public scrutiny, possibly operating in sensitive area, will find public relations absolutely central to trading success. Therefore, it is likely to have to use skilled, professional executives – whether staff or consultancy or mixture of both.

■ First choice must be to appoint a proven professional

Where the decision is to put a professional public relations person on to the staff, the best option must be to appoint someone with proven capabilities. Unless it is to be a big gamble, this experience should be in public relations not in an allied discipline, however useful, such as sales, marketing, advertising or the media. These may seem to those outside marketing to be closely related, but they are distinct disciplines.

Credible companies have not put generalists into senior marketing positions for a couple of decades or more. They want and expect relevant expertise. However admirable, a career in the navy, the civil service or academia will not provide the right abilities.

This is all so obvious that you must wonder why I say this. Simple. Some companies still choose to put a non-public relations person into the public relations slot. And not just organisations where public relations may not have been top of the agenda. A number of the privatised public utilities moved seasoned company servants into the newly-important public relations function. The argument went (how many times have you heard this?) that it needed someone who knew the industry and the company to undertake such a crucial role. The reality is that an intelligent public relations professional can always learn the industry and the company far quicker than anyone in the company could possibly (if ever) learn public relations. The utilities have found that those which recruited good public relations professionals saw their reputations and fortunes rise.

The success of those worthies from other disciplines moved across into public relations range from, at best, adequate to downright disastrous. Some have steered their corporate affairs into arenas of disrepute and their media relations into chaos. However, perhaps I should come off the fence and stop being so oblique; I should declare my view that the appointment of someone to a senior public relations position who has not got the right experience may not be a good idea.

In some of these companies, the old retainer may have a professional reporting to him. Surely that professional can give him the right input? If the line of thinking is that you might bring in a high-profile media personality, say, over the head of your current public relations plodder, think again. You will get the worst of both worlds: a journalist who knows nothing about public relations but will have to pretend he or she does, and a demotivated number two who will do everything possible to make sure his boss does not succeed.

Soon the number two looks for a better job. And once he's gone, there is no one to discreetly understudy either your old retainer/bright new flounderer,. And if you do not believe me, I could give you the names of a couple of ex-marketing directors who thought public relations was easy and paid the price for entrusting this job to a hopeful of various sorts . . .

Appoint a professional. The best man or woman that you can find and can afford.

(There may be a place for an intelligent professional converting from a business area that you value – or an individual you respect and who may have the qualities but not the experience. Someone shifting from the media or another discipline might go into a number two spot for a significant period – both to acquire the special skills and to avoid him or her being the primary adviser before gaining the necessary experience.)

A limited budget is not always a legitimate reason for not tackling public relations properly, particularly in the marketing sector. Often, the reason why the budget is not available is that decision-makers do not rate the public relations function highly enough. Clever buying in public relations is not reducing the budget – anyone can do that – but increasing the expectation and the performance; that takes a real marketing professional.

Effective public relations, ultimately, costs no more than ineffective public relations; the returns from an investment in public relations are usually so significant that a company has to be spending a substantial amount before it reaches the point of diminishing returns.

■ Identify the best candidate for the job

Make sure that candidates for public relations positions have the style and personality compatible with the company. A conservative, cautious environment might not be best served by an extrovert, action-orientated communicator – or vice versa. The right person must have the right temperament, the right brief, the right commitment – and will need the right training.

One of the most important points in the selection process is to ensure that the philosophy of the candidate matches the requirements of the job. Public relations is sometimes seen as a universal discipline in which practitioners can deploy their skills regardless of the sector or framework within which they have to work. Though many principles do translate across business areas, this is not universally true. Public relations is such a personal emotive area that some practitioners can only work in activities that are closely paralleled to their own philosophies.

One reason for this is that public relations activity usually involves some commitment; often, this can only be assured when the aims of the organisation are close to the beliefs of the individual.

Some practitioners have advanced the view that a good public relations professional is like a lawyer – able to present the best possible case for his client, independently of his own views. In contrast, many practitioners believe they would be unable to represent a cause in which they did not personally believe. Rather like the best salesperson, a public relations person who is completely in line with the aims of the organisation, accepts its values and is committed to personal achievements that relate to the corporate achievements is most likely to make a success in the rough, tough world of public relations.

Whatever the selection process, make sure that you have a method to check the capabilities of candidates. Whatever the techniques you may use, testing the skills is always advised, even at the most senior level.

Good practitioners are likely to be articulate, responsive, energetic and have plenty of initiative. Courage is one of the essential qualities; the practitioner will frequently have to make his own decisions, argue them convincingly and must be able to stand by them.

■ Excellent language skills will always be a requirement

Levels of skill may not be the most important factor. However, the one area where you cannot compromise on ability is the use of English – or whatever language in which you have to work. Writing standards will need to be high.

Even great visual ideas have to start with a written presentation. Much of public relations is based on the written word. Someone who cannot write accurately, concisely and persuasively will not have the other skills that you will need.

Never, *never* convince yourself that you can make someone a good writer. It is possible (but unlikely) that you might be able to marginally improve someone's writing – say, from abysmal to merely awful. If they cannot become a good writer themselves, how can you show them how to do it? This can take a dozen years or more of hard work and self-discipline to reach a level of competence in writing. You will not have the time, the training capabilities and the patience, so do not try. I know; I have tried and failed. I can scrabble together a passable sentence and that took me ten years of effort *after* a good education! And I write at least 3000 words daily and I am still learning.

In the selection process, check that your paragon has the right attitudes and motivation. You want someone who is a self-starter, full of initiative; he or she will be mature enough to not have to know it all, but confident enough to know a good deal of it and to learn most of the rest.

Of course, you will not waste time on dullards; there are plenty of companies like Dullard & Dullard Partners, where such good folks can enjoy a satisfying uneventful life. It is not your responsibility to create employment opportunities for no-hopers. Equally, a useful test is to check if you are interviewing someone who complicates everything. You will need someone bright who makes everything simpler. Happily, the business is full of wonderful, talented, ambitious, competent and motivated individuals. The skill is to separate them from the rest. The best technique to do this, sadly, is to suspend your normal generosity and to be ruthless.

■ Buy consultancy to meet the needs you identify

Consultancies can offer a range of expertise. The company can choose the consultancy to suit the identified needs. The best way to handle the public relations activity may not be staff personnel or a consultancy; it may be a combination of these resources. Whether you decide to undertake the selection process yourself or rely on a trusted senior colleague, it is helpful to follow a consistent procedure.

The appointment needs to be right for much will depend on it. Ideally both sides will invest heavily and will be looking for a long-term relationship. An agreed procedure reduces the likelihood of being wooed by attractive but irrelevant aspects that can affect the best of judgements.

As marketing professionals appreciate, public relations consultancies range from one-man outfits to international organisations employing thousands and with turnovers in hundreds of millions.

The first decision is what resources are needed:

1. Do you need special experience of your industry?
2. Do you require national or international representation?
3. Do you need specialisation, e.g. in parliamentary, industrial, environmental areas, or general public relations?
4. Do you want advice or advice and implementation, with or without an internal public relations operation?

■ The start of the selection process is the shortlist

Produce a list of public relations consultancies which appear to be able to offer the services required. To produce a shortlist you may:

1. Talk to companies whose public relations work you admire.
2. Ask key journalists which consultancies offer them an effective service.
3. Talk to a relevant professional communications body.
4. Check established directories.

Much time and money will be spent by both your organisation and the consultancies before the final choice is made. Therefore it is advisable to reduce your list of possible consultancies to perhaps half a dozen before approaching them. Look at their existing client lists. In Britain, this might be published in the *PRCA Year Book*, *Hollis* or *Advertisers' Annual*.

Check on the ownership of your prospective public relations advisers. It may be to your advantage (or disadvantage) if they are members of an international group, or subsidiaries of an advertising agency. It may be important to know that the directors have been in business for two or twenty years, that the consultancy has two or twenty directors. You may eliminate one or two at this stage. Approach the prospective consultancies.

■ Your initial enquiry should be in writing

Try to adopt a consistent approach – and the first contact must be in writing.

This preliminary letter should invite the consultancy to write with details of its expertise and service. You should ruthlessly eliminate all those whose letters are not up to an acceptable business standard. (If they cannot project themselves, they will hardly be able to project your organisation.)

Do not eliminate those whose experience or skills do not appear to match your needs: this may not be a fair test at this stage. From this response, you will have perhaps two or three consultancies you would wish to invite to visit you for further discussions.

Suggest a date for a meeting and clarify your requirements, giving each consultancy the same information and the same opportunity. However, if one asks more perceptive questions and thereby clarifies the brief, then this could be a critical factor.

There is no need to provide the clarified brief to the other applicants who are less enquiring. With one prospective plc client, a small consultancy with special expertise spent days in research, including time on the road with the salesforce. From this, they revised the client's broad brief and produced a substantial and closer-focused document. They were astonished when the client gave copies of this to their competitors, all of whom then realised they had been on the wrong track. Perhaps because of this embarrassment, the client appointed an international competitor with a name, but to whom the business was less critical – another nice name on the client list. Sadly, this consultancy was going through an unstable time and badly let them down within six months.

So, what procedure should your executive leading the selection team follow at the preliminary interview to be sure you are setting the correct course for the ultimate right choice? He or she should conduct this as seriously as a personal job interview. (An appraisal form where you can note responses is helpful when it comes to comparing the strength of the cases presented to you.) Avoid any lunch or drinks appointments unless you extend the same opportunity to each contender.

The next stage will be that your executive visit their premises – assuming that this preliminary interview will have eliminated one or two of your prospect consultancies. Give the consultancies you wish to visit a brief on what you wish to achieve – for example, meeting the team, assessing their facilities, looking at client work and so on. Advise them who will be attending this meeting from your organisation.

■ Evaluate the approach of the consultancy in its own offices

Again, only accept a meeting running over lunch or dinner if this opportunity is given to each public relations company. If you have given the shortlisted consultancies a fair brief then you will be able to assess their response by direct comparison. Factors to be considered might include:

- their research into your organisation
- the physical resources available
- the expertise of the team offered
- the success of other client campaigns
- their investigation of your claims
- their understanding of your aims
- their empathy/compatibility
- the relevance of their observations

Do not expect the consultancy to present a programme to your team or field a particular account executive. It is more important to decide whether they have the skills to contribute to your organisation's public relations aims than to be too concerned with details of staffing. By now your shortlist should be down to two or three. Write to the consultancies you have visited.

Those you have eliminated should be told so and, politely, why. Now, you should be able to give the finalists a written brief expanding your aims. You should clarify to whom they report, when and how.

■ Ask for observations and not recommendations at this stage

With those you have selected for further discussion, invite them to write a short report on how they believe they could assist your organisation. It is also fair to explain to them the position of your selection – 'You are now in our last three consultancies under consideration.'

Do not expect full proposals. These take time to prepare and require a deeper knowledge of your organisation than would be reasonable to expect at this stage. Give each consultancy an opportunity to revisit your offices with the executives they wish to put on your account. Keep your own team constant. Ask each consultancy to discuss their report and their recommendations. Do not pass information submitted by one consultancy to another.

■ Ask for an outline on likely budget and other resources

Points to discuss should include creativity of their work, suitability of the executive, the back-up team, ancillary services (e.g. print, design, house journals, exhibitions), calibre and reputation of existing clients, the reporting and control procedures, fee structure. Relate your company size and needs to their size. It may not be ideal for you to be either their largest or smallest client. If you are too big they may become nervous of jeopardising the business and soft-pedal on their advice: equally you may become wary of moving the account if they do not perform for fear of creating redundancies. Conversely, if your account is too small you may not get the level of service you wish – or feel able to crack the whip, when necessary.

Three main methods of fee charging are followed by most consultancies. All are based on hourly charges for executive time. The most popular method of calculating fees is on a fixed monthly retainer (representing y hours at $£x$).

The other common methods are fees billed monthly according to hours (or days): and a basic fee charged for an agreed programme plus increments for additional work. Additional projects or costs above an agreed level should normally be quoted and approved in advance of commissioning.

Consultancies also tackle projects on an *ad hoc* basis where they quote for an identified activity. This tends to be expensive and the least satisfactory way to build relationships between consultancy and staff personnel. It can be helpful, though, to support staff public relations departments at times of particular need for additional manpower or special expertise.

Do not judge solely on the hourly rate; an average executive at $£x$ may be a poorer buy than a senior man at $2 \times £x$ – alternatively you may not want $2 \times £x$ an hour charges for writing a simple appointment story. Ask the consultancies to prepare a budget – or recommendations on the breakdown of your own suggested budget. This will cover fee, operating costs, media conferences, print, photography and any other items which will involve significant work and expenditure.

Avoid an open-ended fee system and agree a level of expenditure you would allow without prior consultation. Clarify how their invoices will relate to the activity reporting procedure.

You should talk to clients. Ask each consultancy to give you three or four senior client executives with whom you can discuss their public relations service. Talk to key journalists or members of other key audiences to check whether they have any experience of your preferred consultancies.

■ Judge the reputation of consultancies by their references

Should you need more detailed proposals, then agree some fee with your final shortlist of two or three consultancies. This may be nominal. This will also help avoid problems should more than one candidate consultancy come up with similar ideas: this fee can be negotiated to cover such an eventuality. (If they want confirmation of your budget and the names of their competitor consultancies, both are fair requests which should be answered.) Finally . . . make your decision. Write to the chosen consultancy and ask them to attend a final meeting to confirm working arrangements and financial matters.

At this stage, you may well agree a fee for a limited period, perhaps three months, so they can prepare full recommendations; alternatively you could pay them to prepare full proposals and costings; or you can agree an estimate of the work load for the first year, perhaps with an option to review at six months. Some consultancies will offer a contract rather than simply letters of agreement.

Write to the unsuccessful consultancies, thanking them for their efforts and explaining the reasons for your choice.

■ The best client/consultancy relationship is of mutual integrity

Some consultancies talk about their clients as if they were involved in a constant battle of wits with them. And perhaps they are, too often.

Here are a few suggestions for both consultancy staff and clients on how to get the best out of the co-operation. Both parties usually have a team, but, nonetheless, the relationship *does* depend on goodwill and understanding between individuals.

1. *Discuss and agree procedures.* The best relationship will be a partnership, so treat your consultant as a colleague and not a 'supplier'. Agree on regular planning/review meetings. He or she will need your input. Copy him in on all relevant reports and documents. Agree his reporting-back procedures.
2. *Expect ideas and performance.* Ask your consultant to suggest solutions to problems and to offer ideas to take advantage of opportunities – not just to carry out activities. But creativity is not a substitute for action so ask him to report on implementation and expect him to evaluate the performance of the programme, against objectives.
3. *Use your consultant as an adviser.* Always tell your consultant what might be happening *before* it happens. Involve him in policy decision-making. Expose him to other executives and allow him to establish relations with other advisers. Use him to present ideas and opportunities at company conferences and seminars.
4. *Make reviews factual and direct.* Progress must be discussed regularly. Be clear where you are unhappy and allow an opportunity for comment/improvement. Praise good work, preferably in writing, for such letters get circulated in the consultancy and everyone works harder for an appreciative client.
5. *Set and follow fair business terms.* You will get the best return from your consultancy if your account is profitable. Buy wisely but fairly; you should know the income/margin. Expect proper proposals with realistic prices; do not prune down to the last penny. And pay your bills promptly, as in the agreed terms.

CALCULATING THE BUDGET

■ Confirm the resources to be deployed on the action

Public relations activity should be undertaken within an agreed budget. Only rare contingency activity might be outside the confirmed budget. Public relations should be operating within the same disciplines that apply to any other business function. This control not only applies to those running the activity but to senior management; all must resist the temptation to adopt their favourite activity for sponsorship or be wooed, say, by the latest electronic technique and adjust the budget accordingly. If the sponsorship is a cost-effective way of achieving the objectives, then it should be part of programme recommendations. If not, it should not. One company sponsored showjumping because it was the hobby of the chairman's wife; yet all the research showed that the match with prospective customers was limited.

Sometimes disproportionate resources will be allocated to such peripheral activity at the expense of the planned, strategic events; the sales director favours a golf tournament, the international director insists the company is represented at that Hong Kong seminar.

Also, sometimes, there is more excitement in battling through a challenge than there may be in the advanced planning that could prevent it arising in the first place. This has often been true in the world of public relations. Budget is not available for the issues audit but, as soon as a crisis strikes, money becomes no object in resolving the difficulties.

■ Consider the options for budget calculation

However, let us assume that a programme of public relations activity is proposed. How do you plan the budget for this?

There is no one certain method. As public relations is an inexact science, then budgeting cannot be precise. Even if the activities were totally decided, different methods of tackling them will produce different costings. For this analysis, the company must decide which way it wishes to handle such proposed activity. Consider the options in costing.

■ The historical comparison

The most common method is also the least satisfactory. This is based on what might have been spent previously the year before, perhaps adjusted to allow for inflation. Sometimes companies allow this figure to grow in proportion to company growth. This is illogical. If the company grew without the budget, why spend money on more such activity?

More sophisticated planners may make an allowance for factors that might make the task more difficult or easy. These plus and minus factors can be listed and compared – new products are a plus, whilst increased competition would be a minus. From this some weighting can be estimated.

The weakness of the system is that the original figure used as a comparison may be inappropriate. This approach also makes no allowance for a radical option – some great opportunity that may be out of line with the assumed public relations spend. Also those responsible for the public relations planning, knowing that the likely spend is virtually fixed in advance, soon stop looking for such great new ideas – they will never get the budget for them.

■ Resources costing

Under this method, management decides what level of public relations resource it feels it needs and then calculates a cost for this – staff plus overheads plus consultancy plus direct costs plus operational budgets and so on.

This is not too helpful as it gives no indication of whether the resources are at the right level in the first place. However, it does have the advantage that it is starting to introduce some judgement into the budget process – e.g. should we add an executive to handle trade relations or appoint a consultancy for that sector?

■ Action costing

A variation on resources costing is to plan a programme of activity without regard for how it is to be carried out – and then to prepare costings for the various ways it might be run. The programme might include continuity media relations, running the press office, the media conferences, this sponsorship, the annual report and that brochure, the trade seminars and so on.

Cost may be calculated from historical experience or by going into the market to obtain estimates.

■ Competitive tendering

In competitive tendering the agreed activity is prepared as a plan and consultancies are invited to tender for the contract. This is not used often. Although it can be effective in obtaining competitive costs, performance is less certain; many companies that might be eligible to tender are committed to long relationships. Most would be unhappy about a repeat competitive process a year or two later.

This method also requires firm management, as interest in performing can be low – *and* fade as the end of the contract approaches. Experience has shown that good performers may still not win follow-on contracts at a better price, as there will always be someone cheaper and, by the time the client finds they are worse, it is too late.

■ Income proportion

Companies look at sales or margin and allocate a figure as a percentage. Although this has some merit, it still suffers from the somewhat illogical fact that sales is creating the public relations budget rather than the other way round.

In some cases, management may allocate a proportion of the marketing budget for public relations. But how do you compare activity options within marketing? Certainly not by fixed ratios but by the performance return on the investment.

Some 1 per cent or less of sales might provide a usable budget in some large fast-moving consumer goods (FMCG) industries and not in others, such as business-to-business. Similarly, with major capital goods, public relations could be 60 per cent of the marketing spend but in financial services it may be 10 per cent or less. Some idea of a norm can be helpful as a starting point.

■ Industry comparison

One or two trade bodies run an annual members' audit to compile an average spend in marketing and communications areas. Trade and industry journals such as *Campaign*, *Marketing* and *Marketing Week* review spending in advertising and marketing. The comparable figures from *PR Week* on public relations spend are not yet substantial or comprehensive enough but will become so, over time, as managers get used to the concept.

Informal comparisons with others in your business sector or comparable companies of similar size and market position in other business sectors can be extremely useful. Ask your opposite number from non-competing companies you respect to a meeting to discuss and compare public relations programmes, procedures and budgets. You both could learn much at no cost, without risk to your respective competitive positions.

■ Capitation rating

At its simplest, public relations is about changing awareness, knowledge or attitude amongst audiences, most of whom can be clearly defined. From this, one of the more sophisticated and useful budget calculation methods has been developed.

The company identifies, in advance, the numbers in the audiences to be influenced. From this a calculation is made of the acceptable cost to put, say, agreed messages in front of these groups. This can be based on other comparative methods of communicating such information, including direct mail, seminars, conferences, sponsorship or advertising. Some weighting regarding effectiveness needs to be made. For example an advertisement in a national newspaper reaching x potential product buyers will not have the impact per person as on the y potential buyers attending a sponsored event, such as Wimbledon, Ascot or Silverstone. Or will it? That is when the interested focused discussions between the different disciplines within the marketing mix can begin.

■ *Achievement targeting*

One of the best methods developed to date takes the capitation concept one stage further by relating this to the level of achievement that can be expected.

The process is to agree the audiences to be reached. This should be on some numeric basis related to the future performance of the organisation. For example, to increase the take-up this year of our loyalty card by 10 per cent we need to reach A million of whom we would expect B per cent to join. If this is to be achieved through public relations then how would we put a credible message in front of that A million to convince B per cent to take up the offer? If we could do this we could pay £C per thousand as this would be as effective as other options but D per cent cheaper.

The process is repeated across all objectives and the totals cumulated. An estimate of the cost of overlaps and the benefits of scale can be deducted to reach a final figure. This also sets the target against which the activity will be judged at the end of the year. Future budgets would be adjusted according to these results.

■ Develop the budget planning method to suit your needs

None of the above methods offers an infallible or, even, satisfactory method for calculating the definitive budget. All have their strengths and weaknesses. Often the best procedure is to use company procedure and some combination of these techniques.

One rule is certain. Involve the public relations professionals in the calculations and thus ensure that they own the final recommendation. They will then carry the responsibility for achieving and reporting on the level of performance expected from this budget allocation.

Note that Chapter 6 looks at briefing and Chapter 7 at evaluation; these can profitably be read in conjunction with the recommendations in this chapter.

Public relations direction
PLANNING AND WRITING THE BRIEF

Mankind have been created for the sake of one another. Either instruct them, therefore, or endure them.

Marcus Aurelius (121–180), *Meditations*

■ Performance depends on the precision of the brief

The quality of the public relations effort is likely to be directly related to the quality of the brief. However, *any* brief is better than none. There should be no mystery. The brief is an outline of what the expenditure in public relations is expected to return to the investor. It should not be long. It should be focused. It should not propose activity. It should identify expected achievements.

This chapter attempts to outline the central factors in a good brief, with some suggestions on how this might be developed. Of course, developing and writing the brief obviously involves setting objectives, however provisional. And objectives mean nothing unless they can be related to the performance. Therefore, these notes have some synergy with Chapter 7 which looks at performance appraisal. Indeed, there is a little inevitable overlap between the two and it is suggested that these chapters might profitably be read together.

Often, the most helpful brief is the result of much thought and discussion – but not always. Yet, sometimes, a brilliant brief can be scribbled on the back of an envelope. The central factor is simple. What is the public relations supposed to be doing?

Some years back, after a night out with the then marketing director of Vent-Axia, we got into a debate about what public relations could and could not achieve. He told me I could have the business if I could meet his challenge. He then wrote on the back of the restaurant bill, *Make people want to buy our products more than the competition.*

Of course I had to laugh, but I had to accept the challenge. And, together, we did. As a brief it was clear on expectations, with no proposals on what activity should be undertaken. It was precise, but with no detail. It was a formula for success.

We accepted the challenge and put together some recommendations. These were accepted with minimal discussion. This was a management that knew what it wanted.

As a result, the public relations team researched and issued stories about the performance of the products, their reliability and economy in use. The company donated a full modern and historic range to the Science Museum, with a great little presentation ceremony – you can see them there today.

Sales personnel were encouraged to look for (and they found) ancient models, still working, all over the country. The control of one had been sealed up behind a panel in a pub and was still doing its silent job after 11 years continuous running. What a product. What confidence the senior management had in their team. And what a public relations programme. The team generated thousands of reader enquiries, more than the sales force could handle. And we achieved that simple aim in the brief. These fans developed their market leadership position despite some intense competition. Even more important, they became the standard by which all were judged . . . with most of the competition found to be wanting. What a brief!

The world is more sophisticated now and competition even tougher. So, perhaps, just a little more thought may be appropriate in preparing today's brief. Though, in reality, it should not be *the* brief but *a* brief, for there is no set way to prepare the brief for a public relations campaign – as the Vent-Axia anecdote illustrates.

Sometimes bosses or clients are reluctant to prepare any brief, for they feel this might not be to an acceptable standard or conform to some imagined industry format. There is no such standard or format. Of course, there are a quite a few good ways of preparing a brief and many less satisfactory ones. These notes suggest some processes that marketing professionals might consider when preparing a brief. In many ways, this is similar to the briefing process for an advertising campaign or a sales promotion initiative.

■ Brief in-house and consultancy to the same standards

Quite often, in-house personnel do not get a proper briefing and are expected to undertake public relations programmes of activity on behalf of divisions as if they had a total, inside understanding of what was required. This may or may not be realistic.

The briefing process should be more important than that – and it should not be assumed that in-house colleagues have a full understanding of the require-ments, simply because they have worked with marketing over a period of time.

That may give them a familiarity with policies, styles and approaches but does not guarantee that they will be able to read the marketing director's mind on such central factors as objectives, audiences, expected achievements and so on.

In-house professionals deserve the same level of attention that would be paid to an external consultancy during the briefing. Indeed, it could be argued that the in-house professionals are as much consultants as any outside organisation – they are acting as advisers to the management of departments and divisions of the corporation.

In some companies, the selection of consultancies is allocated to the in-house public relations professionals. Where management has full confidence in the staff practitioners, this can be an effective way of tackling the appointment. It should ensure that the strategy and policy are consistent. In addition, the public relations professional on your staff will probably be closer to and know the leading public relations professionals within consultancies.

It is likely that the in-house professionals will be in a good position not only to prepare a short-list but to make the final selection. Even where the marketing department prefers to make the selection itself, it is important that the senior staff public relations people are involved in all stages of the process and participate in the selection decision. Any consultancy that may be appointed will need to work closely with the staff public relations professionals and it is better that there is a positive and constructive relationship right from the start.

■ Produce a written briefing document

However it may be reached, it is always advisable to have the brief in some written form, at some stage. Marketing professionals may prefer to make this the first step but that is not essential. The brief can evolve through discussion; it can come much later than at the first planning stages.

In fact, the first question the marketing professionals might profitably ask is: should we be writing the brief at all? It is certainly practical to prepare the written brief co-operatively with the public relations professionals – or even to ask them to draft this, based on an outline of the marketing requirements or, if it is prepared, the marketing plan.

Ideally, the written brief will not be long – at most, a few pages. However, it may well include references or appendices which identify other areas for sources of information, discussion, input and so on.

■ Circulate a draft of the brief

It is advisable that the briefing document should be prepared initially as a draft. At this stage, it should be copied to all department heads within the organisation who either may have an input into the process or whose work might be affected by the ultimate public relations activities.

If time will allow, it can be helpful to ask for input and, at a second stage, incorporate any agreed changes and additions into the document and then re-circulate this as the final form. This should be done before the document is returned to the public relations department or issued externally to those consultancies on the short-list.

■ Consider nominating a selection team

The approval of the proposed public relations plan of action can be undertaken by one person or by a team. That is entirely the decision of the commissioning executives.

Of course, there are many similarities between briefing an in-house depart-ment and selecting a consultancy, based upon its reactions to the brief. As noted earlier, the same disciplined approach should be taken.

However, it is likely that the in-house personnel may be more directly involved in the development of the brief – sometimes taking sole responsibility for this. To get a clear comparison of the quality of thinking of competing consultancies, it often makes sense to ask them to react to a prepared brief. Their objectivity, commercial acumen and creativity can often be well judged by the comments they make or their suggested amendments or extensions to the client document. For this reason, this section concentrates more on preparing the brief for an outside consultancy.

Whatever steps may be agreed, it is extremely important that the same people are involved throughout the process and in all contacts with the tendering consultancies. If the company selects three companies for the short-list and the sales director only attends two presentations then it is guaranteed that he will not be likely to vote for the third consultancy – and so, the company has put them at a disadvantage, through no fault of their own.

■ Public relations must deliver more than information

If the marketing team view public relations as a tactical communications resource, then the company can happily keep the public relations people down the corridor or on the end of the telephone; tell them when you want information disseminated. If they are any good at this, then you will get an adequate information distribution service.

But, if they are *really* any good, they may actually decline this 'yes-sir' role. Issuing information is only part of any communications process, as every sophisticated marketing person knows. But even communications is only part of the proper public relations approach to the management of both the corporate and marketing reputations.

Clearly, if public relations is to be truly effective then it needs to be part of the processes that the organisation is using to monitor and understand what its key audiences think, feel and want. And processes are what it is all about.

What do we want? Where are we now? How do we wish to move from here to there? What are the processes involved? For in all areas of quality management, the process is the beginning and end of it all.

Many of these processes may be controlled by marketing and the market research professionals. Because, however the strategy is developed, it must involve the public relations people; a central part of their work will be to help shape opinions and attitudes in a way that will be favourable to the organisation sponsoring the initiative.

■ Involve the professionals early

A basic of public relations is that if you want to get the best return, involve the professionals at the earliest moment. Many practitioners will tell you of situations where they have been debriefed on research in which they have played no part – yet immediately can suggest areas where the research could have been developed to gain the knowledge that might have helped to direct, more sharply, the public relations effort. In other cases, the public relations professionals could offer research ideas that could create material that has public relations value itself.

As an illustration, a manufacturer of shirts may be interested to know who buys shirts, who influences the purchase, where they are bought, on what occasions they are bought and what are the factors that influence these purchases.

This might produce an extremely interesting study on shirts; the findings might help public relations people to decide where and how to target their activities. However, adding a question on who washes and irons these shirts – particularly if the study is run on some geographic basis – could produce fascinating information that might form the basis of a public relations initiative that could target both trade and national media. If women are more likely to be given the chore of washing and ironing shirts in the north in comparison with women in the south – or vice versa – this might say something about men/women relationships that could be of considerable news interest.

As noted in the chapter on research, such questions can be added into the survey at the planning stage without incurring additional cost.

And so it is with all aspects of public relations. Involve the professionals at an early stage and the outcome should be better, more focused, with improved cost effectiveness and, quite often, added competitive edge.

For this reason, it is wise to involve the public relations professionals in the briefing process. This does not mean that they always have to write the brief but the public relations people should have an input before the marketing people go firm on this document. Remember that the secret to a good brief is the focus, the direction, the ambitions that are identified. There is no requirement for a volume of information – just the core facts. Though the brief from Vent-Axia was not meant as a serious business approach, it worked better than many expansive briefing documents where exhaustive background becomes more important than simply making a commitment to what should be achieved. Any necessary information can be added later.

If the brief is the prelude to a competitive presentation by a number of consultancies, then each might be given the opportunity to attend separate discussions on the draft brief; additional information can be supplied to each, as they may feel they need more background.

However, it is not fair to invite competitors to revise or develop the brief and then for the client to present this to the other consultancies. As noted in the example on pages 89–90, with one competitive pitch, a leading consultancy felt there were some factors in the brief that needed more investigation. As part of their preparations, they sent a senior executive out on the road for two days with salesmen, visiting customers and a number of the depots that the company operated. They also undertook a telephone survey plus a significant amount of electronic desk research – all with the agreement of the company for whose business they were pitching.

From this, they identified some fundamental weaknesses in the original brief and rewrote this, accordingly, to reflect a sharper, more focused approach that they felt the public relations programme should take. This formed part of their presentation; but they were horrified when the client copied this to the other consultancies.

The reason, as he put it, was that there should be a level playing field with all contenders competing on the same basis. Clearly, the consultancy that had invested all the time and effort (and money) felt that this was unfair.

It was too late to withdraw and the account was awarded to a larger competitor who put up an amended programme of solutions to the revised brief. Perhaps the successful team would have won the business anyway and maybe they would have spotted the weaknesses in the brief. The client would never know because this team had had the opportunity of building on the work of their competitor. Innocently, perhaps, the unsuccessful consultancy had imagined that its investigative work would give it an advantage.

In such a case, the behaviour of the client was not only unethical it was unwise. It wiped out the opportunity of judging to what extent the contending consultancies were prepared to make a commitment in effort to develop an original and soundly-based approach to the public relations in support of marketing. It may not have been a coincidence that the company's public relations failed soon after. Curious marketing thinking (as evidenced by the approach to this competitive pitch) may have been a reason.

■ The brief should set the framework for performance

Marketing managers preparing the brief should resist the temptation to specify exactly what they want in terms of activities to achieve the objectives.

There may be nothing wrong in making some suggestions on areas that they would like to see considered in the proposal but they should not define the programme of activity. A division of GEC once asked my consultancy to produce an expensive video to influence a government audience. The objective was achieved with a briefing document and a meeting at about 10 per cent of the cost of the original plan.

A good brief sets the parameters for performance. So, it may be reasonable to allow the public relations professionals – whether in-house or consultancy – to make a contribution to the drafting of the brief. It should define the basis for measuring the effectiveness of the work. At the end of twelve or eighteen months, or some other suitable period, it is reasonable to go back to the original brief to check: how valid it has proven; whether the direction may have changed (for the better or not); and how the programme has performed in achieving those original aims or objectives spelt out in the preliminary document.

At this drafting stage, it is essential to consider what can be achieved through public relations – and what cannot. It may not be reasonable to expect public relations to compensate for problems over product quality. It may be reasonable to expect public relations to convince wholesalers, retailers and customers that there were understandable reasons for these problems and that they have been rectified with the minimum inconvenience to all.

Whilst it is not necessary to include full company/product information in the brief (headline details are usually enough), any possible source for such additional information should be identified. It certainly is unreasonable to expect the public relations people to undertake investigations into areas of information that already exist within the company. In the briefing process, the marketing people need to involve financial, commercial, production, research and development, human resources and other colleagues whose work will have an impact upon the public relations approach – or where the public relations is expected to support their area of responsibility.

In some cases, if the company wishes to use an outside expert, it is reasonable to negotiate the payment of a fee for the development of the brief. This is particularly appropriate where there is to be a competitive pitch and something at a reasonably developed stage might need to be put in front of the contenders.

Some marketers call in an independent public relations professional to prepare the brief. Clearly, this individual will take no part in the development of proposals in the tendering process – though he or she may be invited to be a member of the selection team. In such circumstances, obviously, such a person drafting the brief must have no links with any of the companies presenting their recommendations against this.

■ Developing an effective brief takes focus not time

If it is an in-house team presenting proposals for this marketing-support public relations initiative, it might be reasonable to expect them to input a day or so of time to ensure that the brief is a useful document. The same level of input might be appropriate if it is to be a competitive presentation with two or three consultancies. As noted earlier, the quality of the development of the brief by each contender may be a factor in making the decision; this does not mean that the consultancies should be expected to make a substantial time commitment in development of the brief, especially if they are only adding information that the company should have available.

■ In the brief, match resources to the challenge

The quality of the public relations performance can be critically important. False economies can destroy the credibility. A developer building a dramatic entertainment complex, with a budget in millions, supplied the newly appointed press officer with a second-grade fax machine which distorted information that was sent. The end result was still readable but journalists receiving invitations or briefing documents began to question the values of an organisation that could not afford proper fax machines.

The launch was a failure, with poor attendance, low public acceptance and poor sales figures. This was not all the result of the fax machine, but the substandard fax machine reflected the attitude of the management towards the public. All the investment was in the hardware and little in the communications. And the public can detect such things.

■ Communications needs are never so obvious that no brief is needed

Consider a recent case where the project objectives seemed so obvious that no communications brief at all was prepared.

The leader of the council of a regional UK city failed to convince the citizens of the merits of a proposed £60 million development in the heart of their city. At a public meeting, he complained that the public had not got the sophistication to understand such opportunities nor the vision to imagine the benefits.

It was significant that over £1 million was spent on the development of the plans; this included a tiny budget for a small advertising agency with talent but limited resources. Supporting public relations was handled by an enthusiastic but inexperienced young person able to do little more than issue media information – certainly not able to take any part in the decision-making or to push public relations into the strategic role it clearly demanded within a public project of this nature.

A more experienced adviser would have insisted on agreeing a brief at the earliest stages; this would certainly have confirmed the critical importance of winning popular enthusiasm for the scheme amongst the citizens.

As soon as work had begun, probably at the first planning meeting, it would have become obvious that something needed to be done to sort out the attitude of the council leader. He would have shown his indifference to winning goodwill long before his disastrous pronouncement. How could anyone credibly blame those whose support was vital to the scheme for lack of imagination? Even fervent supporters might have given the thumbs down to such a patronising attitude.

Not surprisingly, the public rejected the idea and this lack of support convinced the government to decline any supportive funding. If he so disparaged the public whose money he was spending, should it have been any surprise that the communications were not effective? In a more direct marketing example, look what Gerald Ratner did to his company through disparaging his customers. The public can recognise cynicism and arrogance in a nanosecond. After all, remember the public is you and I. And I am not daft. Are you?

In this case, the low priority put to communications and the minimal resources were not directly the cause of the failure, perhaps, but were symptomatic of an attitude towards communications. A single-page brief would have identified the importance of the support of the public for the scheme; from this might have come a clearer identification of what needed to be done to win such community support.

■ Use the brief to resolve differences in views

One powerful argument for agreeing the brief is that it allows differences of opinion to be sorted out before the programme of activity begins. Above all, it can help the communications planners allocate priorities. In the local authority case just cited, perhaps a more significant priority needed to be allocated to public relations. But proper resources allocated does not always mean high resources.

A leading construction company was able to change an important piece of legislation largely as a result of one meeting held over coffee with the right civil servant – previous proposals had included a significant advertising campaign and a £60k video. Either of these *might* have worked, but by laying on the arguments so publicly and heavily, they might have achieved exactly the opposite effect.

The successful change in direction occurred when a consultant was called in to produce the video and she questioned the basic approach. The result was a review of plans and a written set of objectives from which came the wiser and more economic recommendation.

■ Written aims can decide priorities and resources

In another case, the chief executive of a US engineering company sent a note to his public relations head about the plans for a customer event:

> Budgets are tight so perhaps we should abandon a Christmas event this year? I was unhappy that only a small proportion of those we invited last year attended. Perhaps there are too many similar parties, so customers do not have the time or interest?

It was a short memo – but a clear brief. As result the company ran its most successful Christmas customer party ever. The problem produced some lateral thinking. It invited European business contacts to a room over a London pub for a fish and chip supper and traditional bar games – darts, bar-billiards, shove ha'penny and so on. It not only got the best attendance and generated the most favourable comments, it cost a quarter of the previous year's effort held in a Brussels four star hotel.

It is possible to spend too much on public relations. If the content of the argument is not good enough then no amount of budget on the presentation will make it more acceptable. It is possible that lavish expenditure might persuade some people for some of the time but eventually the paucity of the arguments will show through. Such factors are nearly always revealed when the intentions are committed to writing.

■ Plan for an effective briefing meeting

As discussed, a briefing document prepared by the marketing department, might be presented to the public relations people to discuss the implications and to develop any particular aspects that they feel will be important for them to plan recommendations.

However, there is a process that can short circuit these two stages into one; the marketing department simply prepares a single sheet of headlines of the areas that they think will be of significance and then invites the public relations professionals to discuss this.

Areas that are likely to be relevant (which are expanded later in this chapter) would include:

- *The problem or opportunity*: why public relations assistance is being considered to resolve an actual or potential difficulty, or to take advantage of a situation, say, adding competitive edge.
- *Evaluation*: the achievements that are expected from the activity and, therefore, the measures that might be applied to judge the effectiveness and cost-effectiveness of the programme.
- *Financial implications*: the cost of the problem, or the value that could be added by the opportunity, therefore, the potential budget and other resources that could be allocated to a solution.
- *Competition*: the position of the company and/or its products and services in the market place and the relative strength/weaknesses of competitors, perhaps even their plans.
- *Company involvement*: other departments within or without marketing that may be involved in the issue, such as personnel or production, either in inputting or through being affected by any proposed actions.
- *Advisers*: other (external) organisations that may need to be consulted or with whom the likely action may need to be co-ordinated, such as the advertising agency, lawyers or trade bodies.
- *Sources*: where further information can be gained to expand the brief or add essential background to the proposed programme, such as the research department or the merchant bankers.
- *Environmental factors*: other elements at play within the business environment that might be relevant to the situation, but which are not covered in the above headings.

The first draft brief, developed from this meeting, should be close to a final document; this can be circulated, once it has been fine-tuned and edited by those involved in the briefing.

This document will then be the basis for the brief to the internal public relations advisers – or for the selection of competing consultancies. Selecting a consultancy is covered in another chapter, but the fundamentals are simple once an agreed brief has been prepared:

1. Keep the selection team constant.
2. Treat each consultancy equally.
3. Allow them the facilities they request.
4. Use an agreed rating procedure.
5. Expect development of the brief.
6. Select on the strength of the offer – not the details of recommended activity.

■ Individual briefings will ensure the best advice

Collective briefings are not recommended. These are undertaken by some government departments, trade bodies and statutory organisations such as the European Commission. Such processes also often stipulate fixed price quotations in written tenders rather than conceptual face-to-face presentations.

These can be ineffective for purchasing public relations and other consultancy services. The thinking behind many of these rather formal selection processes is understandable and well intentioned; briefing all contenders together eliminates advantage. That may be true, but it also inhibits radical approaches and eliminates many of the factors that help to differentiate the contenders.

If all are briefed together, then the opportunity to evaluate their understanding of the brief or any challenges they might make have made to this, on an individual basis, are lost. Public relations is an organic practice that depends upon relations, judgement, intellect, independence, analysis, creativity, ambition and many other factors that will not be best demonstrated if all the emotion is taken out.

The seriousness of the misunderstanding of these points is illustrated by the comment of one director involved in such a selection process: 'Buying public relations needs exactly the same selection process as buying pallets of bricks'.

Collective briefing simply inhibits the tenderers from asking the really key questions (they do not want to expose the direction of their thinking in front of their competitors) and results in a somewhat superficial proposals with a far greater tendency for them to look alike.

■ Use a planning schedule to get effective recommendations

Explain to the consultancies the stages that the planning should go through and try to put a timetable against this. This might read something like:

1 August	Issue the written brief to the shortlisted consultancies.
7/8 August	Set up the preliminary briefing meetings for them with the selection team.
10/20 August	Allow time and access for consultancies to talk to the advertising agency, sales and other relevant departments.
21/22 August	Second briefing meetings with marketing department.
15 September	Presentation by consultancy to selection team.
18 September	Decision made and consultancy advised.
19/30 September	Pre-planning between marketing and the selected consultancy.
1 October	Campaign start date.

■ Information that will be helpful in the brief

The briefing document, as noted, can be short. But there will still be much information that any effective consultancy will need to produce intelligent recommendations. Some of this will be offered as supporting documents (perhaps as appendices to the brief). Other information will be covered in discussions – or will be developed from access that the company will allow to other departments and even external bodies.

The brief may only require a couple of sentences on each of the following topics – plus any others relevant to the specific circumstances of the company. These notes discuss the options, However, it cannot be stressed too much that the actual brief should be a *brief* summary of such elements.

In everything, the brief must be candid and realistic. The language should be as plain as practical.

■ Review problems/opportunities involved

A central point in the brief will be some form of analysis of the problem they the company, product or the service is facing – or the opportunity that will be opened. At this point, it is helpful to give as much information behind this as may be available or identify where this information might be obtained – but it is not necessary to suggest solutions or activity that will be favoured. The real test of the consultancy's contributions will not be just in its ability to analyse the brief – but in putting together realisable, creative and effective methods of achieving the objectives.

If the marketing professionals tell the public relations professionals they are looking for a programme of media relations targeted towards consumer magazines, supported by regional newspaper competitions and a trade presentation in London with a supporting trade video featuring the television commercial . . . then they should not be surprised if the temptation for some consultancies will be to come back with a recommendation for the activity that has been requested. This may not be the most cost-effective or even the most effective. In some cases, such suggestions may even be wrong; by specifying the type of activity, the brief will be limiting the contribution that the consultancy should make to the programme-planning process.

Try to get behind the problem or opportunity. Suppositions and hypotheses are all valid so long as they are not presented as fact confirmed by research. Clearly any such relevant research should be identified, for example:

- *Developments.* Retailers appear to be misunderstanding the policy behind the low-cost packaging we are adopting. National contracts management tell us some think the plain wrapping was only a cost-cutting exercise not an environmental initiative. Can we gain credit for this, particularly with consumers?

Also, we plan to be the first in the market to offer a 3 year, no-quibble guarantee, with a full cost trade-in on old models. How should we announce this and keep ahead of the competition?

• *Competition.* Our own factory tests (see report from new product development) suggest that our products are superior to competition in most key areas. But this is not recognised at trade levels. It may be that wholesalers are so familiar with our range that they are rating new market entrants higher than they should. Certainly competitors have been winning better trade press coverage. How could we best win market recognition?

• *Customer influence.* Could public relations generate business enquiries to cut wasted sales time on major contracts in new territories? The sales force need support at the retailer level, particularly locally and regionally; a study by our advertising agency (executive summary attached) suggests less than a third of even our current customers see us as the market leaders. Is this a matter of customer relations or should we go public?

• *Corporate relations.* The management buy-out of the company has dramatically improved decision-making but some customers are worried about our levels of debt or our vulnerability to being taken over. Losing the influence of the parent name also seems to make us look a minor player. Also we no longer have the Brussels office to monitor proposed EU directives and we are nervous of leaving this to our trade body. What can public relations contribute at these corporate levels?

Other topics can be tackled in the same way – with a short direct paragraph focusing on the essentials and indicating where further information may be available or where further study/discussion might be necessary.

■ Performance expectations

Why should the organisation invest in public relations? What is to be achieved? How will we decide that the effort and the expenditure was worthwhile? What process will we use to improve the performance, build on success and learn from mistakes?

It may be sensible to allow the consultancies to identify their preferred methods of evaluation; this can be an interesting differentiator. Even so, it is essential that the organisation sets appraisal as a requirement, perhaps with some indicators of the areas where performance might best be measured. It can often be helpful to give an indication of the consequences of good performance – the contract being renewed or the brief extended into other company areas of activity!

An approach to this might be along these lines:

- *Effectiveness appraisal.* The success of the proposed public relations activity will measured by the achievement of the objectives to be agreed. Wherever possible, these objectives should be written in specific terms in the recommendations – to achieve x per cent of this and y per cent improvement in that.
- *Media coverage and enquiries.* Methods to appraise the value of sales enquiries generated through the public relations should be indicated in the proposal. Those elements of the programme that relate to potential media coverage must be subjected to an audit (through some credible or recognised process to be identified) to measure, such factors as the opportunities to see, the projection of positive messages, the changes in awareness and goodwill and resultant action amongst the key target audiences.

Performance appraisal is covered in more detail in Chapter 7.

■ Financial factors

Budgets should not be allocated out of the blue. The most sensible method is to relate the likely expenditure to the likely benefits – or the prevention of costly problems.

Some companies are reluctant to expend what may be necessary to prevent public relations disasters . . . but decide that money is no object when things go wrong.

Marketing should specify the budget that is likely to be allocated. It is perfectly reasonable to bracket this within a minimum and a maximum figure – the level to be determined by the relevance of the plan submitted. Alternatively, a figure for core activity might be suggested with a provisional budget for additional support activity, again, if the arguments for this are sufficiently convincing.

Though it is a common practice, it is not reasonable to expect consultancies to develop plans without a budget indication.

Some consultancies will simply not prepare recommendations unless the resources are allocated. As the chairman of one consultancy suggested, a Mini and a Rolls-Royce will both take you efficiently from A to B. There will be different occasions, perhaps, when a Mini and when a Rolls-Royce will be appropriate. We all accept it is not possible to get a Rolls-Royce on a Mini budget. If the client leaves out budget figures in the hope that the company will get some Rolls-Royce recommendations for Mini figures, the executives are guaranteed to be disappointed. This is the route to over-promising and under-performing.

Consider this. No marketing director of any credibility would go for an interview for a position where there was not at least some indication of the likely salary – so why should a public relations consultancy put all the time and effort in against a supposed blank sheet of paper which may turn out to be little more than a second-hand Mini with Bentley Continental aspirations?

If the marketing budget for the proposed activity is £5000, £50 000 or £500 000 then simply say so; then you will have a fair basis on which to compare the recommendations on how these consultancies will be able to use this sum to maximum effect.

If no budget has been agreed, allow the contenders to relate the sum they feel they need to do the job to the results they feel they will be able to demonstrate. Make sure these relate to public relations achievements and not to the efforts of other company disciplines, for example:

CONFERENCE SUPPORT
- **Visitor levels.** The addition of the public relations recommendations to the programme of support for the exhibition would cost £A. This activity would potentially add B per cent visitors to the stand; calculated against the sales results from the previous year this should achieve £C in direct sales; the proposed public relations budget represents D per cent of this potential sales figure.
- **Media coverage.** We would also estimate that the media relations aspects of the plan should ensure favourable coverage on the new products in perhaps EE publications likely to cover the show. This would put positive messages in front of a potential audience of F, of whom it would be reasonable to estimate some G per cent would be in the company-identified buyer bracket.

  The proposed budget includes a figure of £H to commission an independent audit of the media coverage, the opportunities to see the projection of positive messages and the theoretical value of this.

■ Competitive position

It can be a legitimate part of the brief to the public relations professionals to ask them to check on the competitive position – particularly in relation to public relations and media activity. How this might be tackled would be part of the brief, with the plans for gathering this intelligence becoming part of the proposal. It would not be fair to expect such a study to be undertaken speculatively prior to commissioning. If such information is important to clarify the brief, then a company should be commissioned and paid to undertake this work – preferably not one of the consultancies on the shortlist.

However, if there are known facts about competitive activity or sales figures, these should be included in the brief.

As noted earlier, there is little point in withholding information; at best this wastes money and at worse it can frustrate the relationship. I was once asked to prepare public relations plans for a new product that had been acquired by a leading food company. The marketing director had been brought in from the smaller company with the acquisition and the brief that he provided was lacking much of the essential detail. When we discussed this with him, it was clear, understandably, that he was overloaded with all the work involved in the changes.

Therefore, to ensure that the programme of activity we would recommend was built upon a sound base, we invested considerable time and a fair degree of money in researching all the basic areas that might normally have been covered by the parent company. We believed this would be a service to the client and would reinforce the strength of the proposal.

The first part of the presentation ran through all this background. At the end of it, the client produced a substantial volume and threw it on the table, declaiming that they knew all of this as they had spent the last two months researching this area. We were reassured that our findings were in line with their own ... but had to ask, why had they simply not given us this information at the beginning?

The response was that they wanted to see what findings we would base our recommendations upon. The time and effort that we had spent in duplicating their own efforts might have been better put into the running of the programme.

Briefing a consultancy is not a game. The marketing director is not a ringmaster and he should not be expecting his suppliers to jump through hoops. If he or she treats it like a circus, then he or she will get clowns.

■ Areas of company liaison

In the brief, it is useful to outline possible relationships between the consultancy and the departments that might be involved in the public relations activity – sales, marketing, human resources, production, financial, public affairs and so on.

It is also helpful to note which departments contributed to the preparation of the brief; which have seen a copy of it: and which will be involved in the selection of the consultancy.

Equally important, if complementary briefs are prepared for, say, the advertising and public relations campaigns to support a new product launch, contending consultancies (and the agencies) should each receive copies of both. Some guidance on what co-operation might be appropriate during the planning of related campaigns would be useful.

If the public relations is prepared in support of other plans, these should be appended and the relationship explained. For example, the financial, legal, production and human resources departments may have co-operated in the development of a plan to extend the manufacturing base, perhaps through the opening of new facilities, the expansion of existing plants and some strategic acquisitions. The brief might help fully define the respective roles of each business discipline – so that the public relations planning can benefit from the spread of experience and views, as well as support the various professionals in achieving their respective objectives.

Also, the public relations people contending for the programme may well wish to talk to other management professionals, perhaps, to develop their plans and to fill any gaps in the information that is available. One of the most effective ways of dealing with this will be to copy the brief to appropriate departments advising them that they may be contacted; a note of the names and telephone numbers of the heads of these departments should be appended to the brief. This is far more effective than someone within the marketing department trying to act as an intermediary in gathering information from other departments on behalf of the public relations company.

Public relations is a comprehensive discipline. It will work best when it has the widest input. It should pull diverse executives together to work to meet mutually reinforcing objectives. But this co-ordination and ownership of a collective solution will only become reality if the commissioners of the public relations initiatives *plan* for this to be a collective effort. This co-operation must be spelt out right at the beginning – in the brief.

■ Relations with other advisers

If there are any agreed policies on liaison between the public relations people and other advisers, such as the advertising agency, then this should be spelt out in the brief. If there is no agreed policy, now might be a good time to develop one.

Sometimes marketing works extremely hard at getting the different professional advisers to work closely together – sometimes they are expected to work in virtually watertight compartments and have no contact. Under such circumstances, friction may build up – or, as often happens, these professionals will start holding separate and private meetings without telling the client.

One end result of this is that the arena for development of strategy can move out of the marketing department and into this separate area. If marketing management wants to keep control over strategy then they will ensure that all relationships between all partners representing the disciplines within the marketing mix will be open and above board.

The brief should detail all relevant external advisers – the agency, sales promotion, direct marketing, investor relations specialists and any others.

Marketing management needs to consider what access by candidate consultancies should be allowed to these advisers to help in the planning of the recommendations. This should only be done in co-operation with the advisers. Perhaps the wisest approach is to limit the numbers of the contending consultancies – three should be enough for anyone – and allow contacts to be agreed directly between the respective parties. However, the existing advisers should be asked to treat all the contenders in an even-handed way, giving no advantage to any of them.

After a conversation with the senior person in each, a simple note to confirm the procedures might be sent to them. Do not copy this to the contenders, as it is up to them whether they take advantage of the opportunity:

'As you know, we are inviting three consultancies to contend for our public relations programme which will be looking at sales support/corporate relations/ product promotion (or as appropriate). As you will recall, you contributed to the brief and a copy of the final document, as passed to the consultancies, is attached.

The consultancies are . . . (details of the firms and the key point-of-contact in each, here).

We have advised them of all our external marketing advisers and they will be free to contact you if they wish to obtain any further information. Do not contact them yourselves. However, if they do contact you, please supply whatever information they may request. They have signed a confidentiality agreement.

If they wish to meet you, we would appreciate you allowing them a maximum of an hour each. Please treat all equally; avoid any social contact. As you appreciate, one factor in our evaluation of these companies will be the quality of their investigation into our needs and current activity. You do not need to volunteer anything but should respond constructively to their enquiries. Any discussions should be completed by (date). A short note from you on the results of each contact would be helpful to us by (date), please.'

■ Consider the historical background

For planning, 'now' is what matters but how the organisation got to that position can be important. Consideration needs to be given to whether some history might be outlined – particularly where public relations personnel might be working with the organisation for the first time.

Items that might be covered would include the development of the product or brand, its heritage or pedigree based on factors such as its sales record to date, any promotional support that it might have received including advertising, sales promotion campaigns, media relations and so on. Brand values (or their equivalent) which have been established over time will be particularly relevant.

It is important that this analysis of the background should include the negatives as well as positives.

Sometimes, marketing people leave the brief deliberately vague on the basis that they want those pitching for the business to find out such important facts themselves. If the consultancy (or staff professionals) understand that this is what they are supposed to do, then they will do it. However, this takes time and money and it will be a waste if this information already exists.

Sometimes such research may identify information not in the brief but which might look as if it needs diplomatic handling. A consultancy may not want to risk irritating a potential client by pointing out, for example, a brand development failure; indeed, the researchers might assume the fact that such a failure is not identified in the brief means that there is some sensitivity about it. In such an instance a product diversification or variant which was not successful might influence the handling of the public relations and could be of some significance. Therefore, if marketing management are aware of such facts, they should go into the brief.

■ Check other influencing factors

Other factors that need to be covered in an intelligent brief (and expanded with as much background as can be reasonably added) include:

- the sales and marketing resources deployed
- other marketing/corporate initiatives that might be running parallel to the public relations
- the processes for co-ordinating marketing efforts and associated communications
- the reporting lines and responsibilities for the public relations professionals within the company
- any significant plus or minus factors that could have an impact on public relations effectiveness
- the primary objectives by which the public relations will be judged, plus any secondary objectives which may add some value
- the client liaison and reporting procedures
- the budget
- invoicing, payment and budgetary control processes, either suggested or required

A clear distinction should be drawn between where the company has policies that have to be followed and where it is asking the consultancy to make recommendations.

■ Finally, set objectives that can be measured

The most important element in the brief will be what the activity is supposed to achieve. Often such anticipated achievements will be written in the form of aims – even where they are often described as objectives.

The difference is not mere semantics. An aim is a direction in which the activity should be going, whereas an objective is a specific point that has to be reached. If in doubt – or where it is difficult to set quantifiable measures – then aims may be acceptable, so long as they are recognised as not being definitive. The setting of objectives against which the ultimate performance can be measured is covered in more detail in Chapter 7.

Public relations in action
The management of corporate reputation

The brief is central to public relations for Royal Mail

Ian Bull, head of marketing communications for the Royal Mail, believes that reputation management is a circular activity. Communications managers set objectives and develop plans. Planning and agreeing the objectives provides the framework for all public relations activity. From the objectives, communications management develops the plans, carries out activities and then measures the results that are achieved. From these results they set developed objectives and so it carries on, round to the creation of new plans, new activities and the resulting new results.

In his view, there are five key factors in setting strategic objectives and no intelligent brief is complete without these elements. These are (1) to agree the business goals. From the goals will come: (2) the messages that need to be projected; (3) the audiences that should be targeted; (4) the current perceptions that they hold; and (5) the systems for measuring the changes achieved over the period of the programme.

Major and minor studies can help planning

As an example, the Royal Mail ran a campaign which was particularly targeting opinion-formers with the aim of improving their perceptions of the organisation. The brief identified the audiences as MPs, media, business leaders and City influences. The Royal Mail wanted to develop the level of regard that these audiences had for the organisation; this was particularly in the areas of value for money, its progressive approach and efficiency. A programme was run that included individual briefings, lunches, hospitality, events, sponsorships supported by both corporate advertising and media relations programme.

A mix of subjective and objectives measures was used to evaluate the effectiveness of these efforts including invitation acceptance rates, attendance rates and post-event feedback. The latter included questionnaires completed by both hosts and guests, as well as the tone and comments in unsolicited responses.

External media audits develop the brief

In addition, an analytical media evaluation programme was run and an opinion research study undertaken. This research had set a bench-mark before the campaign and, at the end of the following year, the percentage increases within each audience could be measured.

All categories showed a significant improvement over the period. As an example, though over 80 per cent of MPs and business leaders considered the Royal Mail to be a forward-looking organisation, less than 50 per cent of City opinion leaders agreed with that view – even though this sector showed some improvement over the year.

Clearly, the public relations had had some effect, but the focus for future activity also had been clearly identified. New techniques would be needed to win the acceptance of this message amongst City audiences – or, perhaps, these perceptions reflected a real management rather than a communications problem?

Studies compare Royal Mail with peer organisations

It can often be helpful to consider how one organisation compares with peers in its own sector – or with other organisations held in regard by the public.

Consequently, Royal Mail ran a test to see how it was perceived in comparison with market-leading organisations such as Marks & Spencer, BT, British Gas and Barclays Bank. This clearly showed that in terms of the value for its products and services, Royal Mail with a rating of just over 60 per cent was some way behind Marks & Spencer (considered top performer at nearly 80 per cent) but ahead of the others in this appraisal.

According to Ian Bull, both objective research and simpler studies provide the information that measures the effectiveness of all the organisation's public relations actions. Equally important, this data is essential in the development of follow-up objectives and, from these, the refinements to the debriefing processes; from these come sophisticated programmes of activity that ensure cost-effective performance.

Marketing director of Royal Mail, Jim Cotton-Betteridge, adds, 'The management of corporate reputation critically influences the success or otherwide of marketing promotional activity. Therefore, it is essential for public relations professionals to work hand in glove with their marketing counterparts to ensure business success.'

CHAPTER 7

Setting performance criteria

DEVELOPING AND AGREEING MEASURABLE TARGETS

Progress, therefore, is not an accident, but a necessity . . .
It is part of nature.

Herbert Spencer (1820–1903) in *Social Statistics* (1850)

■ Change is the only purpose of public relations

Few areas are likely to cause more friction in the implementation of public relations programmes than discussions over the achievements. The single most common reason for irritation between the commissioner and the commissioned will be, often, that the measures are applied in retrospect and were not agreed in advance. The consultancy jubilantly negotiates an exclusive interview with the chairman in the *Wall Street Journal* and the exasperated marketing director bitches that the wrong messages are being projected, at the wrong time, in the wrong market, by the wrong person. But, remonstrates the frustrated consultancy account director, you wanted strong corporate support and we cannot get much better than that.

■ Who is right?

The issue has become a matter of subjective debate when it should be a matter of objective appraisal. The who, what, why, where, when and how should be agreed in advance so that the right messages are being projected to an agreed timetable, in the right markets, through the right spokespeople using the best channels of communication. If these objectives are reasonable and specific then the measure of the effectiveness of the resulting work becomes simplicity itself. And, in the course of writing and agreeing the objectives, a clear picture of what is reasonable (and what is not) usually emerges.

119

Chapter 6 looked at creating an effective brief for the public relations programme. As noted there, developing the brief involves setting objectives. And objectives mean little unless they are related to the performance that is anticipated This chapter looks in more detail at writing objectives and the associated methods of appraising performance and so overlaps a little with the previous chapter.

Public relations professionals (in-house or consultancy) may feel they are better off without the exposure that measurable objectives might bring. Clients may think they are not necessary, or may not be prepared to pay the small budget percentage to appraise performance. Both are wrong.

There are five simple steps.

Agree what is to be achieved. Plan a programme to achieve this. Run it, with any fine-tuning that may be necessary. And measure how effective were the efforts. Then back to the start again to revise the objectives and activity.

■ Measure results not effort

Public relations measures normally fall into three broad areas: input, output and achievement levels.

The input levels are the activity undertaken – how many news stories, how many articles, how many interviews, how many trade meetings, how many customer tastings, how many supermarkets visited by the roadshow, how many trade evenings and so on.

Output levels are usually the measure of the direct result of such activities. Theoretically, it would be possible to put in a major amount of effort in issuing news stories or organising a touring roadshow without a word being written by the media or a single customer attending the events organised. Therefore, output measures establish the level of the coverage achieved by the news stories, articles and interviews, or the number of people who attended trade shows, the customer tastings or the roadshows, or the trade evenings.

However, proper performance levels are really the achievements of the activity. Again, theoretically, a million people could be exposed to the news stories in the media, tens of thousands of potential customers could attend the roadshow – and yet not a single one be positively influenced by what the company has to say.

Therefore, the most effective measure of performance will be those that can give a 'before and after' indication of the change in awareness, knowledge, opinion, goodwill, response and so on. Public relations is all about change, and the true indicator of its effectiveness must be the measure of those changes identified in the objectives.

■ Agree measurable targets – and those related only to public relations

The certain way to get the maximum out of public relations professionals (even reluctant performers) in the programmes that they run on behalf of marketing is to set and agree goals that can be measured. As noted, every aim can be rewritten to become a specific objective; this is the starting point for an appraisal method that will be acceptable to both parties and will stimulate the providers of the public relations services to perform ever better on behalf of the company or the client.

Measuring the final results – the changes – does not mean the efforts should be ignored. Appraising the efforts can be a good starting point. After all, if little effort were put in, little might result. Such direct and quantifiable measures (of at least some level of validity) could include: media coverage; editorial enquiries as a result of media coverage; the quantity and quality of attendance at conferences, seminars and similar events organised by the public relations people

In contrast, sales results rarely can be solely directly attributable to public relations – although the craft may have played a large part, in some cases, in creating the environment in which the selling takes place.

There are some exceptions. The insurance service Virgin Direct was launched only using public relations, so the level of enquiries could be recorded and related to the relevant aspects of the programme of activity. Even so, the conversion rate of these enquiries would have been more related to the validity of the service offered. This was not under the control of the public relations planners – though it was certainly a marketing responsibility.

Therefore, normally, the sales alone should not be used as a measure of the effectiveness of public relations – unless the impact of any advertising, sales promotions or the direct efforts of the sales force can be extracted from the equation. Even then, the quality of the product, the price, the service back-up and the many other factors directly produce the sales results.

■ Some measures may simply be all or nothing

In some arenas of activity, the public relations effort can be measured in a direct and simple way. As an example, the UK government at one time was considering dropping its support for the armed forces spectacular, the Royal Tournament, as part of a round of proposed defence cuts. The public relations efforts of the services management team was in place to sell this event to the public and to generate sales revenue. To meet the challenge, its brief was extended.

Briefings to MPs, civil servants, opinion leaders with service backgrounds and current service leaders generated considerable interest. These focused on the measurable contribution the Royal Tournament made to public perceptions of the services, through its show window role.

The government did not make the cuts. It may be reasonable to conclude that the public relations was an influencing factor.

Or, in another recent case, Estates & General, the property developers, planned a £60 million city centre development against considerable opposition – and a number of competitive proposals for a sensitive city centre site in one of the UK's regional capitals. At that stage, the main technique used was public relations. The project won planning permission, public support and corporate funding. Planning permissions, like pregnancy, tend to be all or nothing.

However, in the area of marketing, there are usually many other factors at play and it is not simple to separate out completely the public relations. In such situations, efforts should be made to try to put a measure on an aspect where *only* public relations could have had an influence – this may be a specific audience or it may be particular messages that were projected only through the public relations channel.

French veterinary services leader, Virbac, launched and promoted a feline innoculation product through public relations methods that featured the cartoon cat Tom from *Tom and Jerry* fame. This provided a clear and instantly identifiable 'tag'. Whenever any reference made to Tom or the cat was featured in comments, speeches or media coverage, this confirmed the public relations effectiveness.

Other campaigns have structured different messages projected through, say, advertising and public relations. Surveys of important audiences later can use these differing messages to identify which technique influenced the respondents.

■ Invite your public relations colleagues to propose criteria

Sometimes the public relations practitioners can make constructive suggestions on the factors that could be monitored and appraised to give an evaluation of the effectiveness of the work.

As an example, with a public relations programme supporting a product in a new market sector, the recommendations might identify a dozen key editors and it could become a target that each one of them over an agreed period of time should be properly briefed on the product and the company's activities in this sector. This becomes a simple *output* objective and one that is equally simple to identify whether it was achieved; to be of maximum value, this check should evaluate how many of them carried some form of positive report following this briefing, therefore becoming a performance measure.

■ Control performance in all areas that affect marketing

As an illustration, consider a company where marketing has responsibility for *all* communications activity that could impact upon marketing.

This company's poor community relations may be creating negative media coverage that competitors are using to damaging effect in sales negotiations. One aim for a programme of public relations to counter this might be to improve community relations in all the towns where the organisation operates factories.

This may be a perfectly sensible aim and one that could be reflected sensibly in an action plan. It may even be possible to have some indication of performance without significant research. For example, some success may have been achieved if there seem to be fewer complaints, fewer negative letters to editors of local papers, more people attending the open days and a general improvement in goodwill at meetings that involve the local community. But, above all, if competitors' sales personnel no longer have the damaging news cuttings to use in negotiations – then it might be reasonable to assume that the programme of communications activity has worked.

However, other factors may have played a part. Writing specific objectives and agreeing related, definitive measures of performance will eliminate any doubt about the causes of the improvement.

In this case, there could be several simple means to give a measure of the real development of community goodwill. Year-on-year figures could be recorded. The number of neighbour complaints received in each year could be logged; the number of members of the community attending the open day should be counted; the number of stories that are carried in local newspapers or local radio might be monitored; and the ratio between positive and negative, those projecting company messages or featuring company personnel or photographs, could be calculated.

Any of these historical figures could then be converted into specific objectives which would allow the actual level of performance against these to be measured. Such objectives might be put into words: to raise the number of positive stories in the local newspaper from A to B; to reduce the proportion of these of a negative nature from C per cent to D per cent.

Of course, whilst positive news stories and people attending open days are indicators of what might be happening, they are not direct measures of goodwill. Such simple numbers may be better than no measure at all – and are certainly useful as the initial measure that might be applied to a programme. However, as it develops, there may be need for something more sophisticated, related to attitudes rather than just programme activity. This would suggest the ultimate measure of public relations effectiveness – the measure of the change in opinion amongst the audiences targeted.

■ Objectives should be continually updated – and uprated

The importance of working to quantified objectives is that they can be used as the yardstick for measure at the end of each campaign to assess the success in performance. Where public relations is a new activity within a company, it is sometimes acceptable for the initial aims to be expressed as opportunities. As mentioned earlier, these can be refined and developed into quantified objectives over a period of years. Indeed, once established, objectives can be honed, developed and extended, year on year.

Take some actual objectives for a public relations campaign to support the marketing of a new range of skin care products. These were initially drafted as:

1. To create maximum product consumer awareness.
2. To project the quality and value of the new products.
3. To win national contracts with top retailers.
4. To gain stocking in the top wholesalers serving independents.
5. To explain the environmental and non-animal testing case.

The public relations needs had the benefits of brevity and clarity. But this really was only a first draft and needed development. How could these statements be improved and made more usable?

■ Add measures to aims to create objectives

As part of a brief, these 'objectives' are too imprecise, they are not quantified and so are really *aims*. Because there are no quantifiable parameters set, it would be almost impossible to confirm whether they had been achieved at the end of the campaign. Certainly the *level* of success could not be measured.

In public relations, success is often not a specific point – there can be degrees of success. The *level* of success reached will be important for both marketing and public relations personnel to evaluate the effectiveness and to achieve future, continuing improvements. It would be easy to imagine the arguments that might result later from discussing whether the public relations had achieved 'the maximum awareness'.

But there are other problems with these five requirements.

The national contracts and the wholesaler stocking intentions are not public relations aims; they cannot be achieved through public relations alone. There are other factors of equal or greater significance at play. Yet public relations has an important role to play in the achievement of these.

Therefore, the marketing management (or, at their invitation, the public relations professionals) should, first, convert these aims into public relations aims and, second, put measures on them that will convert them into objectives.

■ Build good public relations objectives from marketing ones

How can marketing aims be adapted to become public relations aims, in support of what marketing is trying achieve, in these five areas? Let us assume for the purposes of this example that:

(a) the other three (numbers 1, 2 and 5) are acceptable public relations aims that we can come back to quantify and
(b) that numbers 3 and 4 are proper marketing aims.

Consider each of these 'marketing' aims:

3. To win national contracts with top retailers.

Public relations can use channels of communication that can reach the buyers within the key retailers. It can present the case for the new products and explain the background to them, the research, the development, the new technology, perhaps even the employment, environmental and non-animal testing aspects of the new products. Therefore, an acceptable public relations aim might be:

To present the business case to the specified executives who influence the buying decision within the specified retail companies.

We can take that a little further to indicate we are concerned about the *effect* of the public relations and not just the effort:

To win understanding and acceptance of the business case amongst specified retail executives.

Note that 'acceptance' is used rather than 'support'. Clearly, support would be better, but the business case may involve aspects of price, quality, competitor loyalty and so on that cannot be changed by public relations alone. This objective, also, wisely assumes that marketing will specify who is to be targeted, so that there is no dissension later.

Consider the other 'marketing' aim:

4. To gain stocking in the top wholesalers serving independents.

The same arguments would apply to the influence upon this audience. Therefore, the aim would become:

> To win understanding and acceptance of the business case amongst specified wholesaler executives.

Now we can go back and attempt to put a measurable element into all these aims. The technique is to start at the end. What might we be able or want to measure to gain an understanding of the effectiveness of the activities we will accept and fund?

■ To create maximum product consumer awareness

Words like 'maximum' give an indication but do not allow for measure. One person's maximum might be another's minimum!
  Try to be specific:

1. By (date) achieve for the new product range A (name), a spontaneous recall amongst our target market of (details) by not less than B per cent of a sample representative of the broader consumer audience. (Respondents to qualify within that B per cent must be able to recall the product name and at least one of the agreed brand messages.)

■ To project the quality and value of the new products

This aim relates to effort and not results. It would be possible to project such messages which either no one received – or everyone rejected! Also, this aim does not make it clear which public is being targeted. Let us assume this group is the intended users of the products.
  In this case, a *spontaneous* recall of several messages about quality and value may just be a little too much to expect. (That could be debated.) But certainly if we want B per cent of our evaluation sample to spontaneously recall the brand name and one of the messages, then a *prompted* response to others may be fair.

2. By (date) achieve a prompted recall amongst potential product users of at least three of the six messages related to quality and value by not less than C per cent.

■ To win understanding and acceptance of the business case amongst specified retail executives

The same approach can be applied. Who are the retail executives that matter? What proportion would we consider to be a success, if the messages are projected so effectively to them that they understand and accept our arguments?

Also the public relations needs to create awareness *before* it can develop the understanding and acceptance. Therefore:

3. By (date), achieve:
   3.1 a *spontaneous* recall amongst specified executives in retail of the brand name by not less than D per cent
   3.2 a *prompted* recall of at least six of the twelve (or whatever) business-case messages by not less than E per cent.

■ To win understanding and acceptance of the business case amongst specified wholesaler executives

4. By (date), achieve:
   4.1 a spontaneous recall amongst specified executives in wholesale of the brand name by not less than F per cent
   4.2 a prompted recall of at least six of the twelve business-case messages by not less than G per cent.

■ To explain the environmental and non-animal testing case

Again, it is not clear which of the target publics is the focus of these messages – perhaps all, in which case, separate objectives may need to be drafted for each. Also is 'explain' strong enough? Surely we want to win some acceptance of these factors to give the new range competitive edge?

Should the environmental and the animal testing arguments be considered together? Skin care products that are not tested on animals may still be produced, for the sake of this case, from petro-chemical sources that are either not sustainable or may have environmental disadvantages. Conversely, products with a good environmental background could be tested on animals.

To keep this example brief, we can look at the environmental argument alone and assume the audience is the potential product users.

5. By (date), achieve a spontaneous rating of product A as environmentally friendly by not less than H per cent of a sample representative of the broader consumer audience. (Respondents to qualify within that H per cent must spontaneously put product A in the top three products in terms of their environmental case.)

Such objectives give more focus to what is required, yet do not limit, in any way, the techniques that might be deployed to achieve the results. In other words, a clear brief allows *greater* creativity in developing solutions.

The wording is only as important as the clarity of purpose that it projects. Indeed, if a marketing professional cannot draft a clear brief it may sometimes be because the process of thinking through what is expected has not been completed.

There is no single defined style for writing objectives and the above are only offered from experience as providing a good working basis.

The first four of these depend upon measuring *perceptions* amongst the target audiences, as a result of the public relations activity. The last introduces the idea of *competitive positioning*.

This may be no assistance in new markets or with the launch of new concepts. However, it can be invaluable in competitive markets where public relations performance, in comparison with other products or services, may have much relevance. Indeed, if wished, all objectives could be written in competitive evaluation terms:

> What percentage of the market rates our product as number one?
> What proportion of wholesalers consider our service puts us in the top three?
> (and so on)

This style of objective defines the method by which the performance will be appraised. Clearly, in these cases, some form of sample survey might be appropriate.

■ Use research to establish true measurement

Ultimately, the best measures of public relations will always be expressed in the same terms as the public relations role is defined. Suppose that public relations is seen as *product promotion*; then its effectiveness should be appraised by measuring how much the activities promoted the products. This might be done by testing amongst the target audiences the increase in awareness of the product messages disseminated through public relations channels – or, better still, the change in opinion towards these products.

If public relations is seen as *the management of reputation* then the rating of the company reputation is what should be checked. Surveys could be run at the beginning and the end of the campaign to measure the regard in which influential audiences held the company – in other words, its reputation with these groups. In addition, such a study will set a benchmark for the activity in the follow-on period. If a study was run at the beginning of one period and then a comparative study at the end of that period, then each study becomes the baseline for the ensuing period.

■ Consider an internal review of media effectiveness . . .

Although media relations will only be a part of the broader public relations effort, it can be a significant part. It can also be a part of the campaign that is relatively simple to measure. It is possible to count the number of positive stories and the number of those of a negative nature.

It is also possible to identify those stories that directly resulted from public relations activity and those that might have happened in any case. Simple analyses of this can be undertaken by staff within the public relations or the marketing function to give a year-on-year rating.

Some consultancies have developed computer-based systems for analysing and rating media coverage. In addition, a number of companies offering an independent media evaluation service are also building their reputations in this field.

■ . . . or look at independent professionals

Measures that only relate editorial coverage directly to advertising costs are not viewed with much confidence within the public relations industry. Such measures give a limited indication.

Many feel that the research on the credibility of editorial versus advertising is not that convincing. Studies have rated editorial as between three and seven times the credibility to the reader, in comparison to a similarly sized and placed advertisement. Such figures must be treated with caution.

Systems used by some of the more sophisticated evaluation companies can balance a complex range of factors to give weighting to media coverage. However, remember that most of these remain a measure of output and not necessarily of the true impact upon the target audience.

How the message is being projected through third parties, notably the media, is not always the same as how it is being received by the target audiences. In such situations, the media evaluation may need to be run in parallel with a process for appraising the impact of the messages – focus groups, opinion surveys and so on.

Such computer-based systems give a rating to the coverage, according to the quality, the tone and other elements within the report. (Comparable criteria can be applied to radio and television reporting of company activities.)

The relative value of an item on the front page of a newspaper in comparison with an item on page three of the business section is not easy to evaluate. An item on the city pages of one of the popular daily tabloids might reach ten or 100 times as many business people as a similar piece in the pages of the *Financial Times*. Calculating the relative value of each of these is difficult. However, the media evaluation technologies are of ever-increasing sophistication.

One advantage of using one of these techniques is that the analysis is produced by professionals who are outside either the public relations or the marketing departments. They are remunerated on a fee basis which means they have no commercial interest in how effective the coverage may or may not have been.

Output measures of media coverage can be calculated relatively simply with these methods covering such factors as:

- press space or radio/television time
- length of the stories
- number of times the company or product name is used
- tone and news value of the headline
- use of photograph or illustration
- position of the item in the publication or the news programme
- validity of the publication/programme
- readership/viewership levels
- total opportunities to see (OTS)
- use of agreed campaign messages
- positive or otherwise tone of coverage

However, media evaluation services can be used with other techniques to gain a better understanding of actual performance, including:

- percentage of the defined target audience that has been reached
- levels of awareness/knowledge that have been developed
- how audience opinion/attitude may have been moved
- (above all) what change in behaviour has been created

Those computer-based systems which evaluate such elements and produce some comparative measure (normally called something along the lines of 'media influence' or 'audience impact'), do have particular value in comparing elements of each programme or the news coverage effectiveness for different products or services – or even the media coverage of one company with another. Another area where useful comparisons can be made include the relative media value of the reporting on two sides in a takeover, or a competitive product challenge.

Therefore, if using one of these services, a helpful policy is to brief the evaluation company to compare media performance with competitors.

Though extremely useful, it must always be remembered that the computer is simply doing some complex calculations using a predetermined formula. It may be more independent but it remains mechanical. Its findings need wise interpretation.

■ Good public relations sometimes stops a negative story

It would not be reasonable to expect such a system alone to measure the impact on journalists of the simple phrase 'I too am a friend of the earth', used by Dr

Keith Humphreys, then chairman of Rhône–Poulenc. It was not directly quoted in all the news reports that followed the media briefing, but it changed the attitude of a number of journalists reviewing the company's environmental policies. Until that point, many had seen Friends of the Earth as the only true voice on the environment; but Humphreys gained credibility by outlining his management's constituency, responsibilities and professional qualifications, comparing these with the unelected, unaccountable and sometimes (well-intentioned) amateurism of the representatives of the pressure group.

The tactics could not be directly measured by the media evaluation techniques – but the difference between the tone of the coverage in the regions where this approach had been and had *not* been used could! The difference was dramatic. And it was up to public relations professionals to use the data to demonstrate that thoughtful preparation and a bold approach could produce measurable improvements in media coverage – even in such sensitive areas where all the odds seemed to be stacked up for the environmental group and against a chemical manufacturer.

Such techniques need to be deployed rather differently on those occasions, for example, when the public relations professional has prevented a damaging story appearing – say, through convincing the journalist that his intended approach was not accurate or fair. An evaluation comparison can be made between how the story appeared and how it *might* have appeared – or between comparable publications, one with whom the public relations professional negotiated and one where he or she did not.

■ Check the effective delivery of the programme mechanics

As already discussed, the ultimate measure must be the change in behaviour, produced by the change in attitude, produced by the effectiveness of the public relations. Yet there are many other factors relating to the public relations performance where checks should be made throughout the campaign. These measures can be helpful indicators of the proficiency with which the work is being carried out and, even, the cost-effectiveness of the activity undertaken.

Some of the simpler indicators to check include:

Reporting	The completion of progress reports to the schedule agreed.
Reviews	The organisation, preparation and running of the planning and review meetings.
Briefing	The understanding and speed of response of staff personnel working on the activity
Input	The proposals suggestions, ideas offered to management to extend or improve the programme.

Monitoring	The review of upcoming issues and coverage of company and competitive activity.
Response	The number of enquiries and/or leads generated by the campaign.
Budget	The completion of activity within the agreed budget and timescale.

■ Consider an independent executive to co-ordinate evaluation

A complementary approach is to use an independent consultant to appraise the effectiveness of other aspects of the programme, according to the achievement of results related to the original objectives. This will have the advantage that the evaluation can be carried out in areas which may be not related to the media. It will also give an independent view – upon which both the client and the public relations professionals would need to make their commitment to support in advance.

In selecting such professionals to assist in the evaluation, it is important that they have no direct connection with either the client company or the consultancy and that they are remunerated strictly on a fee basis related to their work in this area.

■ Watch the timing of evaluations

The quality of the relationship between the client and the consultancy (or the marketing director's team and the public relations director's team) will be of considerable importance.

Any process of evaluation should involve both parties – and each should be happy with the aim of the evaluation and the way in which it is used. If this can be approached in the spirit that the evaluation will help to refine and develop the activity through focusing on those aspects which have worked to the maximum effect, then both parties are likely to embrace this vigorously. If, however, it is used as a basis on which to criticise colleagues, then there may be resistance, even defensiveness in the preparation of reports on activity.

Therefore, in planning the evaluation timing, it is wise not to set this at the end of the programme of activity or the completion of a contract period.

If some form of evaluation is to be undertaken periodically – whether monthly or quarterly or midway through the programme of activity – then this can be used as a basis for a discussion on improving activity.

There will be a far more positive response than if the practitioners feel it is just to be used as a fault-finding exercise. It will also be impossible to get both sides discussing results in harmony if the evaluation is conducted at the end of a contract or salary review period; staff or consultancy personnel will be defensive if they feel the figures might affect their income or welfare.

Even the best planned programme will not work as well in some areas but may work far better in others than had been anticipated. The evaluation provides the base on which to develop the activity; the programme must be sufficiently flexible to allow fine tuning as it develops.

■ Be flexible in developing performance criteria

Although it sometimes startles new clients, I often make the observation at the programme presentation stage that I would be surprised if the programme that is actually being undertaken, after twelve months, is much like that being proposed.

The simple reason is that, at the time of presentation, both sides know the least about each other; the presentation process is often two groups of strangers working at arm's length. After twelve months of working as partners, the relationship has grown; the understanding of the issues has developed; both teams are up to speed; the client has a better understanding of public relations and how it works; and the public relations team have a better understanding of the client, the motivations, policies, philosophies and competitive advantages. It would be surprising indeed if this did not mean that the programme of activity should be far more effective at the end of twelve months. This often means that some ideas have been abandoned and other new ones have been brought in.

■ Use evaluation to update company executives

Another aim of the evaluation of the programme will be to keep those responsible for managing the budgets informed on progress. In the areas that we are discussing in this book, this will be the marketing team. They will want to be assured that the proportion of their marketing budget that they have allocated to public relations is being effectively spent. They may want to make a comparison with the results from other areas of expenditure, such as sales promotion, direct marketing, advertising and so on.

The results of a public relations campaign cannot always be guaranteed in advance, though seasoned professionals can usually predict the results with some accuracy. Therefore, most campaigns might best be appraised on a progressive basis – the level of reader enquiries this quarter compared with the same last year, or the number of attendees at the business seminars compared with the same period twelve months earlier, and so on.

Everybody involved in the development of the public relations campaign – including those responsible for the financial and administrative aspects – should be kept up to date with progress. This is the best possible way to ensure their continuing interest and support.

Six-monthly or twelve-monthly reviews can provide a useful document and this can be circulated to management, or form the basis of a briefing at a management meeting. A regular update on activity, achievements, work in hand, any problems experienced and any failures in performance should be prepared, ideally, on a monthly basis – though it may only need to be formally reviewed every three or six months. (Monthly activity reports should be circulated to all in marketing management involved in the activity.)

In addition, most public relations programmes – even those that are solely focused on marketing support – will be of relevance to other professionals within the organisation. These may include sales (if that is a separate department), production, personnel, international, financial and so on. The public relations progress report and the independent evaluation should be approved by marketing and then refined and edited into a suitable form to be presented to other managers within the organisation.

■ Measure the acceptability of messages delivered

A good reputation is achieved by an organisation through: the constant monitoring of the perceptions of the publics upon whom it depends for success; the development and implementation of policies designed to win their approval; and through the planned and sustained delivery of positive messages about these policies and its related activities.

A measurement of the acceptance of such messages by the publics exposed to them will complete the circle. The reporting of negative messages, or the unacceptability of the positive messages that are delivered, will both suggest that the company needs to change its policies. Marketing directors responsible for public relations should recognise that these are a good indication that the company is not behaving in a way that is acceptable to these publics.

Equally, the public relations professional needs to have the confidence and authority to be able to advise that, whilst the delivery systems may be effective, what is being said is not meeting with approval.

This is one point where public relations shifts from communications into the area of policy – not just what the company says but what it does.

■ Mix formal and informal progress appraisals

Formal research, with a substantial sample, into such matters as perceptions of reputation, awareness, opinion and attitude, remains the best measure of the most significant effects of the public relations programme.

Market researchers will confirm that monitoring the effectiveness of a public relations campaign is not as difficult as many managers imagine; nor need it be an extremely expensive activity. In some cases, a sample of 100 or 200 respondents may be sufficient to get a reasonably accurate measure.

It is essential that the measure is of the public relations effectiveness and that other changes are not inadvertently monitored; other influences in the market-place could include changes in the sales force, the impact of an advertising campaign, a sales promotion initiative, the introduction of new products and so on. Therefore, as the original objectives ideally should have been phrased in relation to some form of quantifiable awareness or attitude factor, it is *this* which needs to be measured.

Attitude surveys are probably the most useful method of assessing the effectiveness of many campaigns. Once a year or so, it is probably wise to monitor different sections of the market at which the public relations is specifically aimed.

Periodically, however, it is valuable to look at overall public attitudes towards the organisation. All public relations programmes are part of a broader corporate effort to build good relations with all audiences that matter. Such a study is certainly useful before the start of a major campaign or periodically, say, every five years.

■ Design attitude studies to be performance benchmarks

Properly constructed, the attitude survey will be of invaluable help to the public relations advisers in their planning. It is essential that it is structured to enable it to be repeated at a later stage. This approach will enable the results to be compared and any advances or declines identified. It may be of less value to research attitudes among retailers then, five years later, to research attitudes among wholesalers, as it will be impossible to draw any comparisons between them.

Similarly, the same research format and, ideally, research specialists should be used. The research will reveal information about other aspects of the company's operations that have an effect on public opinion – literature quality, telephone attitudes, sales force contacts, corporate identity and so on.

A study my consultancy undertook for an engineering company showed that one group that had the most influence on repeat orders was that of the delivery drivers. If they were helpful, punctual and reliable, the salesman stood a better chance of picking up the next order. Yet the drivers had not featured in any part of the marketing or public relations programme. These findings enabled the company to develop suitable policies to bring them into the planning.

Which comes first, the objectives or the brief? As the Royal Mail case study in an earlier chapter suggests, it is a continuous process. A good brief leads to good objectives, which stimulate good ideas, which create good activity, producing good results which, from a good debrief, produce even better forward objectives.

■ Establish methods to appraise personal performances

When undertaking any public relations activity, look at how other people are performing.

With an activity that is so flexible and has so much scope for good people to lift it to new heights or for bad people to depress it to new lows, public relations is an area where it is not always easy to set definitive measures for the performance of individuals. It is not easy but it is not impossible. As always, be certain that you are measuring effectiveness and not just effort.

One UK consultancy that concentrated on media relations used to measure how many stories and articles executives on the account-handling teams produced each week. Each new executive soon learned that their career was more tied to quantity than quality and they responded accordingly. This became a measure of effort, not effect.

Some American consultancies have taken the concept of measuring actual achievements but with a touch more relevance to performance. They use the concept of *strikes* and *hits*. A strike is an attempt to sell a story, article or interview to an editor. A hit is a success achieved in one of these negotiations.

Each week, executives report on how many strikes they made – how many individual editors they spoke to to place a piece – and how many of these produced a result. Such an approach certainly focuses the mind wonderfully. The boss can set a level of 25 or whatever strikes per week and, from this, will soon get a perspective of the success rate. A good operator may convert ten of these to hits whilst a weaker one may only manage five. Immediately, there is a target and an area to focus on an improvement – whether this requires more effort, more application, better news material to work with or training, will be clear once the results are analysed and discussed with the individuals.

One advantage of such a techniques is that the performance – or otherwise – is self-evident. Good operators should know when they are not performing to standard; if marketing has recruited the right people or appointed the right consultancy, then an indicator of performance below standard should be quite sufficient to bring about a dramatic improvement.

■ Good people always assume personal responsibility

When I was working for Allan Woodgates in Dunlop, I learned the critical importance of personal responsibility. I was lucky – for I was rescued from a situation where I should have sunk without trace. In public relations, no one should assume there is any longstop, or anyone to pick up a dropped responsibility.

He was one of the most inspirational bosses that I have ever had. I learned so much from him. He not only had expertise but he had style. I would be waiting on the pavement with a colleague, having come out of a meeting, vainly flagging taxis in a downpour. When he walked out, seemingly, an empty taxi would immediately pull to a halt without him even beckoning. At the end of the journey, he would step out and leave us minions to pay. (Indeed, we often wondered whether he carried any cash at all and, outside office hours, had a valet to look after such mundane matters.)

The most stinging rebuke I have ever had in my career was the mildest of comments that he once made to me – yet I still wake up occasionally in the middle of the night with the shame of it all.

I had been to see an old pal in Fleet Street (when it still was Fleet Street). It was a quiet Friday in the office and we had gone out and had a bite of lunch which turned into a little liquid *après-lunch*. Eventually with the clock well past three, I thought I ought to get back to the office. I was probably not in the sharpest of conditions so decided to walk and at around about four o'clock was back in St James's.

In the press office, there were a dozen members of the team with jackets off, stuffing things in envelopes and manning every available telephone. There were people there I had not seen since the last Christmas party. I could see at a glance the material was about one of the divisions for which I was responsible. Something dramatic had happened whilst I had been propping up the bar. The room went quiet as, swaying slightly, I stepped through the door. Allan looked up and mildly observed, 'I am so pleased you are back. We all thought you had fallen down a hole.'

Clearly, Allan had stepped in and marshalled the troops to cover the crisis that I should have handled. Yet he never raised his voice – just an elegant eyebrow!

I still go red at the thought.

■ Consider a communications audit in tandem with research

One technique which can help establish clearly the present position of company communications and their effectiveness is to undertake a communications audit. This surveys the audiences, methods of communications with them, the effectiveness of these communications channels and where they can be improved – or gaps filled. (This is detailed in Chapter 4.)

A method for establishing the size of the task is to combine this communications audit with the compilation of a corporate reputation 'balance sheet'. The aim behind this procedure is to clearly establish those factors which have an influence on the perceptions of the organisation among the target audiences.

Good products, excellent service reputation and major investment in research may be plus factors to build upon. An unstable management record, foreign ownership, or recent redundancies may be minus factors to be counteracted. Remember that all activity undertaken in the public relations programme is designed to build the reputation of the organisation, its management and the products and services it offers – in other words, managing the corporate reputation.

Marketing directors should remember that success demands as much praise as failure would demand criticism. Where the public relations work of colleagues is successful, recognise it. Praise can be the most motivating aspect of work. It does not cost a lot, but it pays dividends.

■ Relate ethical aims to commercial objectives

When setting performance criteria, most marketing managements understandably concentrate on commercial issues. But there is an increasing pressure on companies to appreciate and respond to community, environmental, human rights and other social issues.

The issues audit, discussed earlier, should identify those social factors coming up over the horizon that might have an impact on company operations. The analysis of these by marketing should show where damage could be limited – or, even, where there may be opportunities to win competitive edge.

To take advantage of this inside knowledge, it makes sense to develop parallel business aims to cover these non-marketing factors. As with other aims and objectives, this will be the first step towards measuring performance in these areas.

A schedule of the marketing plus corporate public relations plans, to cover all eventualities, might be structured thus:

1. Measurable objectives for year one and, possibly, two.
2. Reasonably detailed aims for years two and three.
3. Outline aims to cover those issues predicted to arise during, say, years two to five.
4. Broad aims to cover alternative issues that might arise beyond year five.
5. Draft strategies to position the company in relation to *all* issues.

■ Expect the public relations adviser to be company conscience

Roger Hayes is a public relations professional who moved into general management; for some time, he was director general of the British Nuclear Industry Forum. More recently he was chairman of the IPRA. He believes that stakeholders in the organisation include many for whom the immediate business decision is balanced with broader social issues – these might be consumers, as well as ethical investors. Some, such as environmental pressure groups may be working to a completely different agenda.

These days, it is likely that their knowledge will be greater and their expectations higher, their values stronger and, probably, their cultural diversity wider. Corporations must play a broad role and show leadership of the kind not needed before. Businesses are in the marketplace of ideas not just in the marketplace of goods and services. He believes that strategy is not about reputation alone, it is about bringing management better information about trends and issues that matter to the enterprise – customer needs and expectations, shareholder values, the community culture, environmental impact, product quality and government initiatives for change.

Good public relations must be about positioning the organisation in a coherent way and this can have as much impact in the arena of marketing as any other area of operations. In his view, shared by many, public relations people must look beyond the narrow tunnel vision of the company and have the courage to bring the bad news to their bosses and not fear being shot as messengers. If they are to be effective, they have to be the corporate conscience or they will be nothing.

■ The public controls the issues agenda

If attitudes matter to the organisation, then activity and communications must be managed to create the most favourable attitudes possible. The development of issues, strategies and positioning policies – though not strictly within the scope of this book – can provide powerful insurance.

The discussion of the issues will help focus management minds on the potential these may hold for advantage or disadvantage.

Management does not control the agenda for public issues, so should any of these come up faster or increase in significance, the company will be in a good position to get up to speed fast. Reducing the chances of getting caught out increases the chances of winning public goodwill.

Public relations in action

Strategic planning is a management responsibility

BT takes evaluation into the boardroom

The UK business division of BT, one of the world's most profitable telecommunications companies, is using a sophisticated evaluation system called Mantra to measure the effectiveness of its public relations campaigns. The resulting facts on public relations results are a central factor in strategic decision-making in marketing communications; the information is also used to monitor individual product and agency performance.

Glyn Jones, public relations manager for BT's national business communications, introduced the system to support a new public relations strategy for the whole business division. After putting out a tender, Mantra, supplied by MA Management Services, was selected on the basis of its objectivity in evaluating the press and broadcast media coverage.

Evaluation is fundamental to an intelligent public relations strategy, believes Jones. The aim in adopting the system was to indicate the contribution public relations was making to the overall marketing effort. He feels it has verified the value of the spend and helps justify public relations budgets. Typically, media coverage has been evaluated at three times the original public relations investment, demonstrating value for money and a higher return than is often achieved from larger advertising spends.

The monthly reports on the evaluation were tailored to relate directly to BT's public relations initiatives and to ensure that the reports would be of use to the senior executives who receive them. This included defining a comprehensive framework of messages to be measured through the media coverage.

Summaries give managers the key facts

Each month 'topline' charts show total monthly and cumulative values and opportunities to see figures based on circulation and readership statistics.

Subsequent charts are divided into levels, grouping together on separate pages the public relations campaigns, which are diverse and include: small or large business; new service initiatives; activities that support over 50 individual products and services, such as per-second pricing, data communications and teleworking.

The monthly figures and cumulative charts provide Jones with the information he needs to monitor the success of each public relations campaign and identify any specific negative or positive trends.

The previous year's results are also being used as a benchmark for setting performance targets for the public relations agencies taking on the new campaigns.

At product level, individual programme managers use the reports to see the level of media coverage their products and services are achieving. The media coverage details include a full breakdown of the coverage achieved in each type of media (national business magazines, computer trade press or national quality newspapers), plus details of every article and the relevant journalists' names. These reports are shared with public relations agencies and the information used to tailor activity such as the targeting of news releases, content of media packs or scheduling of media briefings.

Value ratings reflect complex factors

The system produces a value for each individual item of press or broadcast media coverage, calculated by predetermined criteria, which include allocating a rating to each message which appears in the article and then taking into account its size, positioning, prominence, content and the readership, circulation or broadcast audience. Negative and positive results are all identified in the monthly reports.

The software system, developed in-house by MA, shows the client monthly trend charts and management information tables. The software includes up-to-date details of readership and audience figures for every publication and broadcast time slot in the UK, providing accurate OTS figures.

BT public relations managers use the information in conjunction with their own appraisal and opinion research methods. The result, according to Glyn Jones is an objective perspective on performance.

Monthly results against targets are fed into the department's financial reporting system, providing a direct link with strategic planning and the allocation of resources for future marketing communications initiatives.

CHAPTER 8

Marketing: the diverse business discipline

PUBLIC RELATIONS IN MARKETING PLANNING

Times change, and we change with them.
(Tempora mutantur, et nos mutamur in illis.)
Anonymous, quoted by Harrison in *Description of Britain* (1577)

■ Public relations is much more than communications

As public relations is most often seen as a communications discipline, it is understandable that marketing people tend to involve the professionals when marketing communications are being planned – sometimes alongside the advertising or sales promotional specialists.

Of course, public relations has relevance to all aspects of the marketing – and an early involvement ensures that the maximum benefits are gained from the investment. In addition, often a public relations perspective on other aspects of marketing can add both a new dimension and value.

This chapter looks at some of the areas within marketing where a public relations dimension may be more than just useful. Of course, there are few areas of company operations (if any) where public relations could not make a valuable contribution, but this section looks only at some of the more obvious elements within the marketing mix.

■ Get input at the planning stage

Initially marketing evolved as a business discipline separate to sales; more recently, it became the umbrella discipline of which sales is a part. Central to effective marketing is the analysis and planning stages. The first questions in marketing always have to be: is there a market and, if so, where is it?

Only later can such questions as what are the market needs, the competition, the pricing options, the distribution channels, and so on, be addressed. Public relations should be considered at the earliest practical point; the professionals may be able to contribute to the analysis of the opportunities and the markets, both from their experience but also adding their perspective on the possible acceptability of options. This input can help shape, for example, the research development to considerable effect.

As good public relations should be a two-way process, the input from the market, based on the experience of the practitioners, can help in planning.

■ Tailor approaches for consumer and business marketing

Consumer marketing demands public relations support that is sensitive to the highly competitive marketplace. Not only are the products or services in competition, so, in some ways, will be the public relations. Stories will be competing for the available space in publications. Senior executives who carry the important messages will be in competition with others from other companies attempting to win the attention of the editors addressing their key markets.

There can be significant differences between public relations support for the marketing of fast-moving consumer goods (and services) and the marketing of professional or business products (and services) – although both are built upon the same principles.

Sometimes public relations can add an even more substantial competitive edge in the business-to-business sector. Often the more sophisticated techniques developed in support of consumer marketing will not be so widely applied. Sometimes, the product or service differences in industrial or professional markets may be wider or more innovative, giving the public relations more scope to develop, say, news stories, seminars and conference presentations.

In the area of media relations, many business sectors have a wide range of publications and broadcast channels that might follow company developments; as an illustration, a company introducing new services in office systems may find their activities could be of interest on the business pages of the dailies, its local newspapers, regional radio and television, publications in offices systems, management and the end user industries.

The rule must be to tailor the public relations programme to use the most effective communications routes to reach the potential market.

MARKET RESEARCH

Public relations advisers should have the opportunity to be involved in the development of the brief for market research. Where such research might be looking at factors such as awareness of the company, its services, products or its brands in the marketplace, public relations will have played a part in the creation of such awareness. Equally, it is likely to play a part in the development of the activity, following the analysis of the study, so it is reasonable that those whose work will be directly affected by such research should have an input.

■ The contributions of each element may be identified by research

Some believe that a perennial difficulty with public relations has been measuring its contribution. Consider this. The company runs an advertising campaign and it controls exactly where and when the messages appear. The new product moves off the shelf and the connection is fairly direct. But the effects of a public relations campaign may build over time, with influences unfolding across diverse audiences. If sales rise, for example, after the trade and media briefings, how can you be certain this was the public relations investment and not the advertising or sales efforts?

One proven technique is to ensure that one or more core messages are carried *only* through the public relations.

Research can test the acceptance of these by the targeted audiences and, specifically, how frequently these are fed back during the study. A new consumer durable manufacturer developed a special consumer advice line that was only promoted through the public relations. The right question added to the research found that 65 per cent of those respondents who were aware of the new product could recall the advice line.

The finding confirmed that this proportion had been influenced by the public relations activities. Similar approaches with other communications would identify their reach and any overlap.

■ Research can be planned to add public relations value

Another reason for involving the public relations advisers in the briefing for research is that sometimes a question or two can be added that will generate an answer that might be of public relations value.

As an illustration, a manufacturer of ties might reasonably be researching how often men buy ties and where they buy them. The company might also want to know how often ties are bought as gifts. All such information would be useful in marketing planning – but not likely to be of great interest outside the tie industry. Yet add a question which asks how many men have been given a tie that they never wear and who gave it to them – wife, mother in law or office colleague – and you could create a piece of information that will be irresistible to many journalists. Add another question that will draw some comparison between attitudes towards ties in the north and the south of the country, or young and old, or ties at home or at work and the public relations opportunities expand. (See Chapter 6 on briefing.)

Of course, a serious piece of market research should not be spoiled by frivolous public relations questions – but neither should an opportunity to add a powerful element to the public relations programme at no additional cost be lost. Brought in at an early stage, the public relations practitioners may be able to develop complimentary ideas.

They might be able to add an element that can be run in parallel with the research. For example, in the hypothetical survey of ties and tie-buying habits, the consultancy might suggest setting up a charity tie auction with all proceeds being donated to a charity of public interest that the manufacturer had pledged to support. A letter to celebrities asking them to donate an unwanted tie to such an auction would not only have publicity value but could help raise a useful sum towards a good cause.

■ Public relations can design studies specifically for publicity

Sometimes the public relations advisers will suggest undertaking research which is specifically designed for public relations purposes. This will not be a study that is measuring the effectiveness of the public relations but one that produces information designed to make a news story.

Though some would say that this is an overplayed technique which no longer has any originality, it is still true that many such surveys are of interest to the media and can result in quite substantial coverage. Whether they contribute much to knowledge and understanding in the relevant industry sector is less certain.

In the public relations industry, many feel that if a campaign is looking a little thin or a proposal needs an extra edge, then a survey will be developed as a recommendation. There are a couple of leading consultancies who have made quite a specialisation in this area and, although this has not enhanced their reputation for being at the sharp end of the business, it has done their client relations and business trading no harm at all.

The idea of a survey for public relations purposes should not be dismissed simply because it is not a new idea. However, if marketing management wishes to protect and build a substantial reputation for the company, it wants to avoid becoming involved in anything that might be perceived as superficial, manipulative or cynical. In other words, the company should ask questions beyond the simple . . . will this generate media coverage?

Management might ask whether the study reinforces the leadership or authority of the company within the sector. They might want to know if it will add to the body of knowledge within the industry. Will it help position the company or add competitive differentiation?

One simple test of whether a proposed study is a good idea or not is the same one that can be used with any promotional concept, such as a planned sponsorship. That is, ask yourself what your reaction would be if your biggest competitor were to announce that they were undertaking the activity. If your reaction is to curse yourself for not having been there first, then it is probably a good idea. If your reaction is to shrug your shoulders (or worse) then the idea is not worth pursuing.

■ Keep the use of public relations research ethical

In the UK, the Market Research Society has developed a sensible code of conduct, watched over by a professional standards committee. This regulates the use by members and their clients of extracts from research studies. The selective use of parts of the study that do not reflect the overall findings and which might be misleading are not allowed; when research is undertaken to be published, those invited to report the findings must have access to the full report, if they request this.

Interestingly, the society recognises its own public relations needs through a series of awards for best practice which generate both industry attention and media coverage. Chairman of the society at the time of preparing this copy, David Smith, has commented on the move to develop the communications activities of the society. It was the view of some that with the significant growth in market research expenditure there was perhaps less need to promote the use of market research than to communicate the difference between professional (that is, conducted by MRS members) and mediocre research. Public relations of any substance needs market research – but market research needs public relations.

Marketers proposing to use the research as part of their public relations initiatives, are strongly advised to obtain a copy of the code of conduct from the Market Research Society to ensure that they do not contravene some well accepted and sound principles developed by the largest professional body of its type in the world.

■ New product development

Public relations may not always have much of a role to play in the area of developing new products or services, certainly at the concept stage, but the public relations people can be an invaluable source of information and should be involved in planning discussions. Of all those involved in marketing, those who handle the public relations may often have the broadest contact across publics relevant to new products – customers, retailers, wholesalers, trade and professional bodies, government departments, consumer groups, academia, institutional and other investors plus many more. Such perspectives can be useful at product planning stages.

■ Marketplace perspectives are relevant to product development

In a company with a strong marketing orientation, public relations will have played some role in projecting the core values that are associated with the brand

– through news stories, demonstrations, sampling, recipe services and many other techniques. And it is equally likely that the public relations professionals will have a good feel for attitudes in the marketplace. This can be a useful, if subjective, input to discussions of new ideas for revising the product or developing new ones to meet changing needs. (The public relations team that helped the Guy Raymond company develop a leadership position in industrial castors was instrumental in the development of its do-it-yourself range.)

It can be useful to call in public relations professionals at an early stage when the brief is being prepared for a new product evaluation – or on a regular basis when the marketing team are reviewing new product development, or the NPD professionals present their advance concepts.

■ Use public relations to support brand extension or development

Of course, for most companies, new products or services are essential to survival. Technology can outdate some concepts; competitors can close the gap on innovative designs; fashions, styles and needs may change; some products may enjoy a short sales success then disappear.

New public relations approaches can sometimes help extend the life of a product that could go into decline – or help the brand adapt to met new opportunities. Public relations was part of the product mix that helped Cherry Blossom extend the brand from the declining shoe polishing sector into self-shine shoe cleaners and other cleaning products.

Some brands have survived through a continuous process of improvement and imperceptible change. Swan Vestas is claimed to be the only brand of matches in the world that is asked for by name. The red, yellow and green box with a distinctive swan may look familiar but it has evolved through many changes over the years. The brand has been extended into lighter fluids and cigarette papers.

Bisto has been around since man first chewed on a dry, flavourless leg of mammoth. Yet the brand has been kept up to date. The formulation has changed and so has the flavour to match taste. Bisto used to be a floury powder that made it possible to produce gravy as lumpy as your mother used to make. Today it is an instant easy-mix and available in vegetarian, chicken and other flavours. Mars took their confectionery bar brand and built a completely new sector in icecream sales. All have featured public relations to help support sales and familiarise the public with the new lines as they were introduced, building on the established brand values.

■ Communications advisers can feed back valuable views

Public relations can sometimes directly save cost – and possibly embarrassment. One European refrigerator manufacturer proposed to develop the idea of a drinks chiller that could be built into refrigerator doors, allowing the consumer to draw a chilled carbonated drink from a special external tap, without opening the fridge door. Working models had been produced. The idea was simple and attractive.

The public relations consultancy was asked to develop launch ideas. After some investigation, it advised the client that this was not a new idea.The concept had been introduced a number of times in the United States. The advantages compared with the provisional costing had not been well received with the editorial focus group on whom they had tested the idea. As a result of this cautious note, the marketing director commissioned a more detailed study which confirmed this was not a productive area for development.

Fortunately, the company was innovative and moved into products of real promise: coloured fridges; mini fridges; boardroom style fridges; fridges that worked off low voltages for caravans and boats; fridges that could have a replaceable laminated panel on the front to match the kitchen. All of these ideas were suggested by comments from the marketplace – and a number were ultimately launched successfully.

■ Even brilliant concepts need intelligent communications

Potentially good ideas may fail because they are launched at the wrong time, at the wrong price, into the wrong market sector, with the wrong messages.

Public relations may not prevent these disasters. But the experience of the wide world and the market can be useful additions to the planning. And if the public relations people are being paid anyway, why not invite them into launch discussions before the plans have been finalised? Who can tell how many embarrassments have been avoided by the right questions asked at the right time?

The C5 that Clive Sinclair designed and launched proved to be a disaster. It was a tiny, electrical, three-wheeled cycle with a quite attractive body style, powered by a small motor built by Hoover – which, indeed, assembled these machines in a factory in Wales. When a number of consultancies were involved in discussions to handle the launch of this product, one of them pointed out that it was unwise to launch it (as proposed) in autumn in a city centre. One of its key claims was that it was a mode of transport that could be used on the roads without a driver's licence or road tax. Therefore, it seemed probable that journalists would want to use it on the road and, to some safety pundits, the tiny, low vehicle was potentially lethal in city traffic.

The marketing people working for Sir Clive rejected this advice and launched the product at Alexandra Palace one dark, wet autumn day. Journalists were invited to try the vehicle within the spacious confines of the venue. Of course, they wanted to take it out on the roads and were not allowed. Why? As one spokesman said, it might be too dangerous. The product was pretty universally ridiculed by all media and understandably. It failed dramatically – though a handful of these vehicles are preserved as collectors' items and can fetch a price well in excess of what they cost new.

Ironically, I was invited to the launch, representing my client, a transport industry body. When asked about the potential for the C5, I made myself a little unpopular by pointing out that, in my view, there was no real market for sales for on-road use – but there were potential sales for locations off the highway, such as golf courses, airports, universities, parks, sports venues, industrial estates and so on.

Was that a public relations or a marketing or a commonsense view? It does not matter. Even if the public relations professional brings nothing but his or her experience of the company, its products, its markets plus a dash of common sense, he is worth inviting to strategy discussions.

It can also be a good idea to involve public relations people in the testing of any new concepts that are under development. Of course, this can be no substitute for full product testing or proper market research.

■ Product innovation is of increasing importance

Product innovation is one of the most important activities undertaken by a modern company and it must be wise to involve all who have a an expert perspective in the planning and evaluation phases.

In the late 1970s new products were estimated to contribute around 22 per cent to company profits but by 1995 this had arisen to close to 50 per cent. But this activity is also extremely risky. It has been estimated that nine out of ten grocery products do not get from development to launch stage; even then, at least a third of these fail after launch. A study by A. L. Page ('New product development survey', PDMA conference, Chicago, 1991) suggested that for every eleven new product concepts only one achieves any commercial success in the marketplace.

Public relations may have a greater or lesser role to play in the development and introduction of new products and services, depending on to what extent they may be 'new'. A study by Booz-Allen and Hamilton ('New product management', New York, 1982) identified six classes of new products:

- *A new innovation.* This represents perhaps 10 per cent of the sector. These are completely new products which, effectively, create a new market. These often (but not always) have a technology base. Recent examples might include the self-adhesive Post It notes introduced by 3M, roller blades, the video tape recorder (originally developed by Philips but exploited in the marketplace by Sony and others) and sun-blockers.
- *New product lines.* Some 20 per cent of 'new' products are, in fact, the introduction of new lines by particular companies. Such products may not themselves be new to the market. Ashbourne Water from Nestlé followed Perrier and many other well-known brands into the established bottled water market.

- *Product line additions.* These are lines which may be new in the market but are within an existing product line. These represent around 26 per cent of all new product launches and would include items like Yorkie chocolate introduced by Rowntree (and since acquired by Nestlé).
- *Improved existing products.* Some 26 per cent of all new product launches are represented by products that show an improvement of some significance – or not. For example, bleach manufacturers developed techniques for producing thick bleaches which offered the consumer an apparent benefit in that they clung to lavatory bowls and other surfaces and, being less fluid, were easier to handle in use.
- *New positioning.* Existing products are repositioned for new uses, account for some 7 per cent of this sector. As an example, with the decline in smoking in many markets, Swan Vestas used public relations to create a new market where the product was positioned as the handyman's/gardener's match.
- *Cost reduction.* The study suggested that around 11 per cent of all new product launches were represented by products which were either adding value at the same price or actually reducing cost – in other words, a lower-priced product replacing the existing one.

Completely new products represent only 30 per cent of all new product launches but are in the majority of those that are most successful. Part of the reason for this may be the high investment required in the development of completely new product lines and the relatively high risk. This encourages companies to opt for safer choices.

The more original the product or service, the greater the need for public relations to support it and educate the market – but, happily, the greater the public relations opportunities with a concept that will be of broader news interest in the marketplace.

The less innovative the product, perhaps the more creative the public relations and other marketing support will need to be!

In all cases, the knowledge of the market, media and customer opinion, would suggest that the public relations colleagues can contribute at quite an early stage to the processes that produce new products and services.

■ Marketing design

The presentation of the organisation, the products or services through corporate identity, packaging, point of sale and other display elements will be directly relevant to the public relations promotion of the product. Indeed, the design elements will often set the tone for the public relations.

■ Design projects values relevant to public relations

Companies in the food sector, such as Heinz, Bird's Eye and Findus have a consistency of product presentation that runs through a wide range of lines. Indeed, in recent years, such companies have built the organisations' credibility, strengthening the corporate brand – and sometimes reducing the dominance of sub-brands.

This aligns with consumer research into the benefits of brands. Both marketing experience and such research have demonstrated that brand values from one product create a halo effect that can help the sales of another product, whether in the same sector or not.

Surveys by UK market research leaders MORI have shown that a good reputation can be a tangible business asset. Branding can be part of the process that projects the identity upon which reputation itself can be built. Figures from one survey suggest that 7 in 10 of the public believe 'a company that has a good reputation would not sell poor quality products'.

Bob Worcester, chairman of MORI, confirms that studies show shoppers are more likely to try something new from a trusted name; people would be 14 per cent more likely, as an illustration, to buy a new frozen food product if it bore the name Heinz than if it were from a large but unspecified company.

The public relations activity in support of such products also tries to present a consistent approach with a strong emphasis on the values of the company behind each new product introduced. Public relations can reinforce these values through a range of techniques. For example, the information issued to journalists, consumer advisers, trade and professional representatives at any launch might include the results of research and product testing carried out during the development to demonstrate sensitivity to customer needs. Credible public figures that will add their own authority and reputation are often used to make the presentations. For example, with food products a well-known television cook might be appropriate, or a famous restaurateur.

■ Consider launch communications at the briefing stage

Of course, public relations can often have an input into the briefing document that is prepared before the design is commissioned. The public relations professionals will be close to trade, retail, media and public perceptions of the products. This might give useful input to the design process.

My own company helped Station 12, the satellite communications leader of the Netherlands, develop the Altus branding for its new global service, with all design work undertaken by agency, Anderson Lembke. The closeness of this co-operation showed in the integration of the advertising and public relations with the physical branding projected in a consistent way through all communications media. Indeed, the new logo was launched through public relations using video presentations, media briefings and video news releases across world markets, supported immediately after by global television and press advertising. It makes sense. Any other way is inefficient.

If there is this close level of co-ordination, then the design can create public relations and advertising opportunities as a spin-off. Sutton Seeds changed their photographic package design to a stylised and unusual product illustration drawn by a highly talented botanical illustrator. Not only could these illustrations be used throughout the public relations materials – on news release heading, media briefing notes, press packs and so on – but they also helped set the tone for the supporting public relations.

Sometimes companies miss opportunities at this design stage. Consider some ideas:

- Involve a design school in preparing the brief.
- Invite employees to suggest potential brand names.
- Feature the development process in company newsletters/annual reports.
- Use the original artwork as a display in the reception or at the AGM.
- Create a trade competition around the new logo or identity.
- Set up a touring show around factories and other locations.
- Make an enlarged model of the identity for use at company events.
- Build a special hot-air balloon for factory/community open days.
- Issue limited edition lapel pins, car stickers or ties.

■ Using design to add value, projected through public relations

An important function of marketing is to add value to the product or service being offered; both advertising and public relations can help to communicate values that enhance the attractiveness of the proposition and build the perception of a brand. Peter Dart, co-founder of the Added Value Company, has argued that as the media get more difficult and fragmented, packaging can play an ever more central role in adding value to a brand. He suggests that if a label or pack has to be printed, it may as well show something excellent. Indeed, the reverse is true; if the design does not work well then it can act as a damper on the product and the brand values it is trying to project.

Some of this thinking is reflected in the increasing attention paid to all forms of packaging and the design that is carried. For example, traditionally, appliances were sold through advertising and point of sale displays – but the actual product was presented to the customer in a dull, brown box, perhaps with no more than factual descriptive matter on its surfaces. The thinking was that the buying decision had been made by then.

But printing and packaging technology have improved and costs have come down. More retailers display products in the take-home box. And this can deliver a message to family and friends.

Increasingly, such products are appearing in boxes that are laminated and printed in full colour as it is recognised that these messages can be significant –

not just in the initial purchase but in maintaining brand loyalty and building repeat purchases.

As an example, Spillers Bonio dog food is sold in an attractive four colour box. My wife being something of a dog lover, one or more boxes of this product sit in constant view on a table in the conservatory where she feeds the dogs. It contrasts with the plain boxes that she used to buy and indeed, the box is so attractive that when finished, each becomes a useful junk box for children's toys and the brand keeps on spelling out its message long after any impact at point of sale.

■ Design elements create communications opportunities

Peter Dart identifies many options where intelligent design can make a contribution to branding:

1. The shape of the container (for example, Toilet Duck)
2. A distinctive opening device (Grolsch)
3. The packaging material (Ferrero Rocher)
4. The packaging material finish (Absolut Vodka)
5. Any other distinctive physical features (the shape of the Elizabeth Arden Time Capsules, Ceramides)
6. The colour of the packaging (Marlboro)
7. The logo or style (Coca-Cola)
8. The use of a symbol (Woolmark)
9. The use of a personality (Colonel Sanders)
10. Any other purpose-designed feature (simplicity and elegance of Chanel)

Public relations activities should be structured to utilise such values – not just reflecting them in the design of the public relations material but using them in some central way in competitions, sponsorships, sampling and activities.

In practical matters of building the link between the packaging and product design, it can often be helpful – and cost-effective – to ask the same designers to handle the proposed launch materials to a brief from the public relations people. This might include news headings, packs, presentation displays, competition materials and so on.

■ Corporate identity can be taken too seriously

A new identity can be an opportunity for public relations initiatives that, handled well, may build goodwill – or, too often, ridicule from those who enjoy seeing the solemn get egg on their face. Always consider the public relations downside.

Some years ago, when Lucas introduced a new identity, it was launched at a major sales conference. It consisted of a bold letter 'L' in a roundel of dark green. It effectively looked like an arrowhead pointing to the left and downwards. At the launch, so the story goes, in the awed silence when the new identity was unveiled, a lone, quiet but totally audible voice from the back said, 'Perfect. Going downhill and backwards at the same time.'

Of course, reverence is not something that you should expect from sales personnel. It has often been claimed that one major reason why the old BT logo was changed to the nymph figure was the embarrassment that senior directors had over disrespect shown by even the company's own staff over its cherished identity. This was the logo in the shape of a 'T', again in a roundel, where the left-hand, short arm of the cross-piece on the 'T' was replaced with two large dots. Wags would take the identity and rotate it so that the short arm of the 'T' was pointing upwards and proclaim, 'This symbolises a cock-up'. They would then rotate it to show the long downward stroke of the 'T' now pointing upwards and proclaim 'This is a big cock-up', before rotating it to point the two large dots pointing up and to triumphantly announce, 'This is a balls-up'.

A distinguished designer, Robert Vince, revamped the Geest identity and created a logo which faintly resembled two hands cupping the sun. It may have been a coincidence but some of the directors rather liked the idea that the shape of the hands slightly resembled bananas for which the company then was a major distributor. When Vince was asked what this identity symbolised, he explained straight-faced it was two slugs circling prior to mating.

One of the founders of the Geest empire – one of Europe's largest distributors of fruit and vegetables – was Leonard van Geest, a personable and successful business leader, whose Dutch origins left him with a slightly less than perfect grasp of English. The company had successfully negotiated a contract to handle the distribution of a wide range of Florida produce including what were then quite exotic red grapefruit. The advertising agency developed an integrated campaign around the concept of the Greatfruit – advertising, leaflets, posters all putting these splendid 'greatfruit' as the dramatic, visual centre piece of perfect food occasions. All the stunning photography carried the headline, The Great-fruit.

Leonard van Geest was clearly entranced by the whole presentation with one small niggling worry. Right at the end he leaned over to the account director and said how impressed he was. 'Only one small concern – you have spelt grapefruit wrong.'

■ Product pricing

As everyone in marketing knows, pricing the product or service can be a highly significant decision – part instinct and part science. As pricing will be part of positioning the product in the marketplace, then this will have a direct relevance to the public relations support which, itself, will be part of the marketing initiative to position the product in the market.

■ Product pricing will shape communications approaches

Some marketing pundits believe that as many products fail through being underpriced as they do through being overpriced.

Some products that we accept today as being cheap everyday items, such as ballpoint pens, digital watches, printed T-shirts and calculators, were originally introduced as exclusive, premium-priced items. Sometimes this is because the manufacturer is trying to get the maximum return on his investment in product development, minimising the risk of launching an unknown product into the market – but, sometimes, it is a failure to understand the pricing mechanisms at work in the marketplace.

It is unlikely that the public relations adviser will be able or want to make recommendations on pricing but his or her experience in the attitudes of customers to the company and the reputation of competitors can be a helpful element.

■ The credibility of the product promotion plans influences price

The makers of the Mini car should have listened more to both the public relations and sales people in the early stages of its life. British Leyland (then the manufacturing company) failed to recognise the tremendous level of interest in the product and the high levels of loyalty that it engendered.

The makers were limited in the numbers that they could manufacture and should have considered significantly increasing the price. The public relations advisers were not the only professionals to believe that the car should compete on its benefits and not its price. It was presented as a cheap small car and not a unique small car.

After many years of production, the management admitted that they made less than £5 from each one of these vehicles sold; this was at the time when the sales price of each was less than £1000. Putting £100 on the price would have represented a 10 per cent increase but would have multiplied the profits by twenty. The success of the public relations around the launch and introduction of the product would easily have justified such a level. It is doubtful that the higher price would have reduced sales at all. The vehicle is still being manufactured at the time of preparing this copy, is world famous, yet has never returned a decent margin to its makers in over thirty years.

At the other end of the spectrum, a public relations programme run by a small manufacturer of handcrafted harpsichords spread the message of the quality of his instruments across a small market around the world likely to buy such items.

The result of the awareness campaign and the quality performance of the product amongst the first buyers led to an ever-increasing order delay. The craftsman who had set up the business used public relations to maintain product interest and order levels.This gave him the confidence to steadily increase the price, bringing the order time down from four years to a more manageable one year.

In this process, he was able to increase his prices by nearly three times and still be confident that he had sufficient orders booked not to make his business vulnerable. The price reflected a fairer return for the skill and effort that went into the production of each instrument – but, equally important, it gave him the returns to invest in the business and to train young craftsmen to take over the heavy workload of the owner of the small business.

■ Media comment helps establish whether prices are acceptable

Research (and common experience) suggests that consumers often do not have a detailed knowledge of product prices but do have quite well-defined frameworks for these. There will be an upper limit above which the product begins to be seen to be too expensive. Equally important, there is often a lower limit below which concerns about the quality of the product might be raised.

When the consumer considers a new product of which he has no experience, he considers price in respect to comparable purchase, relevance and some abstract perception of benefits related to cost. Imagine a self-sharpening pencil guaranteed to last for life. To someone who uses a ballpoint it may be just a curiosity which he might try if it was comparably priced. To an architect or a lover of fine pencils it might be no more than a cheap alternative. To a teacher or writer who gets through dozens of pencils, a relatively high price might be achievable. In the *Companion Encyclopedia of Marketing*, Katia Campo and Els Gijsbrechts (both of the St Ignatius University Business Faculty of Antwerp, Belgium) discuss pricing. They believe the impact of externally provided reference prices on a consumer's internal price standards depend on whether these external references are seen as plausible or implausible. A positive product review by a consumer organisation might be plausible, for example. With our example, a calculation of how many pencils it might save over ten years may not be.

Public relations efforts in projecting the price *and* value of the product will tend to be more acceptable to the consumer when these are relayed through credible third parties – for example, consumer writers in media trusted by the consumer. The pricing strategy adopted for the product or service will be an important part of the briefing as this will shape the approaches and messages in any proposed plan of action. The campaigns that might be necessary to support the permanent pencil would be very different for different positions in the market – a cheap alternative to everyday ballpoints or a precision, premium-priced drawing instrument.

■ Distribution

Product and service distribution has always been one of the most creative aspects of marketing with new channels being developed right from the beginning of organised commerce. Public relations can be a useful part of the marketing support used to open up new distribution channels.

■ New distribution channels must be sold to consumers

One of the more dramatic developments that helped set a trend for future marketers was the understanding by Coca-Cola in the early 1930s that its product was not a grocery line or a drug store line . . . but a small packaged experience able to give some moments of pleasure often, but not always, associated with quenching of thirst. Therefore, to maximise sales, the product needed to be available where and when people might be indulging themselves, particularly if they were enjoying company – not just when they might be tired, warm or thirsty.

The company helped pioneer distribution through channels that had hardly been used before, such as petrol stations. The development of dispensing machines also opened potential sales at bus and train stations, office lobbies, hotel foyers, hairdressers and countless other locations where people might spend small change for those moments of pleasure.

Today, we no longer think it at all remarkable to buy a loaf of bread at the garage, a tie at the airport, eggs from the milkman, an electronic appliance through a catalogue or even a holiday from the television.

Although public relations has rarely been responsible for the initiative that created such new outlets, it has often helped to develop a level of awareness for the product and its benefits that have made such new distribution channels practical. Indeed, public relations is often extremely effective in helping to build the acceptance of a new method of selling or new methods of distribution. Such innovations have their own news interest and this can often be a central factor in helping the consumer to learn about what is available through such news channels – particularly through news reports carried in appropriate media.

■ Communications supports services through new channels

As an illustration, many financial services are now sold directly to the consumer by the company offering them – rather than through sales representatives, consultants, retail outlets or third parties, such as brokers, banks and building societies. In the UK, the initial major success in this sector was Direct Line, which initially offered motor insurance and, later, household insurance, pensions and other financial services sold via the telephone.

(Though this new development is direct marketing it is, in essence, delivery of the service through a new channel – see pp. 165–6.)

This innovation was paralleled by the development of the First Direct Bank, launched by Midland Bank, which also used the telephone for contact with customers. This organisation took the step one further, enabling all banking transactions to be undertaken 24 hours a day, 365 days a year, over the telephone.

It may be significant that both these pioneering services – and many that followed – were launched through public relations and, in some cases, without other marketing communications.

■ The environment in which decisions are made is vital

Distribution decisions can be of great strategic importance. When Goodyear decided to sell tyres through Sears Roebuck this became a main board decision with the chairman actively involved. Of course, as Burt Rosenbloom, Professor of Marketing at Drexel University, Pennsylvania, has pointed out, partners in the distribution chain are deciding with whom they want to work and this selection is a 'two-way street'. In his words, the manufacturer seeking to secure the services of quality channel members has to make a convincing case that carrying his products will be profitable for these partners in the channel.

Manufacturers must make their case carefully and thoroughly to win the acceptance of such channel members.

As with other areas in the marketing mix, public relations can be used to create the business environment within which the detailed proposition is presented and considered. Company executives are often asked to endorse decisions where they have taken no active part in their negotiation. Attitudes amongst the Sears Roebuck senior executives, in the example, towards Goodyear and vice versa must have played a part in deciding whether they wanted to back the decision.

Of course, the most telling measure of public relations is not media evaluation points, opportunities to see, cost per thousand or other (sometimes pseudo) scientific ratings . . . but, simply, what people say about the organisation when you are not there.

Companies can deploy public relations specifically targeted to support such proposed initiatives – or accept that such situations will be arising continuously and use public relations to build a positive attitude towards the organisation on a continuing basis.

■ Test marketing

If public relations is likely to be part of the national promotion of the product or services, then it should form part of the plan at test market levels to ensure these deliver representative results.

■ Limit the test market communications to the test area

Special care needs to be used in the briefing for the public relations support for test marketing exercises. Clearly, test markets should simulate the likely national position as closely as possible. However, as a new product or service may be of more interest than an established one, the public relations (and, to some extent, the advertising) may attract disproportionate attention and this can bias the results.

It is sometimes difficult to tone down or moderate the public relations; the product or service will have its own level of interest and this can become self-generating after the initial announcement.

■ Local stories can become national stories

If there is an innovative aspect to the new product or it has social or community implications then those talking and writing about it at the local test market level may want to advise colleagues at the national level. In the media, local journalists often have strong relations with national media and news agencies. They not only earn fees for local stories presented at national level, they earn credibility.

Hypothetically, Unilever testing a 100 per cent fat-free margarine in Coventry is as much a national story as a Midlands one. Indeed, with some major product developments, 'public' test marketing may be impossible if the public relations element is to be controlled.

There are other special factors involved in test marketing, supported by public relations, even where the product is not of major national news interest. For example, if a regional area is selected – say Anglia or the south coast – then public relations must only target audiences at a local level.

The national consumer organisations, the relevant trade and professional bodies plus the national media cannot usually be part of the campaign because of the geographical limitation. This usually means that only local bodies, associations, groups and media will form part of the public relations pro-gramme. If anything, this means the public relations effort is probably slightly underplayed which will avoid the risk of an over-optimistic picture of effec-tiveness.

■ There may be only one opportunity for a major news announcement

As with the media, the business organisations that might be involved do not work in watertight compartments, even if only those that have a regional focus are selected. For example, a branch of the Chamber of Commerce might be considered as a platform for a business discussion on a new service to be launched in the region. This could be featured in the branch newsletter and the item might be picked up at national level. Should this be the case, it may well be beyond the control of the marketing planners or, even, the public relations executives. Even controlled coverage might mean that the product or service is unlikely to get a second level of coverage at the time of the later national launch.

The need to provide an equivalent, *pro rata* level of support at a test launch (in balance with the national opportunities for public relations support) must be carefully judged.

In some cases, because there is no such thing as a 'partial' news announcement, the media relations aspect of public relations in support of new products at test market stages is omitted completely. This will enable a full-scale back-up to be provided at national roll-out stage. However, it may be that there are other non-media aspects to the public relations that will be relevant and these should be carefully considered. It would be wise to involve the public relations professionals during the briefing for test marketing so that they can make recommendations on the best strategy to adopt.

The test market is also useful for the public relations team to try out concepts, new ideas, public perceptions and other elements.

■ Corporate marketing

Of course, public relations activity which is targeted at one audience can often have a significant influence upon another. Thomas Coops, head of investor relations for Abbey National, has found from experience that investor public relations efforts that may be primarily aimed at opinion formers (those able to shape views of the company's shares and their value), can also have a direct impact on an organisation's marketing efforts. A company that is well managed in developing investor value is likely to be well managed in the products or services that it sells.

A company like Abbey National finds that investors, financial advisers, analysts, savers and borrowers are not always discrete audiences. The City analyst who recommends an investment may also be a mortgage customer; the shareholder may also be a saver; someone who advises clients professionally may well offer views to friends.

■ Build programmes around personal contact

All public relations activity is effectively a substitute for people talking to people. Clearly, the best relationship is developed where one person is talking to another on an equal and harmonious basis. Techniques such as seminars, presentations, roadshows and videos can extend the audience reach whilst still maintaining some element of personal communications. However, in broad terms, the larger the audience reached, the less personal and the less effective the communications become. One of the skills in public relations is to maintain the personal flavour through all communications techniques.

In a study carried out by Abbey National, the main communications techniques that the company used were rated. One-to-one meetings achieved an 80 per cent effectiveness scoring amongst opinion leaders. This same grouping rated advertising at only 1 per cent – in this case, because it could not present the kind of information they needed to make decisions.

Advertising works well in many areas but not always in the arena of persuasion. Perhaps the rather formal and structured process involved in advertising makes this an artificial technique in this area. In addition it is a one-way information source, allowing no opportunity for a dialogue or, often, response.

■ Corporate credibility affects sales performance

Of course, Abbey National is a little unusual as it holds one of the world's largest share registers with over 2.3 million shareholders. However, the importance of harmonising communications is confirmed by the fact that most of these shareholders are also customers.

Such customers tend to be small shareholders; some 55 per cent of the shares, at the time of preparing this book, were held by less than 700 institutions with over 30 per cent controlled by just 25 fund managers. Information for a major fund holder may be rather different to that expected by a small customer – but the information must be consistent, reflecting different facets of the company's operations and not creating a schizophrenic persona.

A clear definition of what public relations is supposed to be achieving is essential. As an illustration, Abbey National has a focused brief for its investor relations activities.

> To manage the interface between Abbey National and its institutional shareholders and stockbroking analysts. To keep them fully informed as to our strategic direction and business performance in order to build a broad and loyal shareholder base and ensure that share price adequately reflects Abbey National's value relative to the stock market as a whole.

This relates well to the vision of the company to be the outstanding financial services organisation in the UK. Abbey National expands this simple concept by saying that its purpose is to achieve above average growth in shareholder value over the long term by meeting the needs of customers, staff and all the other stake-holders in the business.

■ Public relations can help open international markets

BT is a company that is often seen in Britain as being a national organisation. Yet it has a significant international operation and in Europe, for example, feels that it has the need to raise issues and keep up interest by setting the agenda itself.

Linda Porter, manager of international corporate communications, thinks that the broader the market for any organisation, the more important it is to work to a clear strategy to avoid influences pulling the programme out of shape. She believes that companies should aim for an 'umbrella' programme with a common set of messages and audiences.

The key to success in international public relations is in developing ideas that can be adapted to meet the corporate diversity of markets in which the organisation is operating. This calls for discussion and adaptation rather than control and imposition – though local units should have good reasons for proposing change or delay.

■ Develop productive relationships with local managers

The fact that the local manager does not like the proposal (and there will always be someone who does not) is not a good enough reason for abandoning an essential part of the overall strategy. There is a difference between 'not invented here' and 'it genuinely will not work here'. The best approach is the one which alerts you to political, economic and environmental developments before you decide on elements of the programme.

On way that BT has set the agenda for its public relations within the complex, competitive and sophisticated world of telecommunications has been to try to create an number of its own initiatives. The tools that have been used to do this, amongst others, have included surveys undertaken by the research company, Harris. These have looked at, for example, business attitudes towards liberalisation and competition in the eight European countries where BT has a presence. In addition, a major conference was held in Brussels which developed a number of themes drawn from the research.

The survey gained a large amount of media coverage, she comments, and the results were widely used by the BT chairman and other senior managers in arguing the case in Brussels and beyond. The conference itself attracted a first-class array of speakers, including two commissioners, several regulators and captains of industry and over sixty journalists.

Though she believes that there is nothing particularly original in either of these activities as part of a public relations programme, they are likely to work for most industries and to be exploitable at country levels. With this campaign, for example, BT country managers were each asked to invite a group of their leading customers to attend and this helped to cement their own relationships, as well as demonstrating that BT was committed to Europe.

Porter also urges the necessity for proper evaluation of performance. This is essential to ensure there is a reliable way of determining whether the strategy is working and when to introduce changes that might be needed.

Public relations in action

Community initiatives win goodwill

Unipart integrates marketing and public relations

Good corporate public relations can strengthen relationships with multiple audiences including employees. Recognising community needs and finding common ground with corporate programmes allows companies to involve employees directly. Such was the case when a team of Unipart employees, working with public relations professionals, developed a unique technology event aimed at local primary school children in the Oxford area.

These primary schools were often ill-equipped to demonstrate the importance of IT to their young pupils. Based on their experience in Unipart, the team believed that primary school children would benefit from exploring new technologies in a friendly environment such as Unipart's own technology training and showcase area, The Leading Edge.

A small project team planned one of the most successful community events ever held at Unipart House. They turned the entire Unipart U, the company's in-house university, into a technology showcase for young children, and invited three IT companies to take part. Research Machines, Byte and Software Warehouse were enthused enough to send volunteers to demonstrate their software.

Local schools were contacted with invitations and a group of willing volunteers were recruited to demonstrate the computers on the day. The team designed Active IT to be just what it said: a real hands-on event for young children and their families. That meant it needed to be more than just *interesting*, it needed to be fun.

The team came up with some creative ideas that addressed the special needs of the audience. These included an alien hunt game, a bouncy castle, party bags to take home and a guest appearance by Freddy the Fox, the promotional mascot of local radio station, Fox FM.

Over 350 people attended the Unipart Active IT Weekend. The responses on the survey forms called the event an outstanding success. Dozens of people who attended commented on the innovation and care which had been taken by the organisers and the staff. The patience, enthusiasm and interest shown by Unipart's IT specialist was remarkable. They were able to translate complex ideas about technologies like the Internet so that the imagination of even the youngest child was captured by the experience.

From a simple idea and shared belief in Unipart's stakeholder philosophy came an exciting event which can now be replicated and has been expanded since.

All Unipart corporate public relations programmes demonstrate the stakeholder philosophy in action. 'We believe that building relationships with our surrounding communities through sponsorship and participation in community activities is essential to our business,' says chief executive, John Neill.

Establishing long-term relationships is even more important in times when relationships can be strained. An example of this came from a planning application in which Unipart sought permission to develop a factory on the edge of its headquarters site at Cowley. Initially, local residents were apprehensive about the plans.

The public relations team together with planners and advisers developed an open dialogue with the community to discuss concerns. Literature about the development plans was circulated to the homes of all local residents. A reply paid card asked for residents' views and each card was answered with a personal letter. The team also established a set of working meetings with representatives from the parish council and other interested groups. Four meetings were held during which aspects of the plan were amended to meet residents' needs. As a result, the planning approval for the new factory was applauded by local residents as well as the business community.

The leader in the local newspaper, *The Oxford Mail*, summarised the experience:

Unipart and Horspath Parish Council have proved that civilised discussion can make everyone a winner. The village gets its protection, Unipart its factory and the area 200 new jobs. Not bad, eh?

CHAPTER 9

Marketing: the diverse business discipline

PUBLIC RELATIONS IN SUPPORT OF MARKETING IMPLEMENTATION

The intellect of man is forced to choose
Perfection of the life, or of the work.
W. B. Yeats (1865–1939) from *Coole Park and Ballylee* (1932)

■ Direct marketing

Direct marketing is based upon the concept of putting the sales proposition directly to the prospective purchaser, without a salesman, a sales operation or retail interface in the conventional sense. Public relations might seem to have no relevance in a direct sale, but the truth is the opposite; without a retail operation or other evidence of substantial credibility, the sales decision must be made by the prospective customer on the basis of confidence in the organisation. Public relations can help demonstrate the credibility of the organisation behind the deal.

■ Corporate credibility is paramount in the direct sale

The whole area of direct marketing has expanded in recent years. The sector has moved from being a narrow specialist one, originally associated with low-quality products or services, to one that is very much mainstream. Direct marketing services today are operated to an extremely high standard, handling high-value and high-service items. As direct marketing has improved in sophistication, so have the quality and sensitivity of public relations support for these techniques.

As one of the main factors in the success of the direct marketing operation will be customer confidence, the contribution of public relations can be significant.

One area where this communications craft can add the most is in its ability to demonstrate company or product credibility. This is because most public relations techniques depend upon communications through credible and independent third parties, such as trade and professional bodies and the media.

■ Use the strength of third party endorsements

What the representatives of these independent organisations say tends to be trusted far more than might be sales presentations, direct mail or advertising, which are perceived as being totally under the control of the promoter and are affected by the 'they-would-say-that-wouldn't-they' caution of the members of the target market. But a report by a consumer body, a speech at a conference, an endorsement by a professional association or a news story in a key publication will usually be positively received.

Direct marketing campaigns are often supported by public relations which is aimed not just at promoting the product or service on offer but in establishing the significance and trustworthiness of the organisation behind such an offer.

Direct marketing may be a relatively new area of selling. Of course, some of the techniques have been around for some time and just have to be updated and brought together. Equally, these principles have been applied to more traditional areas of marketing.

The majority of advertising includes some method for prospective customers to respond directly either through asking for additional information or to buy the service or product on offer. *Direct Marketing* magazine estimated in 1993 that these options applied to around two thirds of US advertising, amounting to $142 billion (in 1991, the last year for which figures were available at the time of preparing this chapter). Public relations may play no part in winning the business, but it can be used to build confidence and generate the optimum environment within which the offer is made.

■ Good communications is essential for long term relations

Effective direct marketing often depends on the building of long-term relationships with the customer. Most direct marketing campaigns succeed on their own intrinsic merit. However, parallel programmes of public relations to reinforce and cement these relationships can be helpful. Tom Peters and Nancy Austin observed in their book, *A Passion for Excellence* (New York, Warner Books, 1985) that the sale consummates the courtship, then the marriage begins. How good the marriage is depends on how well the relationship is managed by the seller.

The natural tendency of relationships, whether in marriage or in business, is entropy – the erosion or deterioration of sensitivity and attentiveness. A healthy relationship requires a conscious and constant fight against the forces of entropy. Public relations should be the regular breath of reality that keeps important relationships working to mutual benefit.

■ Advertising

Over a century ago, the prime marketing communications discipline became established and that was advertising. Agencies grew up as 'agencies' for, originally, as everyone in the business knows, they bought space in papers and divided it up to sell to smaller advertisers.

■ Marketing established its credibility upon the success of advertising

In many respects advertising developed its credibility even ahead of marketing. The effectiveness of advertising is well established and this has given it a good level of understanding amongst marketing and other company executives. Public relations generally has not achieved that credibility. These communications disciplines appear to have much in common; indeed, some treat public relations as if it were cheap advertising.

But it is nothing of the sort. These are distinct disciplines that must be planned to work in harmony, reinforcing each other and playing to their strengths. Though complementary, each discipline can cover separate areas. As an illustration, advertising can promote a consumer product, reaching the mass market and stimulating sales, year in and year out – think of Guinness or Fairy Liquid. Public relations cannot. On the other hand, public relations can project and reinforce the values of the company behind these products with the most discriminating audiences. Advertising cannot.

Yet the professionals in these two disciplines have much to offer in each other's areas. Advertising is frequently based upon research which can form a solid foundation for the public relations plan. Shared themes can be developed from a consistent starting point. Messages and the different ways they will be presented can be agreed. The activity timetable can become a shared property. The creativity of the public relations people can add a new dimension to brainstormers; they may also see media news opportunities in advertising proposals. Personalities used in the advertising can be used in public relations events at minimal incremental cost.

Do whatever needs to be done to get them working well together. Start by having joint briefings and realistic budget allocations for each.

■ For maximum contribution, build collaboration

Many marketing directors think they are getting the best from their communications professionals by setting them up in competition. Perhaps the thinking is that if the advertising and public relations people challenge each other, presumably, then they will produce their best; and, equally, if they compete for budget, then they will compete on costs.

Our hypothetical marketing director who goes along with this philosophy might argue that they will be fighting each other to impress him and the company in terms of performance, service and cost control. And that must be good.

No. That must be bad. Difficult though it may be, the skill is to get the advertising, the public relations, the sales promotion and other communications people to work together. In competition, they will be in conflict; the marketing director, unwittingly, may have given them a reason to try to ensure that the other crafts contribute less or even fail. That way, the 'opposition' will be discredited and they will gain.

■ If a launch is to be news, advertising must follow public relations

Take a simple example. How often do public relations advisers find themselves struggling to convince the client that the advertising for a new product or service must nearly always *follow* the public relations? The reason is simple. And it has nothing to do with the relative importance of the two activities.

Logically, any news value in a new product will be because it is new. For simplicity, consider a product that will be advertised through trade, professional or consumer publications (though the principles apply to any product, advertised through any medium).

Once journalists have seen the advertising, they may feel there will be little news value left for their readers; the story has been told through the advertisements.

Most editors are reluctant to write about new products and services that are appearing in their advertising columns in the same issues; they fear that this might suggest that the advertising has influenced their editorial judgement. And, in planning the timetable, it may be unrealistic to assume that the editors write stories for this week's publications and the advertising appears next. Weekly publications (as in this example) go to press on different days. According to the timing of the announcement, some will be able to make that week's issue; others will not. Some will have plenty of time to prepare a full story; others will scramble away halfway through the briefing to get a short paragraph in before the presses roll. Others will want the story in advance – and then you are into the dangerous area of the embargo.

Even if your planning is so perfect that you are confident that the advertising will appear a week after the editorial, most editors will have seen the advertising copy in advance because of their publications' copy dates. Some will feel – rightly – they are being manipulated and may decline to play the game. Whenever possible (which is nearly always) the answer is to have a sensible gap between the appearance of the public relations initiatives and the advertising.

Some of the most successful integrated campaigns have had a gap not of days, or even weeks, but of months.

■ Integrated communications is not domination by the strongest

Integrated or co-ordinated communications makes a lot of sense but the marketers should check that the service they are being offered is *truly* integrated. One advertising agency called in a public relations consultancy to promote its integrated marketing communications service. The consultant was surprised that external promotional support would be necessary . . . until he discovered that the integrated service did not include public relations. 'We call someone in when we need that,' was the explanation! Clearly there is integration and integration.

In contrast, an integrated campaign for the UK mushroom industry mixed pricing and quality strategies with public relations, sales promotion, personal presentations and advertising. Previous *un-integrated* campaigns in the industry had succeeded in increasing sales a little but, as the product was seen as a commodity, by the simple laws of economics, prices declined proportionally. But for this campaign, the professionals worked closely together. This required great flexibility. For example, the plan required individual presentations of the campaign to every multiple, wholesaler, contract caterer and the leading retail greengrocery chains. It took two months to secure the presentations to the 95 buyers identified. Every presentation was achieved, even where it took three or four attempts with some buyers to achieve successful appointments.

These trade presentation meetings were planned over the March to May period for a campaign due to start in September; the lead time was to enable both growers and retailers to get geared up for the promotion. This required the public relations consultancy to develop a complete plan many months in advance of implementation and, even rarer, the agency had to prepare the finished television commercials for private showing to the trade, over six months ahead of them going on screen.

A target to justify this expenditure was set at 6 per cent sales increase without any price fall. The effectiveness of the co-ordinated approach adopted was demonstrated by the fact that the market in the first year rose by over 30 per cent, with a small increase in price to the growers – and sales have stayed at the same level since.

■ Build advertising properties that have news value

Some advertising campaigns have public relations value – not just in the sense that they project the core values of the organisation, but that they are of news interest. This can be because they are topical, controversial or use a personality who is in the news.

If advertising is to be considered part of the organisation's public relations – and it should be – it makes sense to involve the public relations advisers in the planning stages. They will be able to advise on the news potential of any proposed idea. More campaigns might use the multiplier effect of news comment if this were a more frequent practice.

■ Music can have public relations value

Some consumer campaigns have reached wider audiences through using music that is in tune with the public mood of the moment, such as the famous series of Levi jeans advertisements that used classic early rock numbers like 'I heard it on the grapevine'.

Others have created original music (or revived almost-forgotten compositions) that then became commercial music successes; this additional exposure reflects positively on the advertising and the brands being promoted. An interesting example was the theme tune for the Saatchi advertisements for BA – this music was even used on the PA systems of BA airliners before take-off and after landing. Persuasive, subtle reinforcing or not?

In contrast, Brutus jeans commissioned a composer to create an original piece of music 'I pull my Brutus jeans on'. This became a chart hit under a slightly changed title, 'I pull my blue jeans on'. Every time the song was heard – on the radio or on record – it was reinforcing the original Brutus jeans commercial.

■ Advertising dramas can be developed to capture editorial comment

Some advertising has been so apposite or dramatic that it has generated news interest and editorial comment, thereby multiplying the effectiveness manyfold. One of the most often quoted is the series of advertisements created for Gold Blend. The interest in the 'will-they won't-they become lovers' developed over a period of time. Advertising that is designed to create attention should really be planned with the full involvement of the public relations people who would be best able to advise on what may or may not make news. Certainly, a cynical attempt to startle or shock in order to capture a news headline may not always work.

Some advertisers have created posters to attract media comment at a fraction of the cost of television. Wonderbra posters featuring a glamorous young lady greeting an unseen visitor at her door in her bra with the phrase, 'Hello boys', startled the nation. They were talked about and reproduced in many news articles; sales rocketed, again, multiplying the effect of the media spend.

This was wittily parodied – on specially-bought side by side sites – by Kaliber low alcohol lager, with the brand's star, Billy Connolly, greeting his unseen visitor with the cans and saying 'Hello, girls'.

Remember, too, the Conservative *demon-eyes* Blair poster? This generated media coverage which, by the most conservative (sorry!) estimate was thousands of times the value of the cost of the original posters.

■ Plan for any controversy to be in line with strategy

In planning advertising that is designed to generate media comment, consider carefully the influence that any debate might have. Only undertake activities that will generate comment that will support your marketing strategy. That does not mean it cannot be controversial – but it does mean that customers and prospective customers must be likely to be supportive of the advertising's stance in the controversy.

An interesting example would be the advertisement depicting a pile of dead dogs, which the RSPCA presented as its disturbing perspective on the number that they are obliged to put down each day.

Shocking this may have been, but it would not necessarily endear the public to the work of this charity. Indeed, some found the negative image more disturbing than the charity might have imagined. Compare that with the Toys Aren't Us campaign run by the People's Dispensary for Sick Animals. This put over the message in a powerful and appealing way with a photograph which was widely reproduced in editorial columns.

The young person's holiday company, Club 18–30, used a series of provocative double entendres in a poster campaign only to find these censored. The agency was accused of deliberately writing advertisements to be banned – in view of the media coverage that this might attract. As the audience for the advertising of Club 18–30 were young and liberal people, such media commentary was probably seen by the advertiser as being positive and was unlikely to upset them.

Another good reason to involve your public relations people in the planning and approval stages is to get an informed view on whether there may be any potential media negatives.

Budweiser had to axe a cinema and television commercial that showed an American Indian lorry driver in search of a beer. Despite the fact that the advertisement did not run in the United States, it was considered sufficiently offensive for native American bodies to protest. Such controversy did not reflect well on the sensitivity of the brewer. An experienced public relations professional would not have let such an advertisement pass. And even if he or she had then, at least, the client would have had someone to sack for failing in their duty!

■ Balance the advertising and public relations spend

How do you strike a balance between advertising and public relation spending? There may never be enough budget to satisfy all the demands. Therefore the answer must be to allocate funds according to the effectiveness of each discipline. As a simple rule, public relations can be effective where the market needs educating or attitudes need changing. It is less powerful at presenting the same message again and again as may be necessary to support, say, consumer products. A breakfast cereal might be supported by television advertising whilst the public relations focuses on dietary and health advisers, educational data, a cookery campaign, competitions, a youth sponsorship or family initiative. The advertising might need £5 million to reach the audience necessary to achieve the sales forecasts, whilst the public relations efforts might need a budget of 10 or 15 per cent of this.

Yet, in a business-to-business sector the ratios may be reversed, with public relations leading, supported by just a little modest flag-waving advertising.

The largest advertisers in the UK, for example, spend over £100 million, with virtually all of this going through television. The 'smallest' advertiser in the top 100, at the time of writing, was Nestlé which spent just less than £12 million with around 70 per cent of this on television. Television dominates the media-buying of the top advertisers. Of course, there were one or two exceptions in the top 100 with, for example, both Halifax Public Services and Britannia Music spending around £12 million – and in both cases with nothing on television and virtually 100 per cent in the press. It would be helpful if such figures also included the public relations budgets, though in all cases these will be a tiny fraction of the total spend.

There is no validated research to confirm exactly how much these companies might have spent on public relations. Surveys to date by, for example, *PR Week* have only been able to identify expenditures from some major companies and have not yet produced reliable figures.

Normally, public relations professionals find themselves with budgets of just 1 or 2 per cent of the advertising spend. Is this always sufficient?

One major electronics company spent £20 million pounds on acquiring a small company that had technological products that it wanted to add to its range. In the first year it allocated £2 million pounds to the promotion of these, of which just £15 000 was earmarked for public relations. This was to cover the launch of new services and the education of a large and sophisticated market. Such minimal figures make no sense. They are not unusual.

It may be the fault of the public relations people if they do not get allocated a sufficient budget. For the truth often is that however powerful or effective the advertising may be, the launch plus media and opinion leader comments on a new product or service (to quote just one of the more obvious activities of public relations) will always be the most significant in developing a credible environment for whatever is being introduced. Many products and services are launched with public relations budgets less than the production costs of the television commercial. Many companies could afford to be a little bolder in testing what might be possible.

■ Plan for optimum return from marginal expenditure

Consider; what might be the additional impact of increasing an advertising budget from, say, £10 million to £11 million? No advertiser would expect to see less than a 10 per cent improvement in the impact – and might be looking for, perhaps, 20 per cent or more for the £1 million additional spend.

Yet putting that spend into public relations could produce an increase out of all proportion – used intelligently, it might double the overall effectiveness and reach.

Advertisers do not have to take such views on trust, they simply have to test them. Take the overall promotional budget and look at various ways of dividing it. This should not be on the basis of taking money from advertising and putting it into public relations but on the basis of the optimum spend in public relations to reinforce the advertising to the maximum effect. Not having adequate and effective public relations in the marketing mix means missing major promotional support. Editorial coverage alone (and that will be only part of the public relations contribution) can add substantial positive opportunities to see with new products or services that have a news interest.

Sometimes companies pay far more attention or give a higher priority to advertising decisions than they do to public relations – yet public relations is the custodian of public credibility. It was poor public relations that floored Ratners and British Gas, despite major advertising budgets. It has been good public relations that has boosted Virgin Direct and Marks & Spencer.

Some advertisers will produce superb advertisements or commercials that project their products or services to perfection – letting them sit in editorial columns or in broadcast media alongside editorial coverage that relates to the sponsoring company having problems with the environment, battles with its shareholders, an unfortunate environmental record, planning permission disputes and so on.

■ Generate news benefit from advertising initiatives

A famous soft drink company signed up an international sporting hero to front its television campaign yet at the planning stage it failed to discuss this with the public relations professionals. The contract was drawn up and signed which covered the requirements on the star and the number of days that he would allocate. Too late, the public relations people asked for a day for a press conference and a day for a factory visit – both of which could have generated valuable trade, professional and consumer media coverage. This proved impossible, yet if these had been negotiated as part of the original contract, the fee to the star was such that these two extra days would have cost nothing. Not only that, they would have added enormous value to the overall campaign; the star would have loved the personal appearances; staff, employees, neighbours, suppliers, local communities, wholesalers, retailers and countless others would have enjoyed the buzz. All opportunities missed, simply because the advertising and public relations were working in isolation.

■ Avoid using advertising to influence editorial decisions

Marketing professionals should be careful about trying to use their advertising spend to try to influence editorial. Journalists pride themselves on their editorial independence and even those publications that are not as independent as they might be still have editors who do not like being compromised.

A big advertiser may be of interest to a journalist simply through the fact that the company is trying to be a major force in that market sector. Editors will be fully aware of the advertising in their publications and do not need reminding about this. They will also be fully aware that the credibility of their publications is dependent upon the quality of the editorial material; if an advertiser has a good story to tell then it will be considered alongside stories from those who are not advertising.

If the advertiser tries to apply pressure, it will sometimes be counter-productive. Editors will be even more sensitive about appearing (particularly to editorial peers) to have been influenced by a big spender.

Sometimes, advertisers have gone so far as to boycott or threaten to boycott publications that are not pursuing an editorial approach that they would wish. Omega, the watch makers, threatened to pull out of *Vogue*. UK brand director, Giles Rees, criticised the over-use of 'skeletal' fashion models. Later, his boss Nicholas Hayek, the company chairman, overruled Rees, saying that it was not the advertiser's place to dictate the editorial policy of magazines.

At the time of a vital England/Germany football match, Vauxhall removed its advertising from those tabloid publications that the company felt had been excessively anti-German.

■ Public relations decisions are often tougher and riskier

Why do some company executives find advertising comfortable and public relations difficult? Part of the problem may be that public relations is a newer discipline and, as it is sometimes practised, often not disciplined enough. Also, it has not adopted procedures for appraising effectiveness as universally as advertising.

Yet there are other factors, probably, at work.

Advertising decisions tend to be taken behind closed doors, usually in private and amongst colleagues who need to be amiable, even amusing, in order to win company support for the expenditure.

In contrast, public relations is performed in public and depends on third parties that might disagree or challenge the assertions of company executives; it is organic, dynamic, volatile and risky. But that is precisely why it works. Unlike advertising, public relations is two way communications and it helps shape opinion in exactly the same way and through the same channels that form those original opinions.

■ Sales promotion

Sales promotion is usually considered one of the core *below the line* marketing crafts – often, for convenience more than logic, encompassing anything that does not comfortably fit into conventional perceptions of advertising or public relations. Sales promotion is a separate discipline yet one that has many elements in common with public relations. But, much more important, these crafts are synergistic; they really multiply effectiveness when run in close co-operation.

■ Promotions must enhance the marketing offer

In the *Marketing Book* (ed. Michael Baker, London: Butterworth Heinemann, 1994) Sue and Ken Peattie have defined sales promotion as:

> Marketing activities usually specific to a time period, place or customer group which encourage a direct response from consumers or marketing intermediaries, through the use of additional benefits.

The core factor in sales promotions is probably these benefits that are *additional* to the normal marketing offer – whether an opportunity in a competition, extra product, a sample, vouchers, club membership or any of countless ways of offering added benefit. One strong link between public relations and sales promotions is that both are involved in the communications process.

Whilst the primary aim of the sales promotion is to generate addition sales, many of the approaches used also are communicating in the marketplace – a promotion may give customers further information, may present a perspective or profile that could shift opinion and attitude or may simply build awareness. Different promotions may be targeted at different parts of the audience, sometimes projecting different messages.

Some public relations efforts in direct support of product marketing come close to being sales promotional in intent and operation. For example, in the food and allied sectors, many companies run product sampling, tasting and testing programmes as part of an overall public relations activity. Companies sometimes organise a touring circus using coaches, buses, mobile display vehicles (or even trains and planes) to present product offers to members of the public or specialised audiences. Public relations programmes may include competitions, product samplings, consumer tests and other para-sales-promotional activities.

■ Sales promotions can be important in marketing communications

As with public relations, sales promotions can also work in all four sectors of the attention/interest/desire/action concept.

Promotions can attract attention through being unusual, topical or with some other element of interest. They can add interest, certainly to the purchase decision. They will help to build desire through the offering of added benefits and, clearly, they are designed to produce action in terms of purchase.

One aspect of the Peattie definition that has a direct relevance to public relations is the reference not just to consumers but to 'marketing intermediaries'.

At the consumer level, sales promotions can have a real media and marketplace interest. An unusual offer can generate news – the 1938 custom-built Buick, used by King Edward VIII before his abdication, was the unusual prize in a *Daily Mail* promotion that won interest around the world. The use of a celebrity can provide opportunities for editor comment – the Hollywood star of the television commercial visiting the widget factory. The BA executive club was designed to make frequent flyers feel important and created many opportunities for good public relations support.

■ Trade and staff schemes benefit from good communications

But promotions aimed at those who can influence the sales to the ultimate customer can be reinforced with skilful public relations – whether these customers are people buying for their companies or the actual consumers of the products or services.

Shell Oils offered a £150 holiday discount voucher as an incentive for its trade customers as part of a scheme to identify key trade accounts where the company wanted to build loyalty. Such schemes can be briefed to trade media. Leading figures in the industry can be invited to sit on or chair panels of judges deciding the winners of industry competitions.

The annual international event, the Worldcom Young Business Achiever of the Year Awards, was sponsored by British Airways and included the editor of the *Director* magazine on its panel of judges.

Those who help win the sales, build the customer relations, develop loyalty, may be part of the audience for sales promotions, possibly through incentive schemes. Sales and other staff may have the opportunity to benefit from the award of special benefits for outstanding performance.

Companies such as Argos run schemes to help managers control incentive programmes. The Argos Incentive Database was designed to free managers from the headaches of running such schemes. Points can be accumulated for sales performance or any other operational area; public relations can be part of the communications efforts, both internally and externally, to project the concept, build interest and promote successes achieved.

Major retailers, airlines, oil companies, venues and other businesses have introduced loyalty cards that record usage of the stores or services and reward this with discounts, VIP treatment or other benefits. Special offers may be negotiated through local or regional newspapers to introduce or raise awareness of such schemes. Newsletters might be developed for the privilege customers or special social or sales evenings organised. Are such activities part of the public relations or part of the sales promotions? Does it matter, if both groups of professionals are working together to generate the maximum marketing benefit from such creative ideas, professionally implemented?

As some sales promotional campaigns move more towards customer loyalty, efforts often concentrate on the best customers and recognising or rewarding these the most. This demands effective database management; some argue, sales promotion and direct marketing are moving closer together.

Such trends should be paralleled by the public relations activity. This method of communications can focus on specific market sectors, whilst events, hospitality, seminars, receptions and other public relations techniques can also be used to give such customers both recognition and status in the eyes of the company.

Whatever the form of the sales promotion (or incentive scheme) that might be planned, real impact and enhanced performance can be created by involving the public relations professionals. Ideally, as in all other aspects of the marketing mix, it will be better if they are involved in the briefing – and not just when the concepts have been developed.

■ Selling and sales management

There are few areas in marketing where public relations is more effective than in the support of the selling operations. This can work in a number of ways and, as always, a good working relationship between the sales personnel and the public relations professionals can pay dividends.

For example, public relations can help to create the environment within which the sales negotiations take place; it can add authority and credibility to the proposition; it can generate sales enquiries from prospective customers; and, of equal importance, the sales personnel can themselves be a source of positive information and of good story leads for use within the public relations programme.

■ Good communications is a powerful motivating force

Bill Donaldson, author of *Sales Management: Theory and Practice* (1990), has argued that effective communications can be important in the motivation of sales personnel. He believes that people are less motivated if they have negative views about the job, the company or their performance.

If such critical views held by employees are fair, the cause of dissatisfaction must be corrected via product, price, distribution policies or organisational managerial changes.

If the views are inaccurate, then management must improve communications. This can be done by such techniques as review discussion groups, measuring existing levels of satisfaction through the complaints procedures, suggestion boxes, some type of formal survey, exit interviews (with company leavers) and, above all, by keeping close to employees. Whatever the technique or approach, good two-way communications is vital for effective management of the sales force.

Though public relations is unlikely to carry the responsibility for direct communications with the sales force, the public relations professionals may be called in to act as consultants or to prepare communications materials, such as newsletters. However, the biggest contribution may well be in ensuring that all public relations activities relating to the company and the products or services are specifically directed to the sales force. They will be more enthused if they feel that they are 'in the loop', getting information in advance of other audiences; in addition, they will be seen to be a central part of the public relations efforts of the company, helping to build the reputation whenever they are in any form of contact with customers and prospective customers.

The public relations professionals will have a vested interest in good relations with the sales force – they will provide many of the leads for potential public relations stories, case studies, trend reviews and articles. In return, as noted in the performance section, public relations can help generate new business leads for the sales effort.

■ Activities to win valuable sales leads need careful planning

One major European manufacturer of furniture asked a public relations consultancy to develop a programme to improve the number of sales enquiries generated through media coverage. The advisers soon discovered that the public relations that had been undertaken to build market awareness had been quite effective. The enquiry level seemed good.

A little further investigation caused the consultancy to suggest the manufacturer called in a marketing consultant with whom they worked; he agreed that the priority was not to improve conversion rates of enquiries to orders. His review of the procedures established that the company's sales management simply threw out all enquiries if they had not been turned into business within a period of twelve months. What they had failed to recognise was that those enquiring about the product remained the strongest potential customers – even if they had not yet ordered.

The public relations and marketing consultants together drew up a plan both to maintain the level of enquiries and to improve the response to these, not only at the time of enquiry but at regular periods thereafter. After a two-year period, the success of this approach was evaluated. Some 25 per cent of such enquiries were being converted into orders during a period of between one and two years after the initial enquiry. In other words, the company was winning 25 per cent additional business from enquirers who had not actually bought in the first year. Of even greater interest, new enquiries were costing just over £5 per £100 of sales. The conversion enquiries were costing less than £2.

■ Win allies around the customers' board tables

Does every company always get every sales opportunity that it should to present its case? Clearly, even in the best run companies the answer must be no.

The company cannot be expected to win the business if it is not given the opportunity to present its proposition. Therefore, one objective for some public relations campaigns is to ensure that the company always gets the opportunity to present its case, whenever there might be a business opportunity that could be of interest. This is particularly relevant in the area of business-to-business or in big-ticket sales . . . though the principles apply even in the consumer sales sector.

The brief for the public relations professionals can reflect this challenge. Consider drafting an aim for the public relations programme for, say, company ABC. Suppose a relevant tender is issued for which the client board might need to give approval for the final bid, then someone of influence around that board table must say 'Have we asked ABC to quote?'

For many years, IBM used to position itself in exactly this way and it was a technique that worked effectively right up until the time that the company ran into trouble. (The effectiveness of this public relations approach was not any part of the commercial factors that led IBM to lose its way a little.)

Even today, the residue of that philosophy lingers. Right through to the heady days of the mid-1980s, anyone proposing a major business solution from Hewlett Packard, Bull, ICL, Olivetti, Philips or any other player knew that someone around the board table would be asking 'Have you asked IBM for a quote on this?'

IBM competitors had to work hard to overcome this challenge – often in trying to get the specification for the systems written in such a way that it gave them a direct advantage. Even so, though this approach was extremely good for business, it was not targeted towards any direct sales enquiries but, rather, to prevent business going unchallenged to the competitors.

More recently, the AON Corporation of the USA, which claims to be one of the world's largest insurance brokers, set as an objective for its public relations consultants that a public relations effort should be aimed to build at least one interested supporter of AON at every board table where a major competitive insurance broker proposition might be presented. One direct effect of this objective was that the public relations consultancy did not focus public relations efforts directly on those who might specify insurance solutions or even those only that might have the technical expertise to evaluate them but at all of those who might be asked to endorse them – and that would include board members around the table from unrelated areas such as human resources, marketing, production and others.

■ Use public relations to create sales credibility and authority

With most sales-support public relations campaigns, one aim will be to project the authority and capability of the company. Though this might seem obvious this is not always written into every public relations brief.

Public relations can be specifically orientated to create the optimum environment within which members of the sales team will work – ideally, a situation of awareness, understanding and goodwill towards the organisation that will create the best possible basis upon which negotiations can be undertaken.

One description of public relations is that it is all about what people say about you when you are not there.

Imagine the situation where the marketing people have worked well on developing the product or the service, the sales people have negotiated brilliantly and got the best possible deal, those responsible for buying or using the product or service are totally committed. The proposal goes in front of the board – because it's a big-ticket item – for approval.

■ Sales personnel cannot control all influences on sales

Making that decision will be a number of directors completely unknown to the sales personnel; yet these board members may decide whether their company should entrust a major order to a particular supplier on the basis of their knowledge of that company. These unknown influencers around the board table will not have been exposed to the skilful negotiations of the sales personnel. But they may have been exposed to other messages: the company results, news stories, comments from friends. The sales people must involve the public relations practitioners to get as many of these messages under control and reinforcing the sales proposition.

Consider this simple factor. One or more of those directors may well encourage the others to back the wise decision presented to them when they say, 'I've heard of ABC, they've got a good reputation, they have been doing some interesting things recently and I think they are an organisation we can trust.'

Or might these unknown executives swing the deal the other way if they simply profess that they have never heard of ABC and it might be unwise to entrust business to an unknown company? Even worse, they may have negative perceptions of ABC.

If these unknown directors had been reading positive reports of the ABC company in the financial press; had seen a recent television programme which cited its environmental record as a model for industry; had attended a government conference where a senior representative had made an impressive, thoughtful and well-researched speech; had been impressed by the efficiency and friendliness of the telephone operator when calling to check a fact; had seen the sparkling new livery on the well-kept vehicles that the company operated; and had noted the emphasis that the company placed on courteous driving standards – then they might be quite well disposed.

If, on the other hand, they were aware that the local council had turned down a planning application for an extension to an ABC factory because of complaints by neighbours over noise, smell and late night working; if an environment group was critical of company waste discharges to waterways; if increases in remuneration of directors had caused protests at the annual general meeting; and if they had often observed the thoughtless road manners of ABC lorry drivers – then they may well not be inclined to want to put company money in their direction.

The salesmen cannot control such situations. The marketing professional only has a limited influence. But the public relations person has a major influence upon such factors that can swing the sale one way or another.

■ Analyse all audiences that affect sales success

The projection of the authority and credibility of the company can help create the optimum environment within which sales and sales negotiations take place. As noted earlier, plans to influence this sales environment can be part of the brief to the public relations professional. Depending on the nature of the company business and the influences that might be at play, a broad aim of this nature might well be developed to become more specific objectives.

The primary requirement is the analysis of all the audiences that are being reached to ensure that anyone that might be of significance is covered.

The techniques to generate such awareness and regard for the company may be diverse. Spelling out such aims will put an orientation on the public relations that, otherwise, might not have been considered central. For example, public relations may want to talk about the achievements of the company in terms of research and development, awards that it has won for quality of personnel management or for environmental initiatives or other areas that reflect well on its management and its role in the community.

Presentations by senior representatives on conference platforms might have a greater significance. Good factory gate relations, involving consultation, may suggest that the company views winning the support of the community as more than just insurance to get planning permission; positive and enthusiastic factory neighbours can mean dozens or hundreds of ambassadors out in the community talking knowledgably and positively about the company. The same point may apply to employees – good communications becomes more than an unwelcome necessity and turns into something which the company views as part of its responsibility to the team that makes everything happen.

■ Develop plans that create business leads

Public relations can be planned to generate sales enquiries. Though its effectiveness in this area will not be a complete measure of the value of public relations, it can be an extremely good indication of how well the central messages are getting over to an important target audience – prospective customers. This can be particularly applicable where the public relations is in support of major services, capital goods, business contracts or financial services – in all cases, where the source of the enquiry can be logged and the progress can be tracked through the negotiation to whatever the final conclusion.

Take a simple example: a new type of pension may be of interest to writers on personal finance. Perhaps an intelligent public relations programme could present this information to them in a way that they would wish to review this service in their editorial columns. Some might wish to interview the professionals behind the development of the new concept. Trade and professional journals may also follow this up which, equally, can create interest in the marketplace.

Readers may complete enquiry forms in magazines. In other cases, they may telephone or write to the company. To monitor the value of such responses, a programme needs to be set up for telephonists and other staff handling enquiries to record these. Ensure that a check is made of the source of the information that prompted the potential customer to make the enquiry. These can be logged; the response rates from different publications recorded; the quality of the enquiries checked periodically; and the levels of conversion calculated.

■ Build the sales/public relations partnership

Public relations should be part of the consciousness of sales management. For example, an outline of the work of public relations and its involvement with sales initiatives should be part of the induction of every new member of the sales team. Public relations should be on the agenda of every sales meeting and should form part of any national sales conferences. Ideally, public relations will be an issue for discussion at sales conferences and such debate might be stimulated by a paper presented by a senior executive within sales or a member of the professional public relations team. The ideal is to make every member of sales (including the essential sales support staff) part of the public relations team.

Much of the material created by public relations – published articles, speeches, videos and so on – can be used by the sales force; this material should be presented to them with suggestions on how it might be used – in sales presentations or proposals, for example.

The input of the sales professionals should be sought so that such items are being produced in a style and format that is most useful to them

Some form of feedback mechanism should be set up so that the contributional value of this material – or the opportunities that it might have created – can be reported back through to sales management and, from them, to the public relations executives responsible for planning and implementing these activities.

Of course, the sales force will often be the source of some invaluable public relations stories – personality news, case studies, contracts, newsworthy applications, product or service effectiveness and so on.

Some companies use a simple form for sales personnel to complete when they believe that they have something that might be of relevance to the public relations programme. Sales personnel are much more likely to use this in a positive and pro-active way if they have discussed at their sales meetings the support public relations can offer to help them meet budget.

Some companies like to recognise the origination of such stories by members of the sales team – by reporting these in sales newsletters or noting those generated in a regular piece in the company magazine. A simple award can be instituted for the individual, the sales branch or region that in the opinion of, say, the director of public relations, produces the most useful suggestions for such news stories.

■ Use public relations to build the sales environment

Many believe that sales is part of marketing. If marketing is the creation of opportunities in the marketplace, then often sales is the most important link between the organisation making the offer and those potential customers accepting it. Of course, sales is not the only interface.

Many sales take place without any 'sales' personnel at all. Few would describe, say, the checkout assistants in Asda or B&Q as sales personnel. They may be the only company representatives in the shopping transaction, yet they have no influence over the sale. All buying decisions have been made by shoppers *before* this human contact between buyer and seller is established, as this usually occurs at the last moment, not the first – that is, as the customers pay before leaving.

The sale, therefore, of B&Q or Asda must be made before customers visit the store; such influences convince them that this is the store they want to visit for their purchase needs. Increasingly, the sales negotiator, the persuader, is being replaced by organised persuasive communications, notably advertising and public relations. Where these disciplines are controlled by marketing directors, they are taking over at least part of the sales function.

It is true that such checkout staff (and their equivalents in other retail organisations) may offer limited advice. It is also true that companies like B&Q have floor staff to assist customers, but even they do not normally take the sales initiative; they respond to requests for assistance.

The concept of 'sales without the salesperson' is not limited to the retail sector. Countless commercial, business and corporate buying decisions are effected without the input of a salesman or woman. Those sales situations where a sales person is involved may be becoming the exception rather than the rule – no sales person is usually involved in buying air tickets, car hire, books, records and even health and education.

And, even where there may be some negotiation or advice in the purchase, often the person ultimately responsible for the company's offer may not meet the potential customer – he or she may, for example, be more directly involved in running aspects of the company that have no direct sales element. For example, hotel managers will be responsible for the total management of the personnel and resources under their control. Though they may set prices and terms for room hire, conferences, banquets and so on, often they may have no direct role in presenting such sales propositions or negotiating the deal with the buyers. This might be undertaken through marketing efforts – by advertising, direct mail, seminars, conferences, public relations and so on. Yet the face-to-face delivery of the promise may well be made by a receptionist who is full-time involved in business practicalities, not in persuasion – ensuring that all guests get the right rooms, the right services and that they pay the bills for these.

■ All employees should be part of 'public relations selling'

In such cases, the sales proposition is developed remotely from the customer and presented by a third party with no flexibility on negotiation. Public relations can be invaluable in bringing those prospective customers to the point where the deal can be closed.

In any enterprise it is essential that all employees understand the importance of the customer – and understand that the presentation of the product, the service and the support must be of a quality, value and timeliness that will exceed customers' expectations, thus ensuring that the customers come back for more. That may be customer care, it may be marketing or it may be plain commonsense but it is not usually any *formal* part of selling.

And yet, the sales proposition is dependent upon all these factors – and the sales proposition can be significantly different to the marketing projection.

How can marketing, sales, advertising and public relations work together to convert a concept into business for the company?

Marketing is the craft of anticipating what the customers might want, creating or shaping the company offer and placing it in the market. Sales is taking this general offer and putting it to the customer, in the face of competitive challenges, tailored as may be appropriate and presented in terms that meet the customers' needs. Advertising generates awareness through presenting positive arguments about this proposition, generally through media selected to be most likely to reach and influence prospective purchasers. Public relations is responsible for creating the environment within which this sales process takes place and building the most positive attitudes possible amongst customers towards the company, its products and services.

Whether or not there is a direct sales force, public relations (and advertising) should play a central role in helping to deliver these sales proposition messages to the target customer audiences. This role becomes even more important where the communications are not just expected to create awareness or even goodwill alone, but positive action. For example: the hotel in the earlier illustration may have some attractive all-inclusive business packages for sales conferences; or it really knows how to look after families with children; or there are some particularly attractive, themed, out-of-season weekends on offer. None add to the business objectives unless the proposition is presented to customers who buy the deal.

It is unlikely – if not impossible – for public relations alone to win the sale but it can help create the optimum business environment within which the selling process can take place. A MORI study is one of many that has convincingly demonstrated that people tend to prefer to deal with companies that they know and their inclination to buy something is significantly enhanced if it is presented to them from a company in which they hold in high regard; this factor can raise the acceptability by 15 per cent or more.

Whichever executives in the company are responsible for the management of the sales function, they should be involved in the processes of planning and approving public relations activities for the simple reason, as noted, that these can have a significant influence upon the ability of the sales force to generate interest and convert this interest into orders – or even replace the sales force persuasion activity entirely.

■ The creation of sales leads can be a measure of effectiveness

Public relations programmes can be planned to generate sales leads or enquiries from prospective customers. Indeed, the quality of such enquiries can be one measure of the effectiveness of the public relations efforts. If this is appropriate to the sector of activity and the programme being undertaken, then objectives can be written to set this measure as a monitor of performance.

In the Vent-Axia example quoted earlier, sales leads from public relations represented 85 per cent of those created from all marketing sources. (That is, those other than direct referrals to sales personnel from existing customers.) After the first test period, a figure was set as an annual target, with improvement measures each year. As the programme progressed, the quality of the leads and the rate of conversion were also measured.

Such targets should be prepared between marketing and/or sales and the public relations professionals – and put into an agreed format. For example:

Sales enquiries generated by the public relations programme in fiscal A totalled B; we should target to generate B + C per cent in fiscal D. At least E per cent should be from purchasing/line managers/board directors in discipline [as appropriate], from companies with sales more than/employing more than [qualifier inserted here, as appropriate].

The total sales value resulting from such enquiries in the year was £F. The performance target for fiscal D will be set at £F plus G per cent.

Such targets can be refined year on year. Measuring results through sales figures can be a little unfair to the public relations team; they do not directly control the sales. Some companies, therefore, estimate the sales *value* of the enquiries. (This can also give a separate target for the sales personnel to see what level they can convert.)

■ Set performance targets that reflect market reality

An actual example from a recent public relations plan for a company manufacturing office equipment and systems, drafted by the consultancy and agreed by marketing, read:

Enquiries in the financial year just finished which were directly traceable to the public relations efforts totalled 1629, of which 68 per cent were calculated by sales administration to have useful sales potential, with an additional 12 per cent of some longer term possible benefit. The preliminary qualifying process for those enquiries with sales potential indicated that the total sales enquiry value was in the region of £8.4 million. Of the total number of the 1629 enquiries that were recorded, 38 per cent were from companies and organisations with which we have never traded.

Public relations has other objectives which are not directly sales-related; but, looking at sales support alone, we feel the proposed activity would significantly increase both the reach and the impact, as detailed in the recommendations. If this is agreed, the necessary budget for this programme would need to be raised for the coming year by 8.2 per cent to £225k.

Your consultancy believes it would be conservative to set the sales enquiries targets for the coming year to something like twice this percentage level of increase, to reflect the incremental value of the larger budget. This would put the figures for overall enquiries at 1629 × 16.4 per cent (a total of 1896 enquiries) which, at current levels, should show a potential sales value of £9.8m (£8.4 plus 16.4 per cent). Again, at current ratios, the existing level of 38 per cent should be, ideally, from potential new customers.

The sales leads figure is a reasonable target but the sales value cannot be assured, so is no more than an aim. Note that the level of qualified enquiries is a more valid public relations objective for the sales support activities than the percentage that represents new companies. It should be understood that it would be practical for the public relations efforts to continue to generate an increasing level of enquiries (representing an increasing level of potential business) at the same time as the number of new customers with which we might wish to do business would be declining. This might be possible, despite a continuing improvement in the year-on-year public relations efforts.

This apparent contradiction will eventually rise (perhaps this year or the next) because the proportion of the potential market with which the company has not traded before has decreased year by year. When we started the public relations efforts through the consultancy some five years ago, we estimated that we had only ever dealt with or had enquiries from some 12 per cent of our potential market, whereas we would now believe that we have had some form of contact with some 35 per cent of those potential customers that might be of value to us. In other words, public relations can continue to target 100 per cent of the market – but the proportion of the market that represents potential new customers has shrunk over this period, obviously, from 88 per cent to 65 per cent.

In the above example, the approach is not perfect, but it is well considered and well intentioned. One weakness in the measure is that the public relations may have generated a level of interest in previous years from some companies that are still being positively influenced by the public relations but, because they have now established a sales relationship with the company, will not be recorded through the enquiry process. Sales management and consultancy management need to consider whether this is an important factor, whether the continuing business from those who are positively influenced towards the company can be measured and whether this should be incorporated in some way into the targets.

Even with such provisos, most consultancies would accept this as a reasonable challenge; the budget has been increased because the programme of activity is producing results and a better level of results is being expected for the increase in budget. This is quite reasonable as the additional 8 per cent or so of budget does not need to cover any consultancy overheads and can be used virtually 100 per cent on additional results-orientated activity.

Of even greater importance, this structured approach to the generation of sales enquiries is intended to measure the ability of the consultancy to undertake activities that will generate enquiries.

The potential sales volume of those enquiries that are judged to be of value (something calculated by the sales administration team through their initial telephone qualification process for such enquiries) would also stimulate the consultancy to undertake a level and quality of activity that would tend to be more attractive to the larger potential customer – exactly where the organisation wishes to target its sales effort. However, this target does not place any responsibility on the consultancy for sales performance. This is clearly an area over which it can have no direct control; if the performance of the public relations efforts in terms of quantity, quality and value of sales enquiries continues to rise satisfactorily but sales do not rise in proportion, then the problem lies either: in the efficiency of the sales operation; the quality or price of the products or services; or some other factor within the sales offer.

■ Launch new products and services to stimulate sales interest

In its particular role in supporting the sales effort, product launches should be discussed between marketing, sales management and public relations. For example, if the new product is of some news interest, then the launch is likely to include a media briefing element.

Some considerable caution should be exercised in this to avoid the presentation of the product becoming an overt sales pitch – this will be resented by journalists and can be counter-productive. Of course, the media launch is 'selling' the new deal to the media, but the approach must be converted into an information/news exercise. Editors owe a responsibility to their readers, listeners or viewers, not to companies trying to win sales. Be careful about leading the media presentation by anyone with a sales title and do not show that great new sales video.

Similarly, many public relations professionals are cautious about using sales literature in presentation packs. Such material might be available to journalists or, if it is considered to be an essential part of the presentation, can often best be tucked into the back of the media pack.

One technique to reduce the heavy sales impact of such literature is to ensure that every copy has a stapled briefing sheet on the cover which explains that this is information that will be available to customers, that any photographs used in it are available for media use and that such material is available for any reader enquiries.

Even this last point needs to be used carefully as some media, who may be interested in the product and its role or the trend that it represents, will not be the slightest bit interested in the sales impact. This will be true of radio and television programmes. National press will not be impressed by sales literature and neither will many of the professional publications. However, a new product launch is not solely for the benefit of the media.

Consideration should be given to running a series of events with each being modified to meet the specific needs of the audiences to which it will be directed. For example, some factors can be common – the venue, the backdrop, the displays, the sound system and lighting, the catering and so on. The presentation to wholesalers and distributors may talk about the growth in the business sector and the potential benefit to delegates' businesses in using these products to help them ensure that they are at the front of such trends.

Under no circumstances should negative or derogatory comparisons be drawn with competitors. This will not reflect well on the company. Indeed, it is reasonable to expect that many of the delegates will have good relations with the competitors; such comments may upset attendees or may even get fed back to competitors and help to stimulate some level of needle which will be of benefit to no one. Company representatives should talk about their own company and should treat the competition briefly and briskly with some modest respect and move rapidly back on to their own company offer. The furthest any company spokesman should ever go in discussing a competitor will be (and he should even think carefully about this), damning them with faint praise.

Other presentations may well be organised for relevant groups such as retailers, professional and trade bodies, suppliers, company service personnel, representatives of other company divisions and so on.

■ Branding and brand promotion

The success of most of the biggest companies in the world, such as Coca-Cola, General Electric, ICI, Mars, Microsoft, Procter & Gamble, Unilever and Walt Disney, is built around their brands. Brands have a real commercial value and can change hands for major sums out of all proportion to other assets – as, for example when Nestlé bought Nabisco's Shredded Wheat or Rowntree and its Rolo, Kit Kat and other famous names.

Of course, branding is usually taken to be an activity in commercial companies but it is equally important in other sectors. For example, Amnesty International, the Worldwide Fund for Nature, the Red Cross, Oxfam are all clearly brands with their own distinctive values and they need to be managed in the same way that commercial brands might be.

Mark Sherrington, a founding partner of the Added Value Company (and for many years a senior marketing professional in Lever Brothers), has described marketing as the gearbox of the company making the profitable connection between the organisation's core competencies and the needs of the market. In this analogy, he sees the brands as the cogs in the gearbox.

■ Brands work at product and corporate levels

To change the analogy, branding can be a central lever in the positioning of either individual products and services or of the company itself.

As an example, Marks & Spencer may try to position itself as an upmarket brand – though it could be argued that its St Michael brand is more towards the mid-market. Indeed, with the strong branding of Marks & Spencer, many marketing professionals question whether the company actually needs a product brand; some wrestle with the concept that St Michael is an umbrella brand that is applied to underpants and to cheese. Brand segmentation tends to focus on narrower core values that make St Michael the inexplicable brand that, perhaps, proves the rule.

However, the corporate brand of Marks & Spencer has a direct impact upon the likely attitudes of potential customers towards any product or service that might be introduced. Where a company has such strong positioning then this is likely to have a direct effect upon brand positioning; this can clearly be seen in other retailers such as W. H. Smith, Texas or Sainsbury's – or in other sectors with, say, American Express, Boeing, IBM, Mercedes Benz or Norwich Union.

An interesting example has been the handling of the Weight Watchers brand. This was purchased by Heinz in the late 1970s; it had soon absorbed the benefits of the Heinz name in terms quality and reliability – yet added its own distinction in terms of health and, specifically, calorie control without sacrifice of flavour. The success of this positioning approach was demonstrated by the fact that within ten years well over 200 lines were being marketed by Heinz under the Weight Watchers brand.

The development of the competitive marketing strategy is dependent upon a clear idea of how the products or the corporation should be positioned.

Without a clear view on competitive strategy, it is difficult to plan the rest of the marketing support elements – particularly the public relations, which is often one of the most powerful techniques in building credibility. For there are few areas of marketing more closely related than branding and public relations.

Indeed, it could be argued that branding is virtually the direct application of public relations to products or services.

The brand symbolises values that are captured within the product or service and which have an aura that shines beyond. Effective branding demands that the core values of the product are real and promotable but, of course, the brand does far more than this. Often it can add broader values that are tuned into the issues, concerns, or interests of the public in a way that gives a relevance far beyond immediate purchasing satisfaction.

Effectively, this is an area where public relations is at its strongest – though it has to be said that too often the promotion of brand values is achieved without formal public relations support. Perhaps this is because marketing professionals are not comfortable with the function (or performance) of public relations. Equally, many public relations advisers do not understand marketing well enough to be credible with their colleagues in marketing planning. Advertising and sales promotion are two marketing disciplines that can so effectively promote brand values. Consider what public relations can add. What could be more persuasive than the endorsement through respected third parties, opinion leaders, journalists, professional figures, broadcasters, academics and others influenced by public relations messages and, in turn, influencing the public?

Consider an example. A bag of crisps is a low value purchase in both senses of the word. Few people build their day around the purchase of a bag of crisps. A large proportion of sales are either incidental or they are impulse – you are having a few beers with some friends so a bag of crisps will go down well as a nibble. You are having a picnic with the children and buying some soft drinks, some yoghurts, a chocolate bar and – well, maybe, a bag of crisps would pop in well.

For those who use shopping lists (research suggests that less than 20 per cent of us now do) then few would be writing down crisps.

And yet, and yet. The sales of this modest product are counted in billions; virtually everyone eats crisps at some time. A few people eat quite a lot.

When we look for or ask for a packet of crisps by name, that is branding at its most effective. Often we do – where the marketing, the product offer or the advertising has been sufficiently strong to make us want to insist on a specific brand.

However, at many outlets – the pub or the corner grocery shop – we may well only have the choice between whichever brands they happen to stock. Therefore, it can be argued that the strong branding influences the stocking policy of such outlets. In supermarkets, we may have access to all brands and therefore the branding strength will influence what we pick from the shelves.

Take Walkers. Here is a brand that has reinvented itself consistently every couple of years for some little time. It grew from nothing to challenge the then major market leader, Smiths, and it has fought off challenges from many other upstart newcomers. At the time of the 1996 European Football Cup, the Walkers brand managers were perfectly in tune with the mood of the times.

They introduced Gary Lineker – previously a highly successful and credible footballer and, at the time, a credible and highly popular commentator – to endorse the brand in a distinctive series of television commercials. They added even greater impact by drafting in Paul Gascoigne to reprise his emotional tear-shedding role. Indeed, the making of the television commercial itself generated a lot of news coverage on both television and in the print media through the astute public relations activity that was taken in support. The triumphant coup for Walkers was to brand a line of Walkers crisps as Salt and Lineker. The joke was right not just for football fanatics. Lineker was a celebrity and the initiative caught the imagination of the public – and was a graphic demonstration of how to revitalise a brand through tuning into current moods.

■ Public relations is central to the projection of brand values

Mark Sherrington identified that brands have value to consumers as a way of identifying. They provide a consistent level of quality that simplifies choice. This builds consumer loyalty which, in itself, gives a company a level of profit protection for some time. Brands are beneficial to consumers because they represent values on which they can rely; they are valuable to companies because they support both sales and prices.

An intelligent company will use public relations to project such brand values and an important factor in this will not just be the effectiveness of the techniques used to present the messages to the critical audiences but the *quality and tone* of the activities.

We would understand and probably be comfortable with Range Rover supporting county shows or horse trials. We would be startled if they backed national greyhound racing – even if the latter activity could be argued to reach more potential Range Rover buyers. To that extent, Marshall McLuhan did have a touch of sense (not much more) when he said the medium is the message. Clearly, the medium is not the message but sometimes the medium adds a tone to the message that can be significant.

The place that you see the brand and the people you see using it also communicate the proposition, believes Mark Sherrington. As examples, St Honoré in Paris and Bond Street in London command high rent premiums because of the luxury good brands who wish to have their flagship shops there. Sheffield meant so much for quality cutlery that foreign firms set up there to use the city name in their promotional material or bought Sheffield brands to add to products that might be made in Korea.

The six Ps of the brand mix – product, packing, price, promotion, place, people – are all employed consistently and coherently by the great brands to communicate and reinforce their competitive advantage. Indeed, brands use all aspects of the brand mix consistently and coherently to communicate their proposition.

Public relations is all about projecting the personality of the corporation – and, where appropriate, the brand. Consumers in research are often asked who the brand would be if it were a living person, and public relations activities that use personalities need to be sensitive to these factors. It is one reason why the public relations professionals need to be involved in any research – not just to make a contribution but to understand the processes that are going on.

Public relations programmes should promote brand values consistently through the presentation of agreed messages in all editorial materials; the briefing of journalists and other third parties; the selection and use of personalities; the development of policies towards issues; the handling of crises; parliamentary and other public affairs activities; in internal communications; and investor relations.

■ Good marketing communications must also protect brands

What do zips, escalators and aspirins all have in common? David Haigh, director of Interbrand, poses the question. They were all once proprietary brands which lost the right to exclusive use of their own names. They have gone down the slippery slope to generic status; the ultimate nightmare for every brand owner. Many other brands are under similar threat. For example, Jeep, a brand which is synonymous with rugged off-road performance, has had to fight major legal cases to protect itself. Other manufacturers have produced vehicles that they have chosen to call jeep believing that this is a generic name rather than a brand name. Biro, Hoover, Pyrex and BUPA, David Haigh believes, are just a few of the brands which people tend to use generically rather than as true trade marks.

The companies owning these need to ensure they are taking vigorous action to protect them. The company managers would be wise to include the use of public relations in the defence of their brands – letters to editors, journalists and authors who misuse the brand names, articles on the protection that exists, insistence that these words are used with initial capitals and not as verbs: e.g. . . . *The works director tannoyed the factory.* Or that the brand is not allowed to become an everyday expression, as in: *The new machine is the Rolls-Royce of its market.*

It is sensible to keep records of this public relations activity as it could be important in establishing the legal position of such brands and the steps that the owners have taken to prevent misuse.

Brand names may not always be obviously brand names. David Haigh quotes the example where consumers may be under the impression that Granary is a style of bread; it is, in fact, a trade mark and any baker using it must use only Granary bread flour from McDougall in its production. Teflon, Tupperware and Tetrapak are also brands in their own right.

Many of the trademarks which erode to become generics do so in rapidly developing product categories. Often this is because management may be stretched and brand protection seems a minor problem – until it is too late.

New products should be launched with proper protection and this must be continued throughout the life of the brand – and even afterwards, if the name is likely to be used at some future date.

Names alone can have some considerable value. For example, the UK motorcycle industry was devastated by the success of the Japanese – yet names such as Triumph and Norton, which once seemed doomed to disappear with no value, have proven to be of significant interest in the motorcycle market.

BMW acquired a whole raft of valuable motor brands and potentially valuable names, such as Mini and MG, when it bought Rover. In the world of toys, Triang, Hornby, Meccano and Dinky are all brand names that have seen considerable ups and downs over the years. Yet each has retained a value that can be measured – by the simple fact that companies have been prepared to pay a specific price for them. Brand value can be measured by the difference between the tangible assets values and the amount paid by acquiring companies for corporate and brand goodwill. In 1980, tangible assets constituted about 80 per cent of the value of all mergers and acquisitions involving quoted companies in the UK; now that figure is around 30 per cent. Goodwill has risen from 20 to 70 per cent in that short time. Much of this must be a recognition of the value of the brands, as in the Rover or Nestlé deals noted earlier.

It follows from this that an investment in brand protection and promotion can be seen as an investment in the bottom line and not just to promote brands but to protect them from encroachment from competitors.

■ Use communications through product life cycles

Perhaps all products experience some form of life cycle – introductions and slow growth as the market develops awareness; early acceptance and fast growth in sales level; slowing down in growth as the competition begins to enter the market, perhaps with other new products or innovations; plateau as market reaches saturation; and slow decline in product sales as too many producers are chasing too little business; terminal point where return no longer justifies investment and the product is withdrawn.

However, as every marketing professional appreciates, every phase in this cycle can be affected by the marketing techniques that may be deployed. Successful products can be kept alive for decades, generations and, perhaps, centuries. Either the product has a continuing relevance or it may be developed as the market changes or it is extended into new sectors that become of greater commercial significance.

Successful examples are legion. But what about the failures? Ekco was once a market leading brand of radios. A1 sauce was a massive seller. Daimler was range of British-built limousines better known around the world than Rolls-Royce. Force flakes was a bigger brand than Kelloggs cornflakes. All dead and gone. Why? Because of the inevitability of the declining product cycle? Because of some immutable shift in the market? But people still buy radios, sauces, expensive cars and breakfast cereals. The real failure was in the marketing –

and specifically, the market vision. Public relations cannot compensate for weak marketing but it has been an importance influence behind both old brands that survive and prosper – Bovril, Cadbury's, Gillette, Hoover, Oxo, Persil – and newer ones that have risen to take over from the failures – BMW, Bose, Goodman's, Radion, Sharman's.

Many pundits, such as Peter Doyle, Professor of Marketing and Strategic Management at the University of Warwick, doubt whether the classic product life cycle of introduction, growth, maturity and decline exists – at least in any consistent way across product types.

He believes that there is no evidence that most products follow such a four-stage cycle, nor that the turning points are in any way predictable. Many brand histories that do not conform to the cycle theories tend to support his view.

Swan Vestas is a match brand that has always been a match brand and seems set to continue to be a significant brand so long as there is a market for matches. That does not mean that at some stage in the future it could not become something else but that is the way it has decided to position itself – though even within this narrow sector, it has changed significantly over the years. The current relevance of Swan Vesta has been supported by effective public relations over recent years. (It is still the only match brand in the world that is asked for by name, as noted earlier.)

Persil may not mean the same things to today's generation as it did to their parents. But it is reasonable to imagine that Persil may well still be a brand of significance five hundred years from now – when it is applied to the most advanced technology in electrostatic waterless desoilancy.

Bernard Matthews is a brand that started with whole, oven-ready turkeys. It moved from there to turkey portions, turkey joints, turkey products – such as sausages and hamburgers. More recently, it has become a brand for convenient, high-value meat products – pork, lamb, beef included. This is an example of intelligent product development, using tightly focused public relations as part, of course, of excellent brand management.

Atco was a brand associated with the highest quality of lawn maintenance – until, that is, Flymo came along, swept away the traditional market introducing a cheap, efficient lawn-cutting machinery that did not require any skill, expertise or effort. But Atco was not knocked out. It responded with its own development and challenged the new rival largely through public relations channels, with considerable success.

Perhaps brands do not always have a natural cycle that involves automatic decline. As Peter Doyle says, in the *Companion Encyclopedia of Marketing*, managers have to understand that markets are highly dynamic. Successful competitive strategies will be built on anticipating the evolutionary forces involved.

Whatever the strategy and the positioning stance, it will be sensible to include public relations in the mix of marketing efforts to support and promote the products and services, particularly through projecting agreed, credible brand messages.

■ Retailers have become significant brands in their own right . . .

Across most developed countries, both the size and influence of retailers have grown in recent years. The average size of a retail outlet has grown significantly, largely only controlled by local or national planning requirements. Over the same period, many of these have moved from city centre to city periphery or even further afield. Many factors have influenced this change: the increased mobility of the buying public, the cost of city centre space, the inconvenience and difficulty of stock deliveries, public and staff parking, and so on. All such changes have affected both marketing approaches and the supporting public relations – for example, the greater need to communicate at national and not just regional, local, or city levels.

Parallel with this, in many countries, there have been moves to mergers and acquisitions, so that upwards of 60 per cent of major retail business may be controlled by half a dozen large chains. Product manufacturers and producers have lost influence as retailers have become the closest interface with the public. Therefore, public relations in support of retailing activities has become increasingly important.

One of the factors that influences the buying decision is the attitude of the consumer towards the retailer of the products and services (as well as the producer of these). It is significant that in the UK all the major retailing groups are heavy users of public relations – at the same time, of course, they are often convinced users of advertising (indeed, amongst the largest spenders in the country). However, advertising spend may be used on a tactical basis to position these stores and to promote them, whilst public relations is used on a continuous strategic basis to develop goodwill.

A survey of the larger spenders in advertising shows that retailers occupy most of the top positions. Whilst public relations is important in supporting the marketing of products, it is invaluable in supporting the development of the brand credibility of services. This is because public relations is all about reputation and service brands tend to be more about perceptions of values and other aspects that might be likened to reputation rather than the delivery of specific benefits that come from product marketing.

■ . . . and own brands continue to increase in importance

The three largest companies in grocery retailing in the UK – Sainsbury's, Tesco and Safeway – gain an average of 50 per cent of turnover from their own brands, according to the latest available figures. (Of course, one major retailer, Marks & Spencer, wins almost 100 per cent of its sales from its own brands.)

Clearly, own brands have become brands that are synonymous with the retailer. Perhaps this explains why much of the public relations efforts undertaken by high street names (though many are no longer solely in the high street) are targeted to presenting the company *behind* the products or services.

■ Services are increasingly branded, today

Services are often treated as products, with their own names, identities and value branded. For example, the Cooperative Bank has developed its position in financial services through adopting and promoting an ethical strategy. This is designed not only directly to earn goodwill but to build policies that earn goodwill. It is an interesting example of public relations becoming the organisation rather than just a facet of the organisation.

Perhaps the differences between services marketing and products servicing are less pronounced than the similarities. Many of the rules that apply to the FMCG area could be applied to the fast-moving consumer services area.

■ Marketing matters to non-profit organisations

There used to be a massive marketing gulf between profit activities and non-profit organisations. This has been closing over recent years. In many respects, the non-profit sector has to be just as 'commercial' as the profit sector. Consider, for example, the work of Oxfam, Friends of the Earth, Greenpeace or Amnesty International. All have strong commercial objectives and all are promoted with marketing techniques that are remarkably similar to those that might be deployed in the profit businesses of products and services.

Of course, the non-profit sector is extremely diverse. Charities, pressure groups, social organisations (such as hospitals, schools, trusts, trade associations, professional bodies, trade unions) have business objectives to achieve, many of which require effective marketing and public relations skills.

Of course, some non-profit organisations, such as local authorities and statutory bodies, are more involved in the arena of public affairs. Others are extremely commercial as they compete in open markets; the mutual bodies, such as some insurance companies and building societies, operate in hard-nosed commercial sectors, with the only real difference in their operations being that they are not designed to generate profits but to return benefits to members. The mutual bodies compete with those that have turned themselves into public companies. Some people would not be aware when buying an insurance policy or pension from Norwich Union or the Prudential whether either is run for profit or for the mutual benefit of its policyholders. Similarly the mutual or non-mutual status of Abbey National or the TSB has little impact upon the financial services that these institutions might offer.

■ Sponsorship

Business sponsorship in the UK exceeds £300 million per annum in direct funding, perhaps three times this figure if supporting costs are included. Yet, probably only a proportion of this money is spent in a disciplined, measured way. Of course, this does not mean that the money is wasted; much of it may well be delivering benefits. But unless real objectives have been set for the activity, it is impossible to calculate how well it has performed.

Some marketing people believe that the inability of some parts of the sponsorship industry to organise itself in a way that it can deliver measurable results is one of the reasons why sponsorship activity in the UK lags so far behind the United States – which is spending at least ten times the UK level. There are many honourable exceptions, where the research has been undertaken and the sponsorship fully rationalised – the Royal Tournament, the Science Museum, Wimbledon and the London Marathon are all good examples, amongst a steadily growing number.

The complexities of managing the event (or the support for it), the messages and their projection to direct and indirect audiences, mean that sponsorship is often, and wisely, viewed as an aspect of public relations. If it is viewed as an alternative communications medium, a subset within advertising, say, then there may be problems ahead.

Whilst it will be legitimate for the audience reach to be calculated in advertising terms and compared with other advertising media, sponsorship is much more. For example, the environment around the activity can be extremely important, something that is less critical in advertising media decisions. The sponsor usually is seen as being central to the activity, whereas the readers or viewers of advertisements know the advertiser has no editorial responsibility or control.

Imagine this. If horses were maltreated at the National Horse Trials the sponsor would be embroiled and, probably, would from suffer negative comments. If the *Daily Telegraph* or *News at Ten*, say, make an embarrassing mistake, no one expects the advertisers to explain. The reason is that often the sponsoring organisation is bigger and has a higher profile than the event organisers. But the advertiser is seen as a buyer of time or space on a communications channel.

Increasingly, those seeking sponsorship and those considering this as a marketing option are becoming more professional. Organisations seeking sponsorship know that they must offer something tangible to any sponsor that is going to fund this activity. The potential backer will want to know the audience being reached, exactly how the sponsor's name will be used, entertainment and publicity options and so on.

Equally, any organisation that is seeking a sponsor has to be able to answer clearly the question of what will be in it for that company putting its name on the event.

For the sponsoring company, an acceptable starting point may be to identify in the most general terms what might be expected from the sponsorship. (Later, these can be converted to more precise objectives.) Such requirements might include:

- We want to back projects/initiatives with which we feel comfortable and which relate in a positive way to our business and our customer interests.
- It is important that anything to which we add our name will be understood and accepted by our employees and reflect our involvement within the local and business communities.
- Any suitable event must allow us to allocate staff who will benefit from the experience of managing the relationship between the company and the event organisers so that they gain the maximum experience.
- Measurable business returns must be the most important element in any such support, in that we need to be able to see a direct return on our investment . . . with goodwill and other less quantifiable benefits seen as no more than a bonus.

Of course, sponsorship can create name awareness but, even more important, as noted, it can create positive associations. Some sponsorships give excellent entertainment opportunities and others give access to senior people who may be influential in the development of the company.

There are some simple basic rules to be decided in running a successful sponsorship:

1. Clarify your objectives.
2. Agree these before looking at options.
3. Do not be persuaded to adjust the objectives to meet the attractiveness of the offer.
4. Allocate a senior member of the company team to be responsible for this activity, ideally reporting to the chief executive.
5. Be very specific in what you expect, particularly when agreeing procedures with the event organisers (who may or may not be experienced in sponsoring). Do not allow any grey areas or agree anything 'in principle' but get the detail clarified at the start. If in doubt, write clauses into the agreement that give you, the sponsoring organisation, final control over everything that cannot be mutually resolved.
6. Ensure that all relevant professionals within the sponsoring organisation are fully involved, including public relations, marketing, human resources and so on.

Sponsorship can be a powerful way to project messages to important audiences, with the incidental benefits of good entertainment opportunities for major clients, plus the association with an event that reflects well on the organisation. When sponsorship is well thought through it can effective; if marketing professionals intend to venture into this area, they simply have to ensure that they review all activity with an independent, performance-orientated perspective.

■ Customer care

Increasingly, the product or service that is offered is a total package. This may include such factors as: the quality of experience in dealing with the company; the service support; the reputation 'halo'; added value in services offered; and the continuity of contact.

■ Skilful communications must build competitive edge

Regular customers expect regular contact and this helps to build loyalty. Indeed, as competition stiffens, more and more companies will be looking to tailoring their offer so that it is more directly related to the individual customer. This customer-orientated approach is really the basis of marketing. Customer care may be a relatively new term, but the concept is central to a marketing approach to doing business – no one matters more than the customer.

At one end of the spectrum, say, buying a standard airline ticket may involve all sorts of incentive schemes and loyalty efforts; these could include frequent flyer schemes, executive lounges and the personalisation of all contact – so that the customer's name is used in contacts.

In the manufacturing sector, companies are realising the considerable benefits that can be offered in tailoring products precisely to meet customer needs. Technology has helped in this area. For example, computer systems can show the customer the range of options and confirm the order in every detail, linked directly into production processes. This means, for example, the production line is not turning out regular blue models for stock but specific items, each of which is individually identified to a customer.

The timescales on this are also considerably shortening. Some motor car manufacturers now claim to be able to get a model through the production line, built exactly to specification, within a week. But even with popular models of cars, there may well be a choice of half a dozen different engines, three or four body styles, a dozen paint finishes, a dozen interior finishes, all sorts of options like air-conditioning, power-steering, sunshine roofs and others; models are literally available in a million variations.

■ Customer focus can add competitive edge

Competitive edge becomes increasingly important; public relations can be a valuable technique in projecting this service capability. If a company can build a product to the specification of the customer then it may well have the advantage. All other things being equal, this means the company has a better story to project than those that can only supply from stock.

With such techniques as on-line terminals linked to a central computer or CD ROM, the whole range of custom options can be seen and checked before the order is placed. From its origination in the motor industry, this trend is now moving through into kitchens, bathrooms, domestic appliances, furniture, holidays, pensions, bank accounts and many other areas.

Increasingly, there will be many people able to have an influence upon the service reputation of the organisation. Remember the classic John Cleese Video Arts training film that showed the service engineer destroying sales with his standard response to every problem with his weary 'Who sold you this then?'

This seminal example of old-style insensitivity still has validity, but has become somewhat outdated.

■ All employees are part of customer care public relations

The concept that the service personnel are not part of the sales team and have no connection with marketing would be viewed as illogical today. Even lorry drivers and van delivery salesman are being trained to see themselves as part of the marketing effort. Indeed, they are really essential to the public relations of the organisation, as they often represent one of the most influential direct points of contact between customers and the company.

There are some central points that need to be decided in managing the quality of service; the marketing functions should be central in this area but public relations professionals must be involved in the process to ensure that they are providing maximum support at all points possible.

To what extent does customer loyalty contribute to the profitability and the development of the organisation? This question can be best answered if the following points are covered:

1. Define customer loyalty and, perhaps, set different levels of expected commitment for different types of customer.
2. Measure sales profitability achieved from such clients including business that may be recommended from satisfied customers. To achieve this measure, there should be incentives for referrals.
3. Run a comparison between the cost of winning new customers and maintaining the custom of existing customers.
4. Identify the key points of contact between the company and both existing and potential customers.
5. Set up processes at as many of these levels as possible for getting feedback – and report to management on customer attitudes and comments.
6. Evaluate objectively why customers become ex-customers and transfer their business loyalty to someone else.
7. Research and appraise customer satisfaction – and, if to have any value, ensure that this is always undertaken independently.
8. Make sure there are processes for using all information to improve the proposition that is offered and, therefore, the customer satisfaction.
9. Check customer expectations against company performance over a relevant recent period and identify methods for improvement.
10. Relate all proposed changes to the personnel dimension of customer care and consider the communications needs.

There is an old marketing adage that the company will succeed and grow if it always exceeds customer expectations. Yet too many companies fail to measure what these may be. Know what your customers expect and exceed that – and you have a successful business. It is that simple.

Public relations can play a vital part in each of these points of contact. Public relations personnel should be invited to join such discussions and invited to make observations on how they propose to support the development of customer satisfaction. In some cases, this will require new initiatives. In others, it will require the tailoring of existing activity to ensure that it is directly supporting the customer care drive.

■ Public relations can set customer expectations

Concepts are not good enough. In effective customer care programmes, it is the implementation that is important. If a policy is developed, then the experience of the customers at point of contact will be critical in deciding whether this is a programme that works or not. Customer care must be developed so that all of the approaches are natural to the members of the organisation who have to follow these through. They should spring from a real desire to be positive and helpful towards customers – rather than being jolly and artificial actions imposed on a possibly resentful team.

It may seem obvious, but customer care programmes must also be orientated towards dealing with customer care issues – and not with coping with fundamental flaws in the structure of the organisation. For example, at one stage in its transition from a nationalised body to a group of privatised organisations, British Rail introduced a programme to help train platform staff to deal with unhappy travellers. At that time, there had been much negative media coverage about the attitude of British Rail staff in their dealings with the public. They often seemed negative and defensive.

Conductors, porters, ticket office staff and others were put on courses to help them improve customer relations, particularly in handling complaints.

The newly-enthused staff soon found that the techniques they had been taught in training simply did not work. Indeed, sometimes the friendly and positive attitude actually created more antagonism. If a train is half an hour late and business travellers miss a key meeting, they are not looking for charm and warmth from those they confront about the issue. They want an explanation on why it happened and what is going to prevent it from happening again. British Rail did not have the machinery in place to provide that information to those dealing with such recurring problems.

In reality, a customer care programme was being used to try to paper over the cracks in an inefficient service that had fundamental problems in communications. If the staff did not have the information, then no amount of training on human relations techniques would be of any value. The core problems of British Rail needed to be tackled before those at the interface with the public could hope to do a credible job.

■ Care programmes must be followed by all in the service chain

At a different level, I used to make a regular journey that required me to fill up with fuel at an Esso station at a convenient point. I had changed my car to a diesel model and, although the engines no longer smell, the fuel has a unpleasant lingering odour if it gets on your hands. Esso – along with other companies – had introduced a system whereby little disposable plastic gloves enable motorists to handle the pump without getting any trace of diesel on the hands.

The first time that I used this station after buying my diesel Audi, there were no disposable gloves in the little dispenser by the pump. I filled up using a wrap of paper around the nozzle.

I commented on the lack of plastic gloves to the cashier; she acknowledged this without any explanation or apology. Nor did she seem to be taking any action about it. I asked her what she proposed to do and she said that she would ask the maintenance man to replace them when she could find him. I pointed out that there would be other customers who would have similar complaints and that she should treat it as a priority.

A week or two later I called again at the petrol station and, whether by chance or not I do not know, but there were again no disposable plastic gloves at the diesel pump. Again I pointed this out to the cashier – a different young lady. Again she did not seem concerned. 'We do not handle that', she explained. 'There is some chap who comes round every so often to fill the dispenser.'

Presumably Esso employed her, and whatever arrangements Esso might have made for filling this dispenser with gloves was really nothing to do with the customers. It surely was everything to do with the cashier, who is the only point of contact that the customers have with the company. I said to her that this was a service the company offered but which it was failing to deliver and she should treat it as a priority.

She dismissed my concern with a shrug, so I explained that I would not be calling again at her service station. This produced an irritated sigh from her. I explained that if she, and everyone else, failed to meet customer needs, she would be out of a job and it would be no good at that point to blame the unknown bosses. In my view, she was letting down both the public and her employers; she could not take the money under such circumstances.

As you might expect, I was underwhelmed by the wave of indifference. Of course, one should not expect much else. But how is it possible that the retailer/ franchise holder does not train or supervise their personnel to even understand and follow fundamental customer care policies? First rule, almost any problem can be overcome with a smile and some attention to the customer.

I now consciously try to avoid Esso stations. Why? Not simply because of a failure of a simple service but because of a failure of training of the personnel or possibly recruitment of the right personnel. Few people enjoy making complaints; if these are handled negligently the discomfort is so intense that many people will not expose themselves to embarrassment.

If an organisation makes a promise then it has a responsibility to make sure that it delivers this promise. It would be better if the garage made no effort at all to provide these disposable gloves. At least, people then buying fuel at their stations would be those who did not care whether their hands smelt of diesel or not.

■ Expect your public relations professionals to monitor performance

Any public relations professional of any ability should be constantly checking all aspects of the company's relations with its main publics, particularly customers. This might well also be a marketing responsibility and there may be professionals involved in undertaking this work.

However, if public relations might be considered to be reflected in what people say about you when they are not there, companies need to remember that stories of their poor service get recounted by many people, many dozens of times in private and in public.

Withdrawing custom may be of little consequence, but if millions of people are unhappy about the service and they withdraw their custom, then the company may pay the price of seeing sales decline, and may begin to take the customer more seriously.

■ The best policy is total focus on the customer

Richard Whiteley is an author and founder of the Forum Corporation (TFC), a Boston-based consultancy that specialises in helping businesses to become more customer-centred. His first book, *The Customer-Driven Company*, was a bestseller and voted by *Fortune* Magazine as one of the year's four best business books.

He believes that customer care is much more than customer magazines and loyalty cards. It is really about putting a total focus on the customer. He believes that companies should decide what they are good at and concentrate on it ruthlessly.

The simple rule is that you should identify which customers you want to build with and identify what they really want. Sometimes the answers are surprising. In the book he gives some examples. Dominoe dominated the US home delivered pizza market by offering customers basic pizzas and a guaranteed $3 off the price if delivery took more than half an hour. Customers were offered a basic range of pizzas with standard Coke – and not even Diet as an alternative.

Yet this approach kept the company leaders for thirty years. Their market share slowly declined, and eventually it had slipped from 50 per cent to 33 per cent and they found themselves with the same market share as their down-market competitor, Pizza Hut. The original initiatives had been overtaken by the market. For example, consumers had come to accept the half hour delivery guarantee and this had been adopted by many competitors. But the product range choice was simply too narrow. The company broadened the choice, winning back customers and returning the best profits ever in 1994.

■ Use an analysis of customer needs to improve service

Prism is the pest control subsidiary of Johnson Wax. Researching the concerns of pest control customers running restaurants and hotels, it discovered that the biggest concern was rows with their own customers and the potential for court fines if insects got into the premises. Broadly, they were not worried about Prism's effectiveness, but the risks if something went wrong.

Prism's response was to extend the guarantee to include the repayment of any service charges, plus an apology to any complaining guest, offering reimbursement of the bill and any court fines, should something go wrong under one of their service contracts.

Whiteley believes that most companies have invaluable research data on the attitudes of their customers and yet continue to ignore this. Some research seems to suggest that a company needs to achieve more than just having satisfied customers, believes Whiteley. 'Satisfied customers will leave you. If you are not top rated, then people will say you are good but you could be better. And they may turn to competitors.'

■ Attention to needs can build repeat business

In the early 1980s the US motor industry was under severe attack from the Japanese. General Motors chairman at the time, Roger Smith, launched the Saturn model, which was promoted as a low-priced, sub-compact car. It was intended to create as much discussion about the way the company treated its customers as it did about the actual vehicle itself. The Saturn achieved the highest sales per dealer in the country and the highest customer satisfaction rating, with 90 per cent saying they were very satisfied.

The car also achieved a higher retention rate with 61 per cent of owners saying that they would buy another Saturn. Indeed, when General Motors held a rally at the Tennessee factory where the Saturn was manufactured, some 40 000 people turned up, completely overwhelming the little town of Springhill, where the car was built. Whiteley believes that a company can only become truly customer-centred if it has true hands-on management leadership from the top. Richard Whiteley believes that expectations are set by world-class companies, irrespective of industry.

People believe that if McDonald's can serve the customer quickly and pleasantly then this should be the standard that should apply at the bank. In the UK he believes that First Direct has carved out a special market niche through placing great emphasis on service at all levels. The airports authority, BAA, listens to its customers and is responding – even in simple things, such as putting more clocks in airport lounges because people are time-conscious in that environment.

■ Set standards at the highest in your industry

Retailers like Tesco not only offer fine products backed by good service but try to make the shopping experience so pleasant that people will want to come back.

Sir Colin Marshall rates highly as a leader as a result of getting British Airways from a sluggish loss-making organisation into a service leader; he made sure he understood customer needs and concerns. For example, he would turn up at Heathrow at 5 am to talk to customers coming off his planes.

Companies sometimes need to consider new ways to reach customers and potential customers. When Vauxhall introduced the Cavalier replacement, the Vectra, they needed to reach both fleet and individual buyers to build sales if the Vectra were to repeat the success of the popular Cavalier.

With its event agency, Spectrum Communications, the company decided on a corporate-style day out. This was built around the concept of the chance to drive a Vectra round a major British racing circuit. They chose three venues (Silverstone, Alton Park and Brands Hatch) and planned three weekends to hold eight race days. The highlight would be to drive a Vectra round the circuit with a professional racing driver, who would then take over and show how it should be done. There were also opportunities to try go-kart racing, quad bikes, clay-pigeon shooting and helicopter rides. The brave-hearted could also be the passenger in a highly tuned, racing sports car.

Questionnaires collected at the event showed that 88 per cent thought the event was good or excellent whilst 92 per cent thought the Vectra was a good or excellent car compared to their existing vehicle.

■ Internal communications are essential in effective programmes

When Barclaycard introduced a customer magazine as part of their campaign to get closer to their customers, they found it achieved several objectives. Shaun Powell, then commercial director of Barclaycard, said 'Our magazines have improved consumer awareness of our services, increased customer retention and, through improved turnover, have paid for themselves.' But it must be remembered that customer magazines are just a technique – part of the mechanics of customer communications.

Craig Waller, managing director of Omnicom-owned Premier Magazines, believes that it is critical that the performance of these is properly measured.

Customer magazines are intended to fulfil criteria in terms of maintaining loyalty but we have to get better without proving their effectiveness, he believes.

The company practises what it believes. For example, *Your Choice* which is produced for the Coop retailing group is delivered to homes, not distributed in-store. It aims both to maintain loyalty among Coop shoppers and encourage store visits by customers of competing supermarkets. Research commissioned from Taylor Nelson AGB found 83 per cent of respondents (including 81 per cent of regular Tesco shoppers and 77 per cent of Sainsbury's shoppers) believe the magazine encourages them to visit Coop stores.

■ Handling complaints is an art in itself

Some UK companies, like Somerfield, have particularly well thought-out procedures for dealing with complaints. Traditionally, dissatisfied customers talk about the problems they have experienced and, therefore, amplify the problem. Satisfied customers are less likely to project the good news to a wider audience. Yet the positive response of Somerfield to complaints has set a standard that many in the industry are trying to follow. Not only does the company refund money without question where appropriate, it will also offer a replacement. The letters in reply to complaints are issued extremely promptly and, although by necessity have to be computer-produced, are carefully personalised and individually signed.

Any effective customer care operation has to have immaculate procedures but it also needs to have people that really do care. When Sodastream called in the professionals to look at its complaints handling procedures, the consultancy found that there could be a lapse of six weeks before there was a response to some problems. Research suggested that nearly 90 per cent of complaints were focused around the same recurring six or so problems; the 10 per cent that were complex were slowing down the ability of the department to respond. The need was to separate complaints into those that could be resolved easily and those that needed fuller investigation. And this sorting process needed to be under-taken as each phone call or letter arrived.

Processes for recording and dealing with both letters and telephone calls were introduced, using the best technology available at the time. These systems would have been of little value were it not for the enthusiastic personable professionals, well-trained and well-motivated, who dealt with every enquiry individually. These were real people (not, as with some companies, made-up names) dealing with real problems and able to trace any customer enquiry in seconds on the computer screen. This is now the norm but was quite innovative when originally set up by this consumer-orientated company.

Of course, customer care is much more than dealing with problems. The collation and updating of the database and the keeping of the customer records and enquiries can become an invaluable marketing tool for the company. Public relations will also be an essential element within any customer care programme.

Public relation in action

Public relations and marketing working together

Kwik-Fit try to project core values

Some businesses have been built through the intelligent use of public relations. Tom Farmer, founder of Kwik-Fit, recalls how he learned about the value of public relations very early on in his business career. Long before Kwik-Fit days, he sold tyres at a discount from a store he had rented. He explains that he was having trouble getting supplies as the big boys tried to keep him out. A reporter from the Sunday Post wrote an article, called 'Tyre King Tommy'. He told how Farmer was selling discount tyres and of the difficulties he was facing. The next day, when he got to the shop, there was a very long queue of customers waiting to buy tyres. His business had lifted off, and, he says, he never looked back.

'In that one instance, I learned the value of having a good press and I have worked hard at it ever since.'

Good public relations begins with good policies, and Tom Farmer illustrates the point well. The company moved into child safety products in the late 1980s. At the time, there was no law about using child seats. So, to encourage their use, Kwik-Fit introduced its unique scheme in which fitters would fit the seat free; the entire cost would be refunded when the child outgrew it and it was returned to the company. Thus the company got over the two main obstacles to their use, namely getting them properly fitted and the price.

The scheme received enormous publicity and brought thousands of parents into Kwik-Fit centres. Company advertising and marketing people worked in parallel with the public relations people, and the seat scheme was heavily advertised and marketed. As parents came in, they also saw the discounted prices for motoring products.

This scheme was public relations led, but by running parallel advertising and marketing campaigns, Kwik-Fit was able to turn the campaign into solid new business.

As most motorists in the UK know, the company spearheads its marketing with the slogan 'You can't get better than a Kwik-Fit fitter', but there are drawbacks in having such a slogan, explains Farmer. Fitters have to be able to live up to it in real life. That means the company must train them better than anyone else; it must have better customer service policies than anyone else, and as people, fitters must fulfil the expectations raised by the television commercial – friendly, reliable, trustworthy and willing to go the extra mile in order to delight customers.

'You can't get better than a Kwik-Fit fitter' is not just a slogan, believes Tom Farmer. 'It is a declaration that we must live by, in all our activity. It must live and be seen in our advertising, but also in our public relations, our marketing and, indeed, in the way in which we go about our business.'

When he started out, on the very first day, he wrote a sentence on the notice board, 'Our aim is 100 per cent customer satisfaction.' In the quarter of a century since then, Kwik-Fit has grown from one centre to one thousand, yet he has only made one change in that statement, by altering the word 'satisfaction' to 'delight'.

That statement, he believes, sets the tone of the organisation; in all public relations and marketing, it is the core thought that must come through. Customers must be delighted with the prices, with the service, with the people – and when they report a problem, they must be delighted with the way in which they are treated to put things right. 'Caring for people is good for business. If you care for them, they will come back to you.'

Farmer is convinced that public relations can be a fundamental company philosophy reflecting real core values. 'I believe in what our company offers and so I have always worked closely with the media. People believe what they read in the papers. Often, it is not what actually happened that is important, it is what the media says has happened. When a customer reads in the editorial section of a newspaper that Kwik-Fit is a good firm, then he or she is more likely to believe it than if we make the same claim in an advertisement. So we work hard to tell the media about the way in which we go about our business.'

'If the editorial is praising the company for customer care, the advertising is saying that you can't get better, and Kwik-Fit marketing policies are saying our aim is to delight customers. Then, as long as we can live up to the claim there is a good chance of success' explains Tom Farmer.

CHAPTER 10

Marketing: international communications

I look upon the world as my parish.
John Wesley (1703–1791), in his *Journal* of 1739

■ International operations

To manage communications at a local level is difficult enough. To do so across the globe is highly problematic. Marketers will need local public relations expertise in every market in which they operate. And their advisers will need to understand the culture of the different markets – particularly the local and head office countries.

■ Always get good advice on the local business culture

I once undertook a confidential study on behalf of a major Japanese carmaker in the UK. In the course of this, I remember meeting one Japanese executive who was unusually outgoing and affable in style. Most Japanese are friendly and polite but rather restrained. This man was full of joy and confidence. However, he completely took the wind out of my sails when he greeted me, 'How the f*** are you?'

I told him I was fine and hoped he was well – but my startled expression must have shown. 'Is there something wrong?' he asked.

'Well, that is a most unusual and outspoken greeting – certainly not one I'd expect from a Japanese business executive.'

'Ah', he confided with a wink. 'I am very well knowing the English customs as my friends at the factory have taught me much useful phrases. They have been most delighting and charmful.'

I smiled. 'That is a very forthright greeting,' I explained. 'I am not sure that I would use it in a business context, if I were you. In fact, I am not too sure that I would use it in any context!'

He looked puzzled. 'I have been all over your country, meeting and greeting many people and they all seem delighted. Many laugh out loud, so I must be getting the expression right.'

'Well it is certainly unusual but I think they are having a joke at your expense.' When I explained the joke, he was not so happy.

Later in our discussions, he suddenly brightened up. 'I know, I will repay their naughtiness,' he proclaimed. 'I have a friend who will help me. I will tell my colleagues that he is an honoured visitor from Japan and I will invite them to my home to meet him. He will give a long, boring speech in Japanese for half an hour or more during which those rascals will not get a drink.'

Who said the Japanese do not have a sense of humour? Though I have yet to find out if he carried out his threat.

■ International public relations must be managed to a central strategy

Boots is a business that seems to be quintessentially British. There is no high street of any consequence that would not be complete without a Boots. The retailer is part of the life of the nation. Indeed, it has been proven from research that well over 90 per cent of the UK population will go through those familiar doors every year. And an astonishing 25 per cent of British adults visit a Boots retailer every week.

The strength of its UK business has perhaps overshadowed its international activities. Could such an essentially British operation trade on a major global scale? Ian Wright is head of public relations for Boots Healthcare International, which operates across fifteen countries with over £200 million sales across over a hundred markets. The company sells over-the-counter self-medication products including market-leading international brands such as Nurofen, Strepsils and Optrex. To support this business, Wright spends over £4 million a year on worldwide public relations, most of this targeted at supporting the company in its markets.

He stresses that the company is run to the primary objective of managing shareholder value. 'In the end', explains Wright, 'It's the shareholders' money which I'm investing in public relations. Responsible management of that investment demands that we measure the impact and effectiveness achieved.'

■ Project core brand values globally

Really effective co-ordinated global brand and corporate public relations campaigns are rare. The success that Boots International has achieved in integrating marketing and communications comes from a philosophy that runs through the company, believes managing director Barry Clare. 'To be effective, management must share a commitment to flexibility and to the rigorous application of performance management, feeding back into the programme. This allows the company or the client both to identify concerns that might need rectifying and to celebrate success.'

All benefits to other stakeholders spin out from this – an interesting philosophical contrast to, say, Richard Branson's Virgin, which has its focus on employees. Two different but highly successful companies, but that is a debate for another time and place.

The Boots International marketing strategy is centred on brand objectives. Public relations takes the lead in both corporate activity and internal communications, controlling both international brand presentation and corporate identity.

■ Continuous evaluation can strengthen relationships

Ian Wright believes that any evaluation that is effective must be a continuous development process which not only identifies failure but also acknowledges success. Relationships have to be strong enough between communications management, public relations advisers and the marketing brand managers to allow honest and open discussion of those achievements and failures so that these can be built upon for future success. In his view, the way to balance conflicting demands for immediate profit and market share growth is to work to a long-term vision but with well defined short-term milestones.

Not all measures of performance need to be either complex or expensive, he believes. For example, when looking at qualitative editorial measurement, there are a number of factors that can be appraised reasonably objectively and which will help to improve future performance. The method and quality of contact with editors and journalists will have a considerable influence on the ability of the organisation to achieve positive coverage and get over its messages. The effectiveness of this editorial contact, its frequency and the perceptions of the journalist towards the organisation can be appraised relatively simply.

One way to achieve an intelligent appraisal of performance is to ensure that the brief is written with a performance orientation. It is wise to try to define what potential results might be viewed as being successful and to agree the measures for evaluating the actual results in both marketing and reputation terms. In addition, a programme should be appraised during the course of running so that any fine-tuning can be considered – as well as at the end when both the effectiveness and the cost-effectiveness can be judged.

His department uses an editorial measurement form which is completed for each major media activity within the programme. On a periodic basis, competitive activities are also reviewed so that comparisons in performance can be made.

■ The professionals must participate in appraisals

Benefits of this method are that the most effective techniques can be used and the value of the activity identified to management. At the same time, Ian Wright believes that effective appraisal, which includes the direct and active participation of the public relations professionals, will also help to strengthen both their desire to perform well and their commitment to meeting company business objectives.

The results of each editorial discussion or negotiation over an interview, story or feature, can also be measured and scored against potential. In other words, some measure of success should be determined in advance and then the final outcome checked against this. Finally, the quality and quantity of the audience that would be reached through the item can be measured through an informal appraisal process or through one of the computer-based media evaluation services.

■ Mix global policies with local know-how to ensure success

International public relations is just like marketing – the same around the globe, only different everywhere. Some would argue the different cultures around globally change all the ground rules. This is rarely, if at all, true. The ground rules remain largely the same but the interpretation and, particularly, the implementation must be adapted to suit local needs and sensitivities. My own Worldcom Group summarises this in the phrase *Global access, local focus*. Less than ten years ago this was an original concept but has since been widely adopted across business, perhaps because it is a logical summary of a sound approach.

As noted earlier, the central element for success will be to have local experts you can trust. They must be nationals. They must work in the relevant market. They must have international experience – to know what is the same and what is different in their market. Above all, they must be pragmatic and not obsessed with re-inventing everything. Here are some suggested guidelines to developing an international public relations programme to support international marketing:

- Ensure that you have agreed business objectives for each market, from which the marketing and public relations plans can be built.
- Ask your home market public relations professionals for their views both on the possible plans and how to achieve them – they may have contacts or local resources.
- Together, draft a public relations brief from this that clearly identifies what you want to achieve, not how you want to achieve it.
- Check this out with your local marketing professionals and ask for their views on suitable local public relations resources.
- Look for this local public relations partner you can trust to advise on the practicalities of your objectives – staff colleague, independent, consultancy executive, possibly the partner firm of your home consultancy.
- Ask for recommendations against this brief – ideally from 2 or 3 sources.
- Involve group and local marketing professionals in the selection process.
- Agree the reporting lines at group and local levels, trying to ensure that these allow a long term relationship to develop.
- Apply the selection criteria, monitoring, appraisal and fine tuning processes detailed earlier, (Chapters 6 and 7).
- Organise regular face to face briefings locally on a monthly basis, say, and as frequently as practical at group level, ideally involving public relations partners from across as many markets as you manage.

Appendix: sources of information

Advertising Association (AA)
Aberford House
15 Wilton Road
London SW1V 1NJ
Tel: 0171-828 2771

Advertising Standards Authority (ASA)
Brook House
2-16 Torrington Place
London WC1E 7HN
Tel: 0171-580 5555

British Association of Industrial Editors (BAIE)
3 Locks Yard
High Street
Sevenoaks
Kent TN13 1LT
Tel: 01732 459331

Central Office of Information (COI)
Hercules Road
London SE1 7DU
Tel: 0171-928 2345

Central Statistical Office (CSO)
Government Offices
Great George Street
London SW1P 3AQ
Tel: 0171-270 3000

Chartered Institute of Marketing (CIM)
Moor Hall
Cookham
Maidenhead
Berks SL6 9QH
Tel: 01628 524922

Communications, Advertising and Marketing Education Foundation (CAM)
Aberford House
15 Wilton Road
London SW1V 8PH
Tel: 0171-828 7506

Confederation of British Industry (CBI)
Centre Point
103 New Oxford Street
London WC1A 1DU
Tel: 0171-638 8215

Confederation Européen des Relations Publiques (CERP)
Rue des Petits Carmes 9
B-1000 Brussels
Belgium
Tel: 00-32 25112680

Direct Marketing Association (DMS)
1 Oxendon Street
London SW1Y 4EE
Tel: 0171-321 2525

European Parliament Office (EPO)
2 Queen Anne's Gate
London SW1H 9AA
Tel: 0171-222 0411

Incorporated Society of British Advertisers (ISBA)
44 Hertford Street
London W1Y 8AE
Tel: 0171-499 7502

Industrial Society (IS)
48 Bryanstone Square
London W1H 7LN
Tel: 0171-262 2401

Institute of Directors (IOD)
116 Pall Mall
London SW1Y 5ED
Tel: 0171-839 1233

Institute of Export (IOE)
Export House
64 Clifton Street
London EC2A 4HB
Tel: 0171-247 9812

Institute of Management (IM)
Management House
Cottingham Road
Corby
Northants NN17 1TT
Tel: 01536 204222

Institute of Practitioners in Advertising (IPA)
44 Belgrave Square
London SW1X 8QS
Tel: 0171-235 7020

Institute of Public Relations (IPR)
The Old Trading House
4th Floor
15 Northburgh Street
London EC1V 0PR
Tel: 0171-253 5151

Institute of Sales Promotion (ISP)
Arena House
66-68 Pentonville Road
Islington
London N1 9HS
Tel: 0171-837 5340

International Association of Business Communicators (IABC)
One Hallidie Plaza
Suite 600
San Francisco
California 94102
USA
Tel: 001-415 433 3400

International Committee of Public Relations Consultants (ICO)
Willow House
Willow Place
London SW1P 1JH
Tel: 0171-233 6026

International Public Relations Association (IPRA)
Cardinal House
7 Wolsey Road
Hampton Court
Surrey KT8 9El
Tel: 0181-481 7634

The Marketing Society (TMS)
St George's House
3-5 Pepys Road
London SW20 8NJ
Tel: 0181-879 3464

Market Research Society (MRS)
15 Northburgh Street
London EC1V 0AH
Tel: 0171-490 4911

Newspapers Publishers Association (NPA)
34 Southwark Bridge Road
London SE1 9EU
Tel: 0171-928 6928

Newspaper Society (NS)
Bloomsbury House
Bloomsbury Square
74-77 Great Russell Street
London WC1B 3DA

Periodical Publishers Association (PPA)
Imperial House
15-19 Kingsway
London WC2B 6UN
Tel: 0171-379 6268

Press Complaints Commission (PCC)
1 Salisbury Square
London EC4Y 8AE
Tel: 0171-353 1248

Public Relations Consultants Association (PRCA)
Willow House
Willow Place
London SW1P 1JH
Tel: 0171-233 6026

Public Relations Society of America (PRSA)
33 Irving Place
New York NY 10003
USA
Tel: 001-212 995 2230

Publishers Association (PA)
19 Bedford Square
London WC1B 3HJ
Tel: 0171-580 6321

The UK European Commission Office (UKECO)
Jean Monnet House
8 Storey's Gate
London SW1P 3AT
Tel: 0171-973 1992

▌Selected Bibliography

■ Introductions

F. Jefkins, *Public Relations*, 4th edn (London: Pitman, 1992)

H. and P. Lloyd, *Teach Yourself Public Relations* (Sevenoaks, Kent: Hodder & Stoughton 1989)

■ General communications

P. Bartram and C. Coulson-Thomas, *The Complete Spokesperson* (Brighton: Policy Publications, 1990)

Q. Bell, *The PR Business* (London: Kogan Page, 1991)

S. Black, *The Essentials of Public Relations* (London: Kogan Page, 1993)

A. Cadbury, *The Company Chairman* (Hemel Hempstead: Director Books, 1990)

R. Haywood, *All About Public Relations*, 3rd edn (Maidenhead: McGraw-Hill, 1991)

R. Haywood, *Managing Your Reputation* (Maidenhead: McGraw-Hill, 1994)

F. Jefkins, *Planned Press and Public Relations*, 3rd edn (Andover: Blackie International Thomson Publishing Services, 1993)

B. Penn, *Be Your Own PR Expert* (London: Piatkus Books, 1992)

Public Relations Consultants Association, *All You Need to Know about PR* (London: Public Relations Consultants Association, 1991)

D. Ross, *Surviving the Media Jungle* (London: Pitman Publishing, 1990)

J. Smythe, C. Dorward and J. Reback, *Managing the Corporate Reputation, New Strategic Asset* (London: Century Business, 1991)

N. Stone, *How to Manage Public Relations* (Maidenhead: McGraw-Hill, 1991)

J. White, *How to Understand and Manage Public Relations* (London: Century Business, 1991)

P. Winner, *Effective PR Management*, 2nd edn (London: Kogan Page, 1993)

■ Financial public relations

K. Andrews, *The Financial Public Relations Handbook* (Hemel Hempstead: Woodhead-Faulkner, 1990)

R. Bing and P. Bowman, *Financial Public Relations*, 2nd edn (Oxford: Butterworth-Heinemann, 1993)

J. Graham and D. Lake, *Investor Relations* (Plymouth: Euromoney Publications and Dewe Rogerson, 1990)

■ Government relations

J. Connelly, *Dealing with Whitehall* (London: Century Business, 1992)
I. Gilmour, *Freedom of Information* (London: Central Office of Information, 1993)
G. Jordan, *Commercial Lobbyists* (Aberdeen University Press, 1992)
C. Miller, *Lobbying – Understanding and Influencing the Corridors of Power*, 2nd edn (Oxford: Basil Blackwell)

■ Public relations techniques

S. Black, *Exhibitions and Conferences from A to Z* (London: Mondino, 1989)
M. Bland and P. Jackson, *Effective Employee Communications* (London: Kogan Page, 1991)
N. Ind, *The Corporate Image*, 2nd edn (London: Kogan Page, 1992)
W. Olins, *The Corporate Identity* (London: Thames & Hudson, 1990)
D. Phillips, *Evaluating Press Coverage* (London: Kogan Page, 1992)
P. Sheldon Green, *Reputation Risk Management* (London: Pitman Publishing, 1992)
M. Walters, *What about the Workers?* (London: Institute of Personnel Management, 1990)

■ Case histories and studies

S. Black, *International Public Relations* (London: Kogan Page, 1993)
D. Moss, *Public Relations in Practice – A Casebook* (London: Routledge, 1990)
M. Nally, ed., *International Public Relations in Practice* (London: Kogan Page, 1992)

■ Marketing

T. Ambler, *Marketing from Advertising to Zen* (London: Pitman Publishing, 1996)
M. J. Baker, *Marketing – An Introductory Text*, 5th edn (Basingstoke: Macmillan, 1992)
M. J. Baker, ed., *Companion Encylopedia of Marketing* (London: Routledge, 1995)
R. Bennett, *International Marketing* (London: Kogan Page, 1995)
T. Cram, *The Power of Relationship Marketing* (London: Pitman Publishing, 1994)
T. Griffin, *International Marketing Communications* (Oxford: Butterworth-Heinemann, 1993)
N. Hart, ed., *Effective Industrial Marketing* (London: Kogan Page, 1994)
N. Hart, *The CIM Marketing Dictionary*, 5th edn (Oxford: Butterworth Heinemann, 1996)
G. Humphrey and N. Hart, eds, *The Professional Advisor's Guide to Marketing* (Didcot: Mercury Business Books, 1990)
T. H. Nilson, *Value-Added Marketing: Marketing Management for Superior Results* (Maidenhead: McGraw-Hill, 1992)
P. R. Smith, *Marketing Communications: An Integrated Approach* (London: Kogan Page, 1993)
J. Wilmshurst, *Below-the-line Promotion* (Oxford: Butterworth-Heinemann, 1993)

Index